IMAGES
of America

AROUND CHELSEA

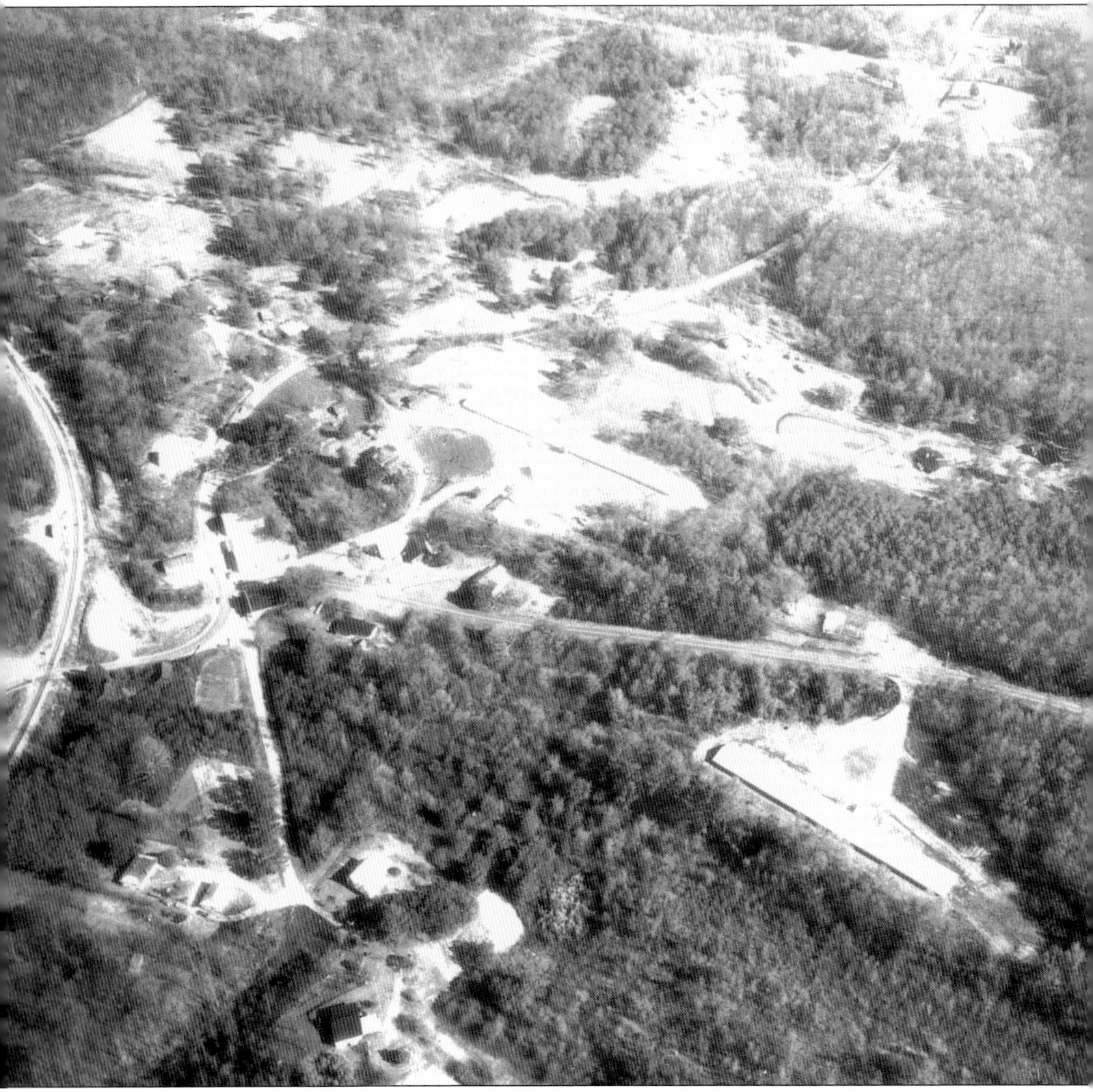

Sky View. This 1980s aerial view of Chelsea, Alabama, was taken from an F-4 jet. Homes are shown sprinkled within the town; this photograph is vastly different than the Chelsea of today. (Courtesy of Olean Kenny.)

On the Cover: Liberty Baptist Church Vacation Bible School, 1950s. Liberty Baptist Church's vacation Bible school has continued to grow from when it held its first class in the 1940s. Among this group of children standing outside the original church building is future Chelsea mayor Earl Niven. Unfortunately, he is not visible on the cover, but can be seen on page 43. In the original photograph, he is in the second row, second from the left. Liberty Baptist Church dates to the early 1840s. (Courtesy of Olean Kenny.)

IMAGES
of America

AROUND CHELSEA

Christi-Ann Bono

ARCADIA
PUBLISHING

ISBN 978-1-4671-1641-1

Published by Arcadia Publishing
Charleston, South Carolina

Printed in the United States of America

Library of Congress Control Number: 2016932141

For all general information, please contact Arcadia Publishing:
Telephone 843-853-2070
Fax 843-853-0044
E-mail sales@arcadiapublishing.com
For customer service and orders:
Toll-Free 1-888-313-2665

Visit us on the Internet at www.arcadiapublishing.com

This book is dedicated to the community of Chelsea and to those who strive to preserve and pass on these treasured stories and snapshots of days gone by.

Also, I dedicate this book to my children in hope that you be inspired.

Contents

FOREWORD

Preserving and learning our history gives us a deeper appreciation for this wonderful community we call Chelsea. *Around Chelsea* tells the story of the families and events that paved a way for the future of this city. My family has deep roots here of which I am thankful. I married and raised a family here. I have worked in Chelsea and have been blessed to serve as mayor. I have seen the magnificent changes that took place over the years. Although travels have taken me to many places, Chelsea is what I call home. It has been an honor to witness this town blossom, grow, and thrive. What began as so little has reaped great gains. There are remnants of Chelsea's past peppered throughout the city; however, some are only in memory. *Around Chelsea* shares those experiences and shares the story of how our city became the community it is today.

—Mayor Earl Niven

ACKNOWLEDGMENTS

This was an immense project. My best effort was put forth in the interviews and research it took to convey the unique history of the growing city of Chelsea and its neighboring towns.

I first thank God for the opportunity to write this. Next, many thanks are owed to my loving family: my husband, Carl; my father, Ray; and my three boys, Brock, Tal Matthew, and Noah. Thank you, Mayor Earl Niven, for your willingness to embrace this project for the city. To Councilwoman Juanita Champion, I am grateful for all your help in locating contacts and sharing your time with me. A thank-you is given to Olean Kenny for preserving Chelsea's story and the precious few photographs that remain from years ago; I truly appreciate your willingness to happily contribute in any way possible. Thanks go to the Shelby County Historical Society (SCHS) and Bobby Joe Seales and to Earlene Moore. I also thank Jim and Judy Bailey. I am appreciative of Walter Savage Jr. for sharing with me the untold story of the Hargis family. Mary Fogo encouraged me to discover Chelsea's history in the first place. I want to thank Arcadia editor Sarah Gottlieb for her offers of help and support at any time needed. I also want to extend a special thank-you to the late Shelba Nivens and her son Tony Nivens. Without her desire to preserve the past and her graciousness to share facts and photographs, this project would not have moved forward. To my misfortune, I met her only once before her passing, but the inspiration she gave to me is enduring.

Introduction

The history is rich in Chelsea, as well as in the small towns that surround this booming area. As I began thinking of introducing the idea of *Around Chelsea* to Arcadia Publishing for the Images of America series, I wondered what I would uncover from the past. What stories would be unveiled? What could be learned so others could have a better appreciation for these Shelby County communities? There is pride among those living in the hills and hollows of this region. Many of them remember the days gone by. They knew the towns before modern business, before the bustle of Highway 280 traffic, and before the town names were commonly spoken. They desire to preserve history. They want to see the story unfold through photographs that captured a moment that is no longer.

In the early 1800s, Creek Indians lived on the vast land where Chelsea is today. Through the actions of Andrew Jackson, the Battle of Horseshoe Bend changed the Creek Indians' way of life and allowed pioneers to explore new areas and to establish the State of Alabama. Soon after that battle, General Jackson and several Indian chiefs signed the Treaty of Fort Jackson. The treaty ceded 23 million acres of land to the United States. In 1819, just a few years later, much of the land became Alabama. Pioneer families began to settle what would become the towns of Chelsea, originally called "Melrose," Harpersville, Wilsonville, Sterrett, and Vincent. At that time, the Kendrick family was settling in K Springs, located down the road from Melrose.

The beginning of the 20th century, however, brought great change for Melrose. In 1908, the Atlanta, Birmingham & Atlantic (AB&A) Railway laid track through the area. This proved to be a substantial catalyst for growth. The railway renamed Melrose to "Chelsea," and a budding town was born. The AB&A Railway was consolidated in 1967 and became part of the CSX Railroad System that runs through Chelsea today.

As settling families began to move close to the train tracks, businesses began to develop. Some of the first to plant seeds in Chelsea were a gristmill, sawmill, general stores, a drugstore, cotton gin, planing mill, a barbershop, and a post office.

Chelsea slowly began to grow. Incorporation in 1996 ensured rapid progress. At the time, Chelsea's population was just a little more than 900. After incorporation, Earl Niven was elected mayor, and within 10 years, Chelsea grew more than 200 percent. The latest census showed Chelsea's population at more than 11,000.

There is evidence of Chelsea's past sprinkled around the town. The Weldon Store still stands, although how long it can stay in its current spot is unknown. The Chelsea Library was once the home of the Crane family and sits adjacent to city hall. Liberty Baptist Church has been perched on Highway 47 since the late 1800s. In 1931, K Springs Church built its white building that still stands today but is leased by another organization. Old Quinn Burying Ground is also located in Chelsea. It was established in 1849 by War of 1812 veteran Loftin Quinn. It is the burial ground of many of Chelsea's early settlers and some Revolutionary War veterans.

Likewise, evidence of Chelsea's growth and progress is abundant. A new school, Forest Oaks Elementary, opened in January 2014. New neighborhoods are under construction. Chelsea's new senior center recently opened on Highway 36. There are restaurants, fast-food chains, gas stations, two major grocery stores, and a Walmart, just to name a few examples of a growing community.

The town of Harpersville, which neighbors Chelsea, is one of Shelby County's oldest cities, and it precedes the establishment of Shelby County and the State of Alabama. In 1815, the Harper and Kidd families settled "Big Springs," as Harpersville was originally called. Some of the first businesses were a blacksmith shop, a store, and a steam-driven cotton gin. The community even ended up with a regular stagecoach stop. Eventually, Elmhill Academy would open in the growing area, which attracted both in-town and out-of-state students for boarding. Harpersville became known for its educational facilities. The town has also produced some famous faces. Henry B. Wathal became a stage and silent-film actor in Hollywood. NBA stars George McGinnis and Warren Kidd, as well as baseball player Ernest G. Carter, call Harpersville home.

In 1925, Highway 280 was constructed and became known as the "Florida Short Route," bringing more traffic through the small town. Harpersville was incorporated in 1945. Today, the town offers well-known winery Morgan Creek Vineyards; festivities at Old Baker farm, which withstood the Civil War; private schools; a drive-in movie theater; and a library. Harpersville's motto is "Rich Past, Bright Future."

In 1812, Wilsonville got its first settlers. Henry W. Robertson brought his family from South Carolina to the sprawling land. Then, in 1821, a man by the name of Sam Wallace took a horseback ride with Robertson to Tuscaloosa to claim 1,000 acres each from the land offices. The name, however, came from a man named Adam Wilson. He was farmer in Wilsonville, and his son was not only a farmer but also a physician. By the turn of the 20th century, the town was the trading point for the two rich farming areas of Fourmile and the Kingdom. Around 1865, the first depot in the county was erected in Wilsonville. At the end of the 1800s, J.F. Pope built an expansive store in the middle of town. Pope is thought to have been the largest individual taxpayer in the county during that time. Wilsonville was incorporated in 1897. A significant development in the 1950s was the Gaston Steam Plant. Electricity is produced there and is used throughout the Southeast.

Not far from Wilsonville is the neighboring town of Vincent. Settled on the Coosa Valley, it is known for rich and fertile soil. First called "Propel," Vincent was incorporated in 1897. When the railroad came through in 1898, the name was changed. The town boasts the oldest-living Christmas tree in the state, which is lit annually in a ceremony during the Christmas Parade.

Sterrett has a unique history not many know about. With a population today around 700, the city got its name from a prominent family in the area. Alphonso A. Sterrett, a member of that family, served in the Alabama state legislature. The town was once the focus of a massive production of pottery and was known as "Jugtown."

One

"It's All about Family."

The view looks much different today than during the meager beginning of Chelsea. A wooden sign denoting Chelsea greets drivers topping Double Oak Mountain. It does not take long to notice the evidence of a growing city. Once traveled by horse and buggy, dirt roads are now paved. Gas stations, specialty shops, grocery stores, and fast-food chains run up and down this stretch of Highway 280. Traffic lights hang over what was vast land once cared for by a few pioneer families. Where log cabins stood are now brick homes for the thousands who call the area home. In more than 100 years since the area was first settled, the sense of family and community has not changed. Pioneers headed to the area and began to settle in the early 1800s. Some of the founding families of Chelsea are the Blackerbys, Chessers, Cranes, Kendricks, Nivens/Nivenses, and Weldons. Most Chelsea Kendricks can trace their heritage back to Abel Kendrick, a Revolutionary War veteran. Many Kendricks served in the Revolutionary War as well as the Civil War. In 1861, the nation plunged into the Civil War, and two dozen Kendricks and their in-laws enlisted in the Confederate army. Some of the men who served are buried at historic Quinn Burial Ground of Chelsea. Other pioneering families followed and have descendants remaining in Chelsea today. From the beginning, families helped each other, lived near each other, and depended on each other, creating a community that still stands strong. In fact, the motto of Chelsea, which is hanging on a wall in city hall, is "It's All about Family."

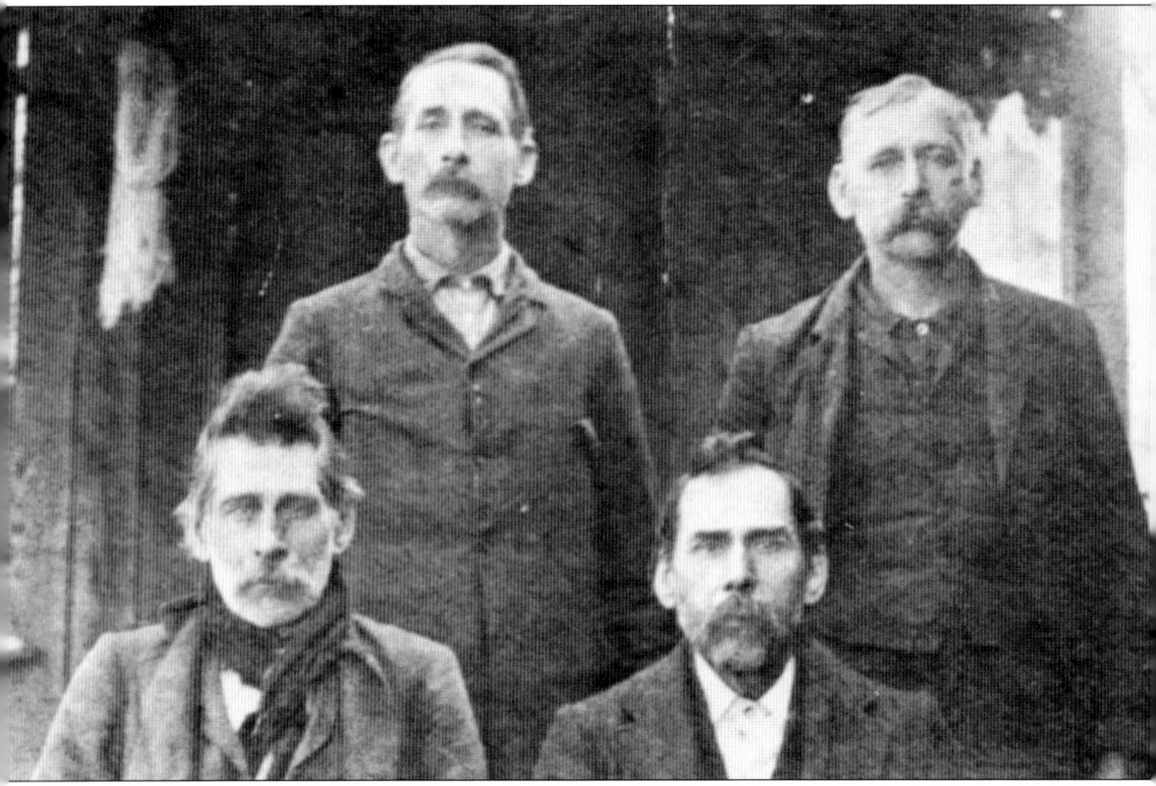

KENDRICK FAMILY, PIONEERS. Pictured from left to right are Kendrick brothers (first row) Luther and Jud; (second row) Bob and Elbert. The Kendricks were pioneers in the Chelsea area. Most Kendricks can trace their lineage back to Abel Kendrick, a Revolutionary War soldier. Abel's son married the daughter of Lewis Turner, who was also a Revolutionary War soldier and pioneer to the area. Together, these families settled in the Chelsea area in the mid-1800s. (Courtesy of Shelba Nivens and SCHS.)

LUTHER KENDRICK AND FAMILY, 1901. Next to Luther is his wife, Martha Spearman Kendrick. Also pictured are children Clifton, Birdie, Flora, Walter, and Ruby. Cecil is the baby in the mother's lap. Luther built a cabin in 1867 when he was just 15 years old. He constructed it on what was eventually called Kendrick Springs. A story has been told that several springs were discovered after clearing brush from the cabin. The area was surrounded by a group of sulfur, mineral, and pure water springs. The name was later shortened to K Springs. Luther Kendrick later donated land for a school around 1896. Later, on that ground, the K Springs Church of God was built. (Courtesy James and Judy Bailey.)

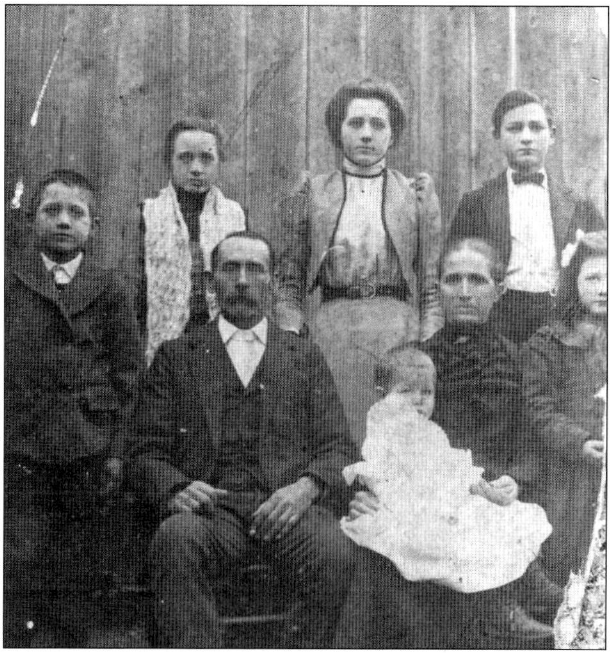

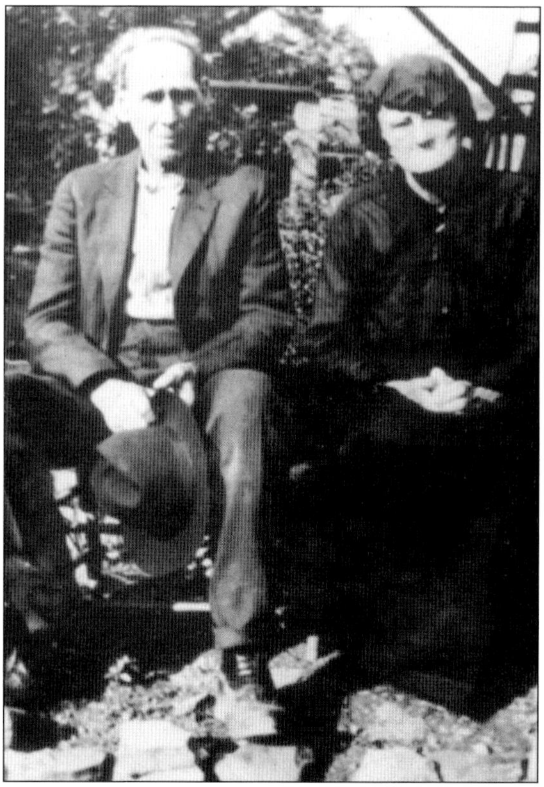

JUD AND CARRIE KENDRICK. Jud Kendrick is pictured with his wife, Carrie, in the early 1900s. Jud was born in 1850 and died in 1939. Carrie was born in 1851 and died in 1932. The couple had eight children, at least two of whom passed away at a young age. Their son Oliver became a minister and pastored to several churches in and around Chelsea. (Courtesy of Shelba Nivens.)

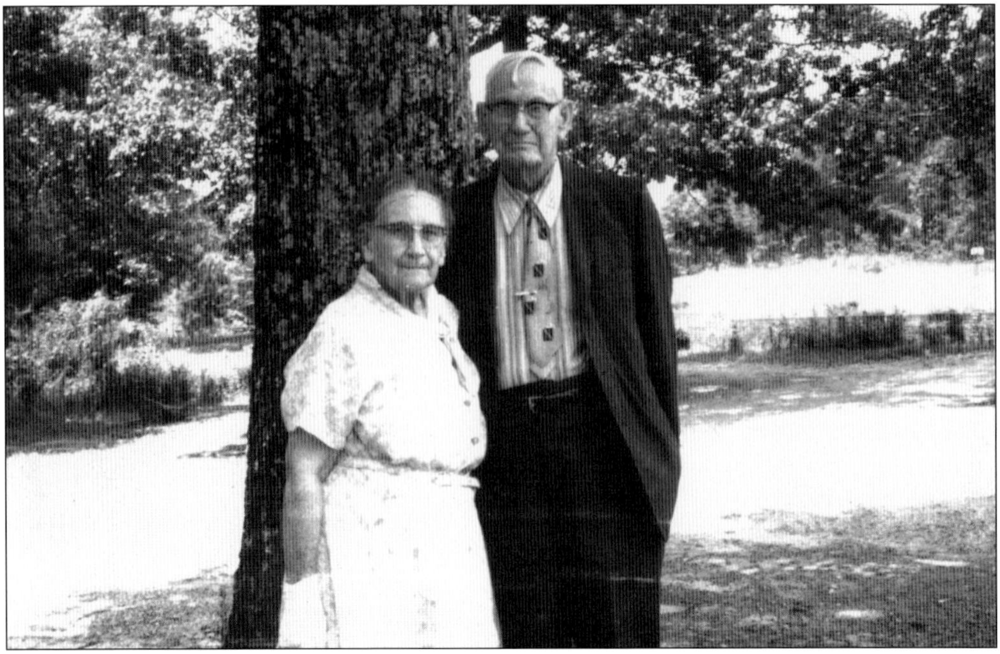

FRANK AND RESSIE KENDRICK. O. Frank Kendrick, son of Jud Kendrick, with his wife, Ressie, are pictured in the 1940s or 1950s. Frank and Ressie celebrated a 50th wedding anniversary in Chelsea. They knew each other since they were children. Both Frank and Ressie died in 1978. Together they had seven children: Lillian, Elvie, Barney, Bernice, Wilton, Freddie, and Jean. (Both, courtesy of Shelba Nivens.)

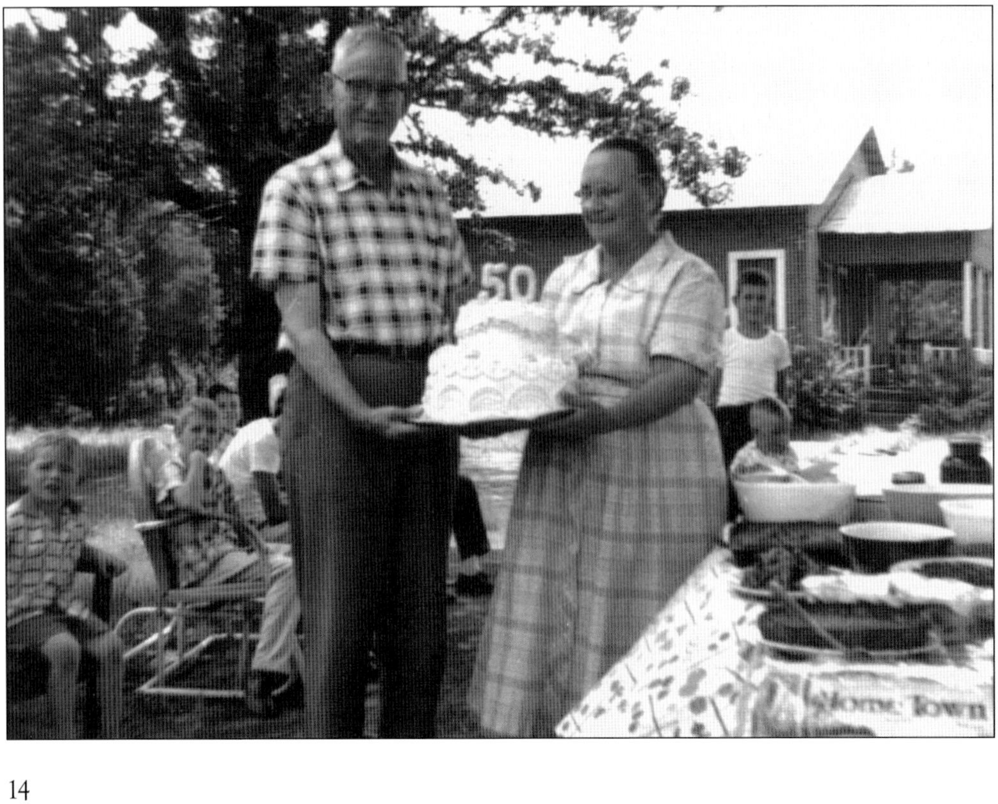

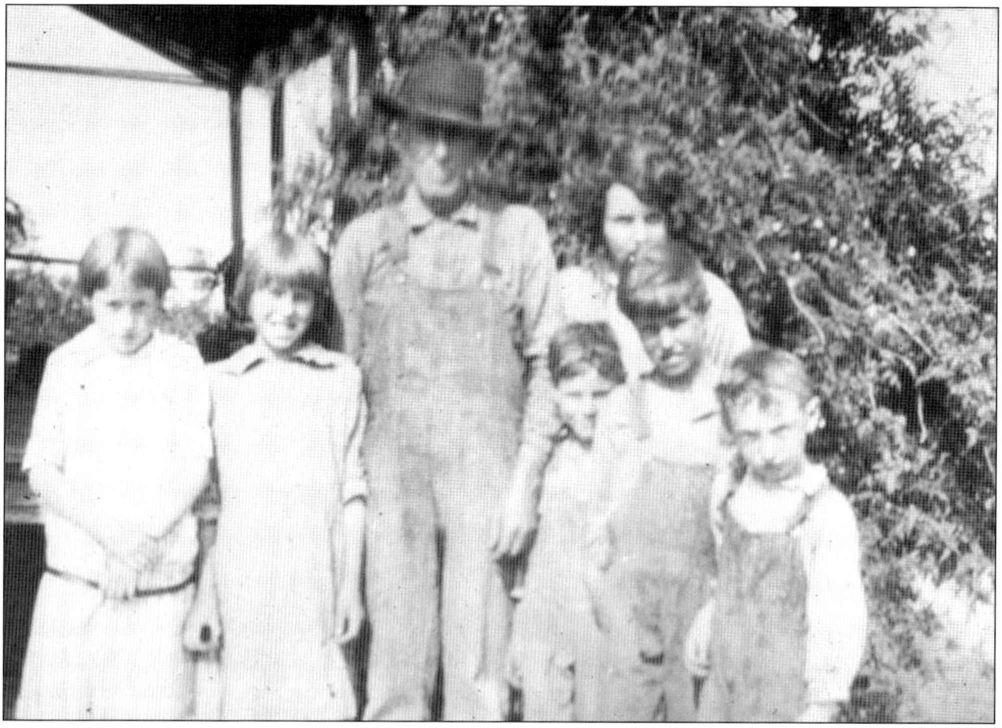

Jud's Grandchildren, Frank's and Elra's Children. Jud Kendrick is pictured standing with his grandchildren Elvie, Verna, Myrtle, Elra, Floyd, and Barney. Elvie and Barney were Frank and Ressie Kendrick's children; the others were the children of Jud's son Elra and daughter-in-law Jemima. (Courtesy of Shelba Nivens.)

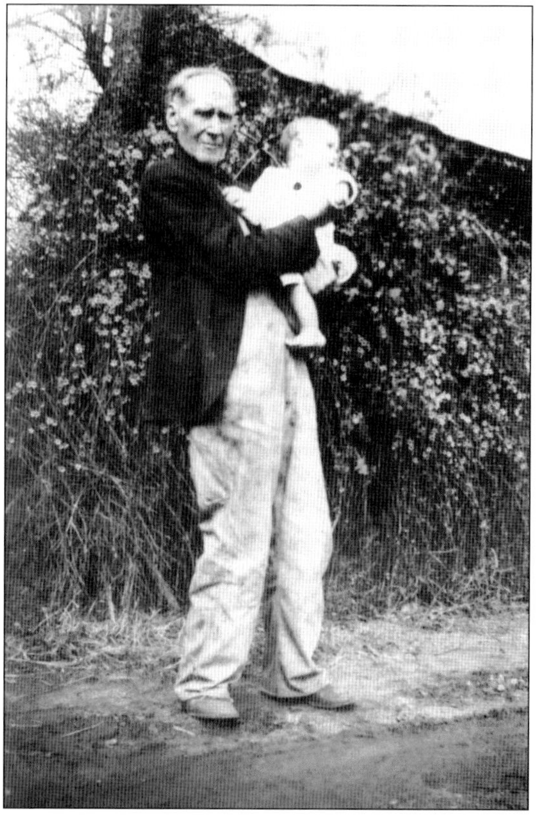

Jud and Grandchild. Jud Kendrick is seen with his grandson in the K Springs/Chelsea area in the 1930s or 1940s. Even after the Civil War, with promises of free land in Texas, most Kendricks stayed in Shelby County, and well over 150 years later, descendants still occupy the land in the area. (Courtesy of Shelba Nivens.)

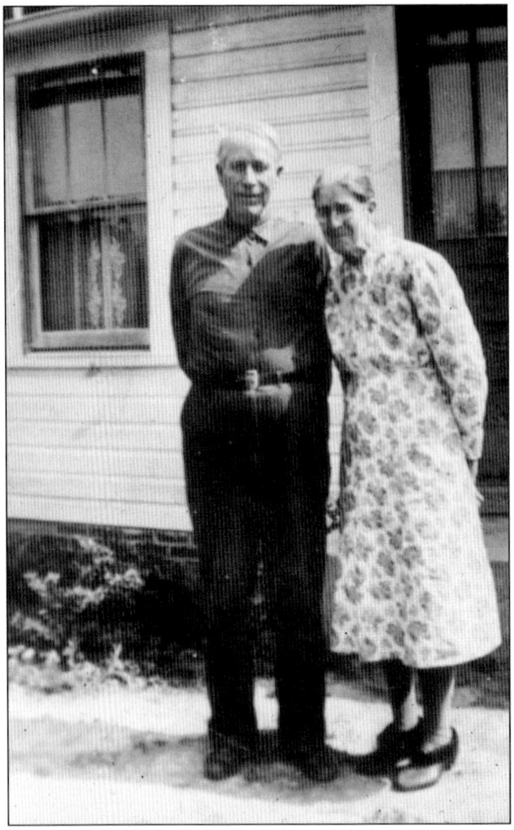

Tom Kendrick. T.L. "Tom" Kendrick was the son of Jud Kendrick. He married Louisa Shirley. "Uncle Tom," as he was called by some, was known for his "loud praying." In *Early Settlers of the K Springs/Chelsea Area* by Shelba Nivens, Tom's daughter Eunice recalled that he could be heard from the church throughout the community. (Courtesy of Shelba Nivens.)

Eunice Kendrick. Eunice Kendrick is seen singing at K Springs Church of God. Many of Uncle Tom's descendants, as well as other Kendrick relatives, have been active in the church for decades. Some of Tom and Louisa's other children are Gertrude, Luna, Aubrey, Oren, Donna, and Ozelle. (Courtesy of Shelba Nivens.)

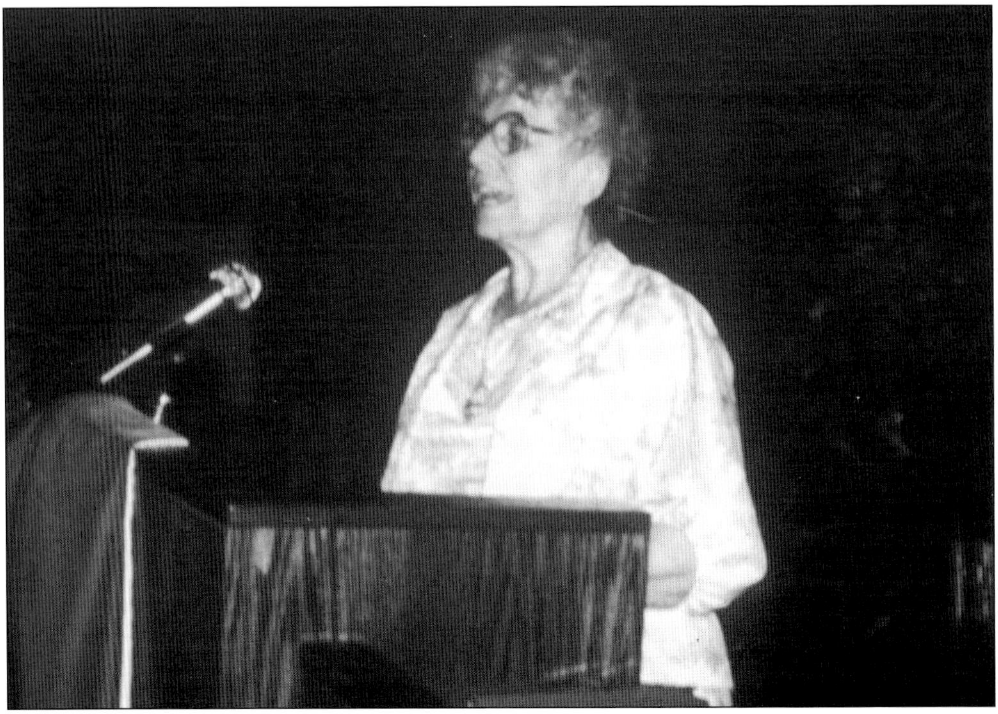

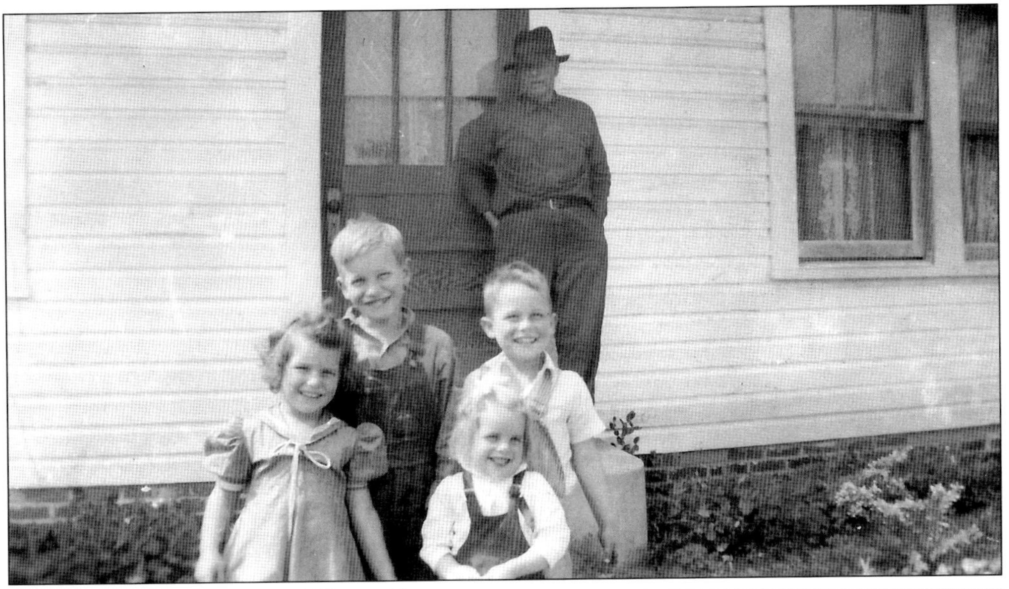

Tom and Grandchildren. This is Tom Kendrick with a few of his grandchildren, Donald, Craig, Rena, and Juanita. Around 1911, Tom Kendrick deeded two and a half acres of land for further work of the K Springs Church of God. Tom died in 1944, and Louisa died in 1962. Both are buried at Pleasant Valley Cemetery. (Courtesy of Shelba Nivens.)

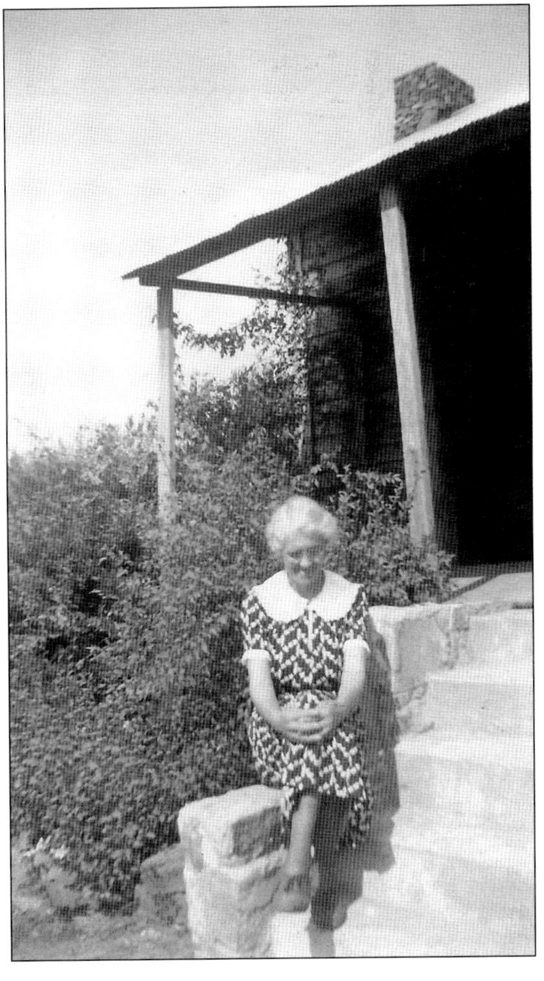

Jemima Kendrick. Jemima Kendrick is sitting outside of her home on Highway 39. Jemima was the daughter-in-law of Jud Kendrick. She and her husband, Elra, had three young children and a fourth on the way when Elra died of typhoid fever. She is quoted in a newspaper article by her daughter-in-law, the late Shelba Nivens, saying she conquered her hardships through her faith. (Courtesy of Shelba Nivens.)

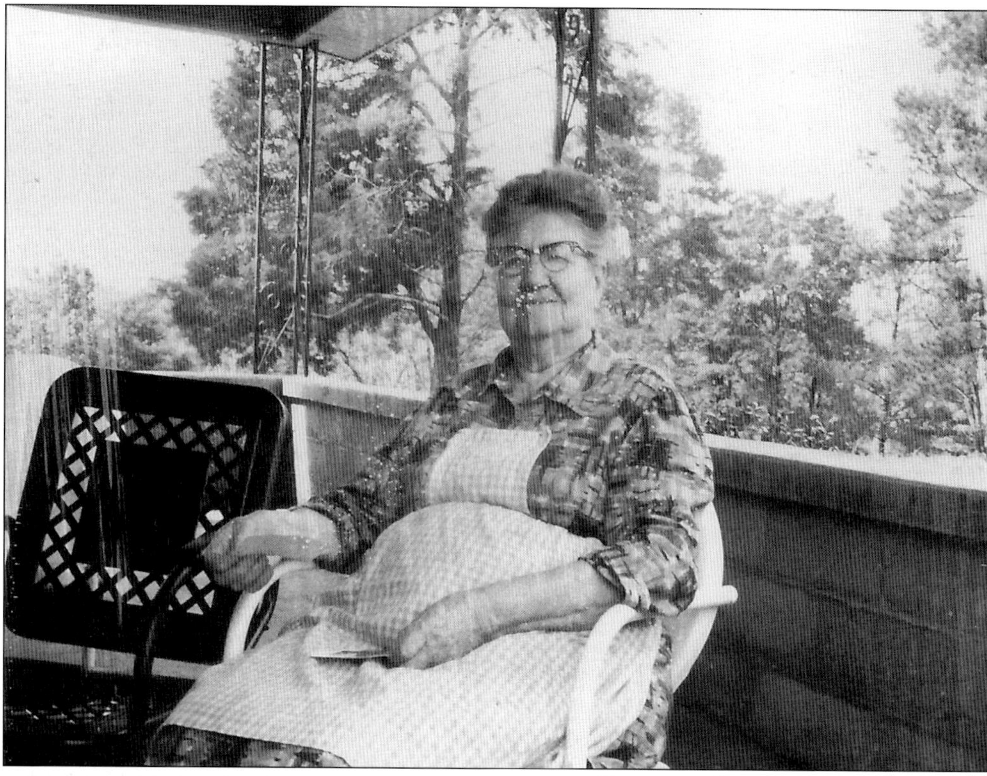

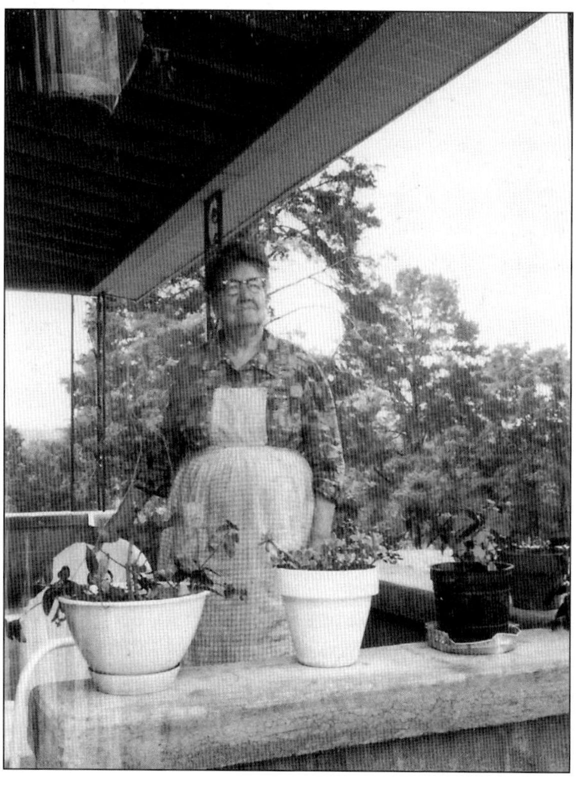

Dovie at Home. Dovie Chesser is pictured on her back porch in Chelsea for her 86th birthday in the 1970s. John Franklin Crane was Dovie's grandfather. The Chesser and Crane family have lifelong roots in Chelsea. Some Chesser descendants still live in the area. (Both, courtesy of Shelba Nivens.)

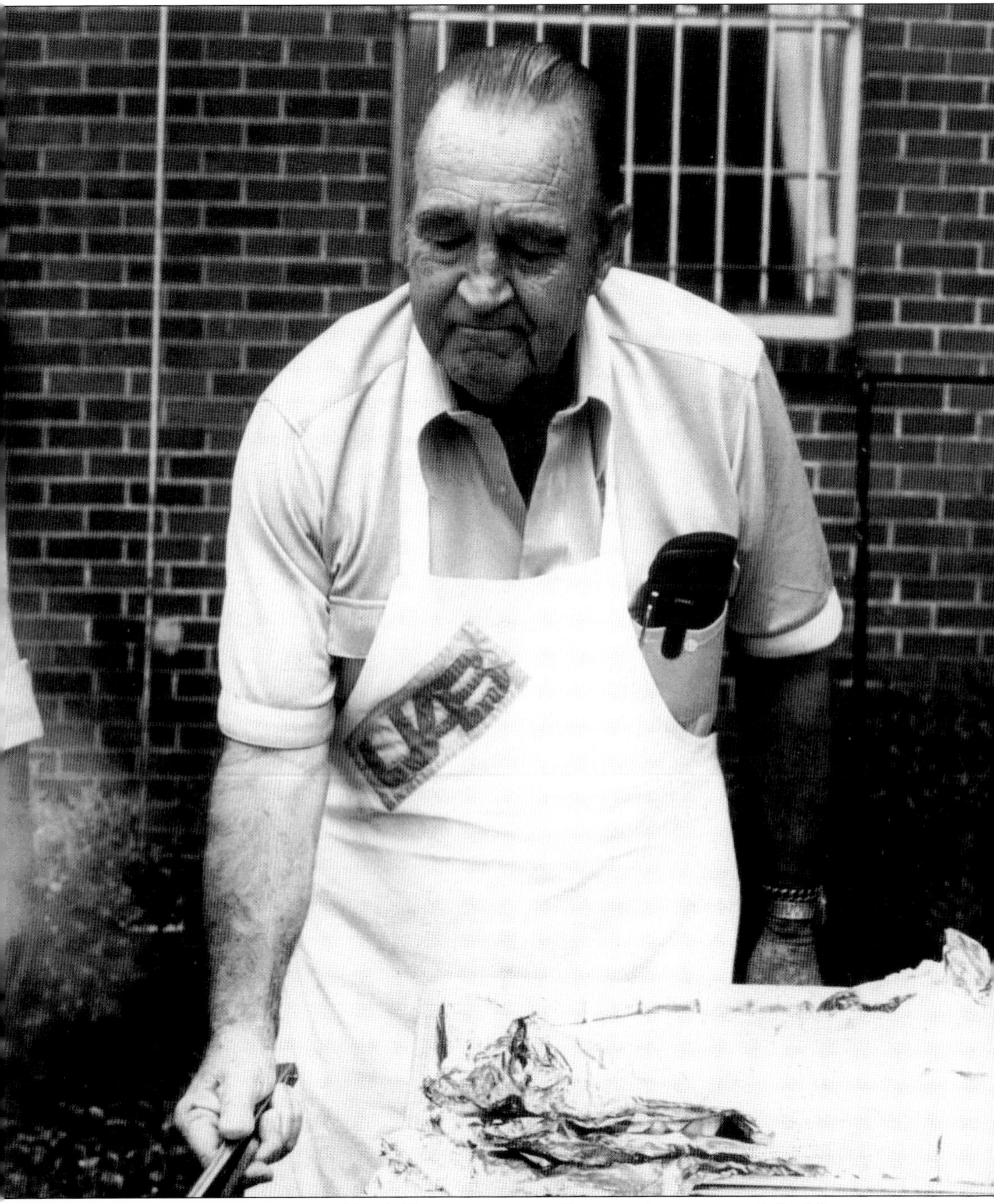

Lloyd Chesser, Grill Master. Lloyd Chesser is seen grilling on the campus of the University of Alabama at Birmingham. Stanley, the son of Margaret and Lloyd Chesser, was the director of campus services and grounds. Stanley Chesser died when he was 67 and is buried at Liberty Baptist Church Cemetery. (Courtesy of Olean Kenny.)

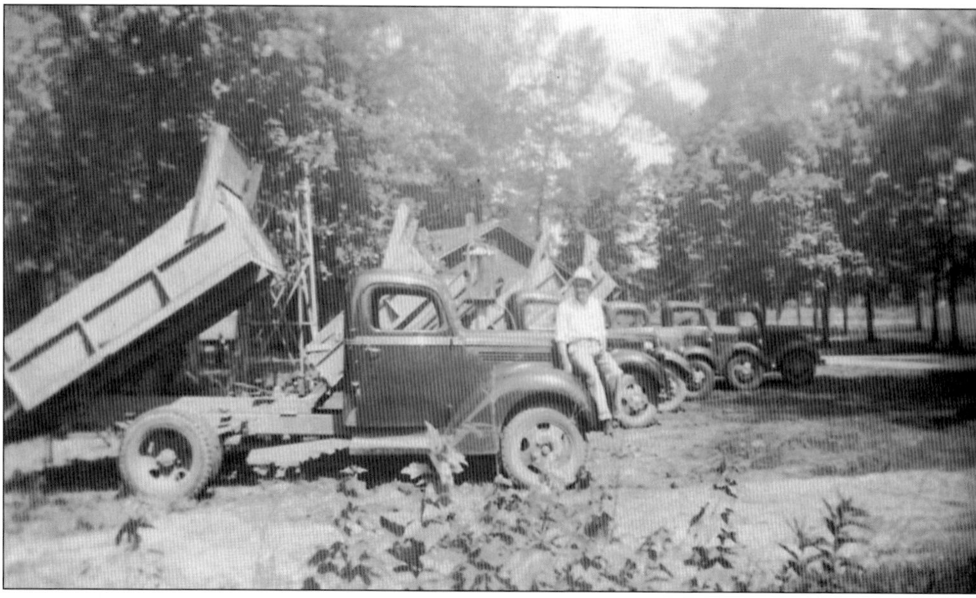

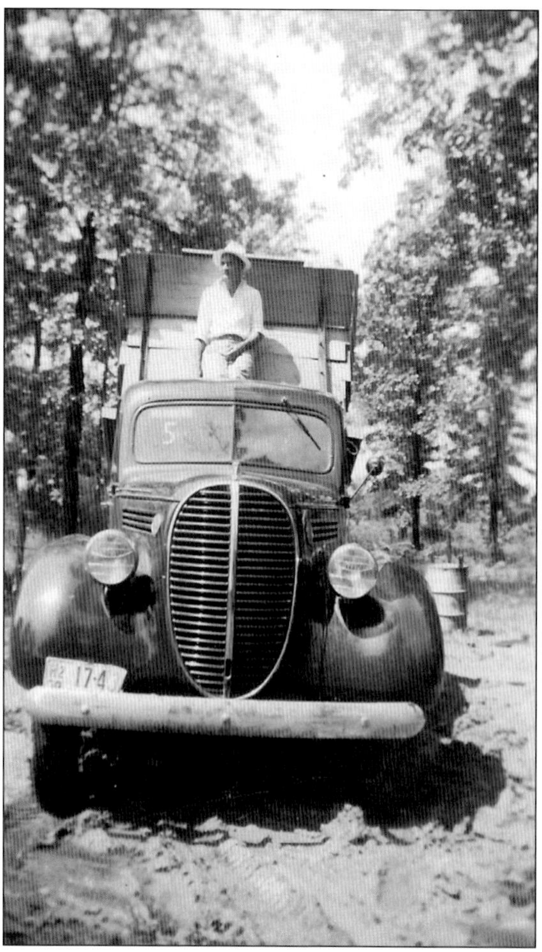

MURRAY NIVENS AND CHESSER CONSTRUCTION, 1930s. Murray Nivens is posing with trucks he used while working for L.P. Chesser Company. In the 1930s, Nivens constructed roads throughout the state for the company. He also once helped operate the Coalville Mine in Chelsea. The Nivens/Niven families in Alabama trace back to 1843 and in Chelsea to around 1848. Susan Nivens is recorded as marrying Daniel Wilder after the death of her first husband. Daniel Wilder received land in the "little narrows" area as well as the K Springs/Chelsea area. Some members of the Niven/Nivens families served in the Civil War. Some are buried in the Quinn Burying Ground, which was established in 1849 by Loftin Quinn, a War of 1812 veteran. (Both, courtesy of Shelba Nivens.)

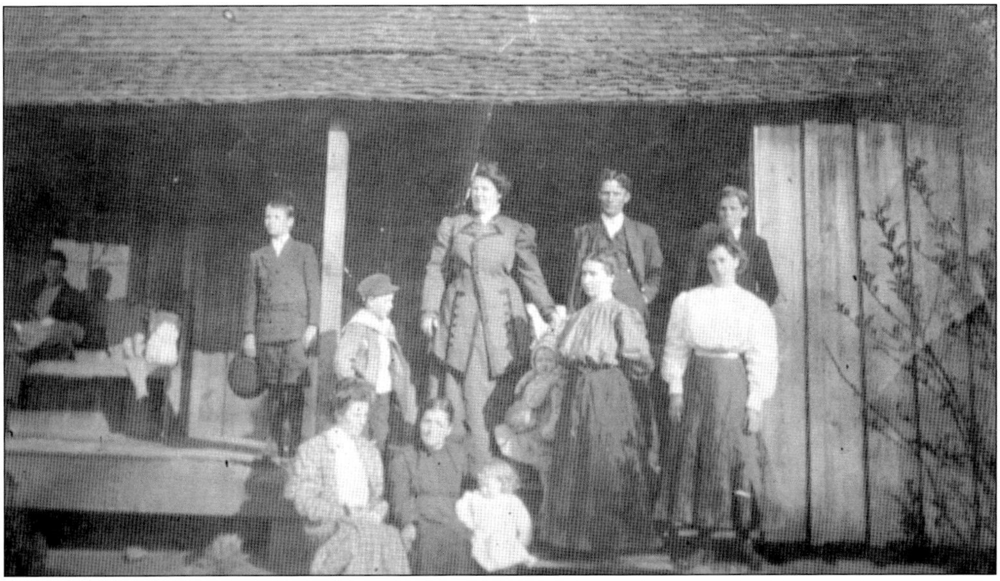

The Moore Family. Here, members of the William Riley and Frances J. "Fannie" Moore family are gathered on the porch of their home for an early 1900s photograph. Descendants of the Moore family went on to become influential teachers and administrators in the Chelsea school system. Riley and Fannie's grandson Lavonne Moore was a successful owner of Mountain View Lumber Company in Chelsea and was elected to the Shelby County Board of Education, where he served for 18 years. (Courtesy of Shelba Nivens.)

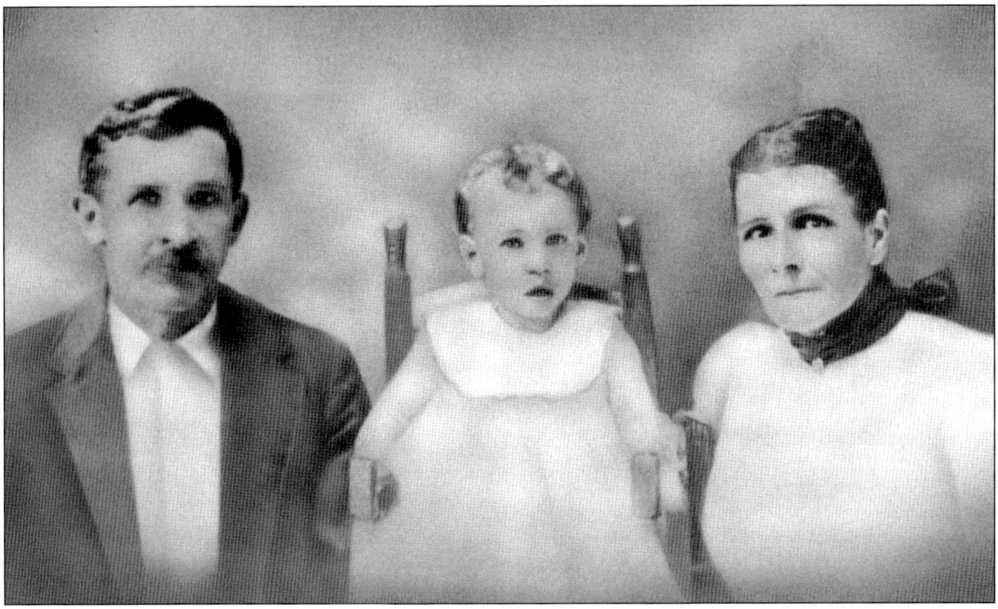

Riley and Fannie Moore. Riley and Fannie Moore are pictured with one of their children, Winfred. William Riley Moore married Frances J. Hadaway in 1877. Descendants of the Moore family still reside in Chelsea. (Courtesy of Shelba Nivens.)

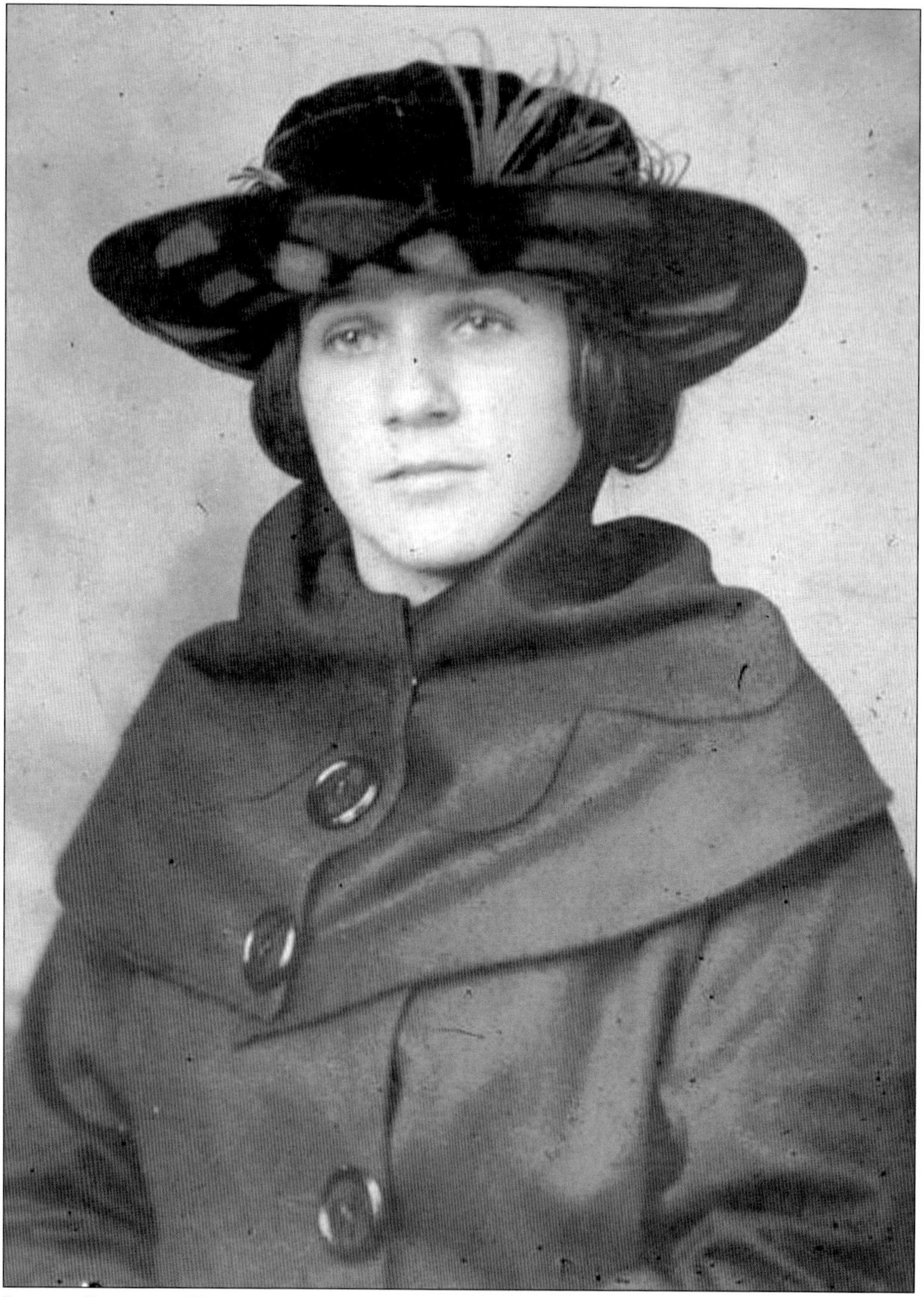

LILLIAN, LONGTIME TEACHER AND ADVENTURER. This is Lillian Tuttle Moore, who married Willis Moore, son of Riley Moore. Lillian taught school for decades at K Springs, Saginaw, Fourmile, Harpersville, Vincent, and Westover. She retired in 1967, and another journey began when she joined a church group that traveled around the world. When substitute teaching, she shared her adventures with students through photographs. (Courtesy of Shelba Nivens.)

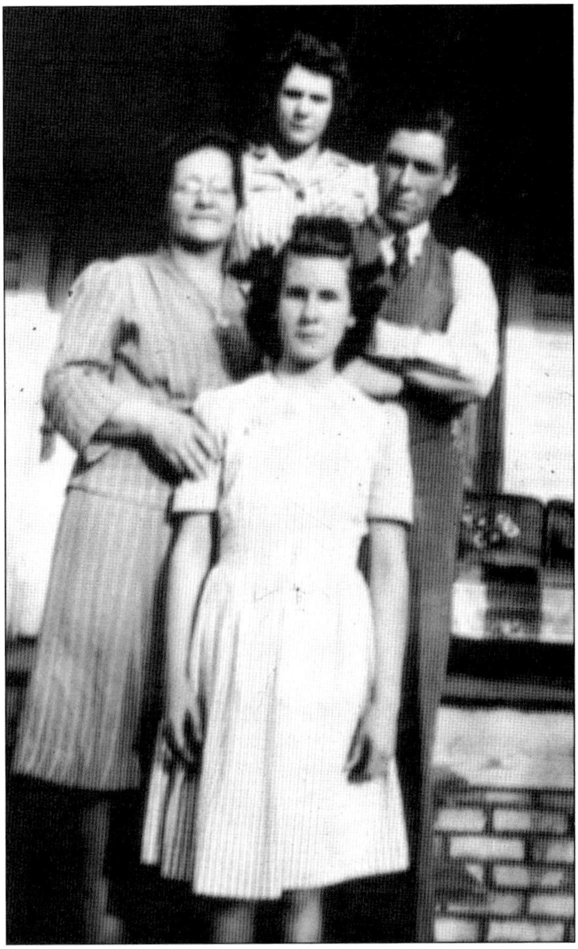

Lillian and Children. Earlene Moore is pictured with her mother, Lillian. Earlene, who lives in Chelsea, followed in her mother's footsteps and devoted her life to teaching for more than 30 years. In 1985, she was named Teacher of the Year in Chelsea. Earlene was later elected to Chelsea's first city council after the town incorporated in 1996. (Courtesy of Shelba Nivens.)

Herman and Charlene Moore. Herman and Charlene Moore are pictured shortly after their wedding. Herman was the brother of Earlene Moore. He joined the Navy near the end of World War II but was never deployed. Many Moore family members served in the Revolutionary War, War of 1812, the Civil War, World Wars I and II, and the Korean War. (Courtesy of Shelba Nivens.)

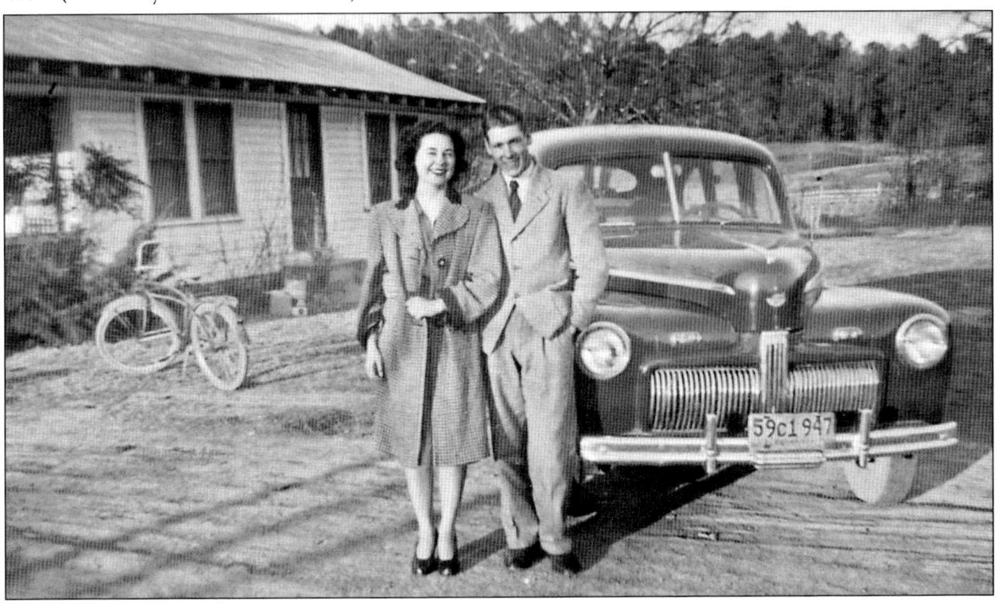

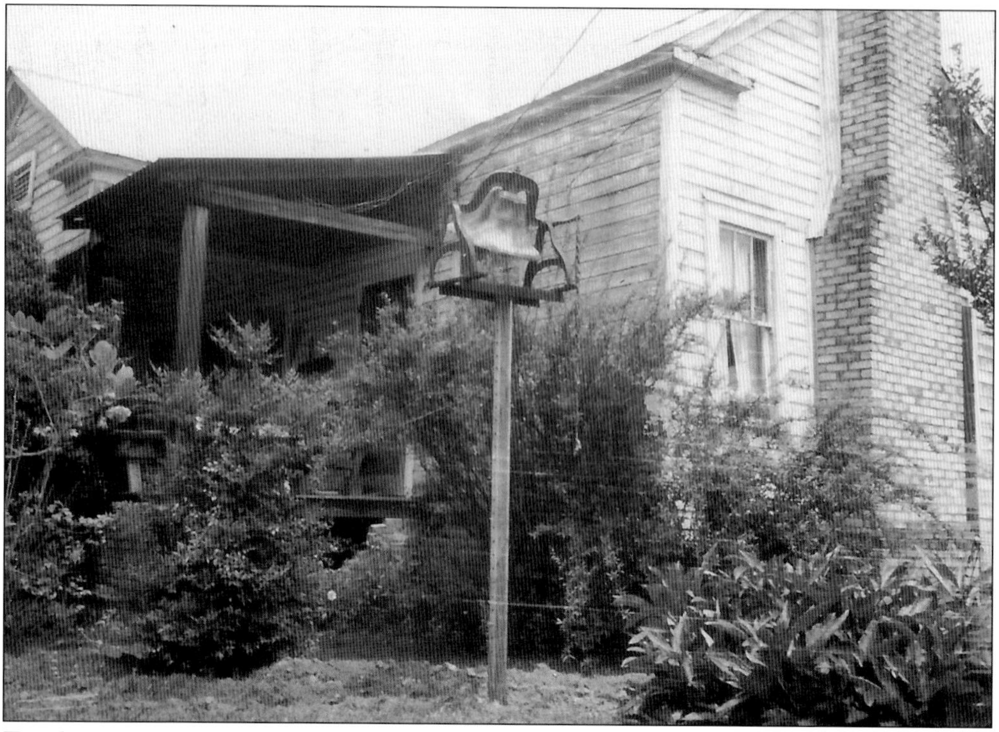

The Old Coalville Post Office. Pictured is the old Coalville Post Office on Highway 39. The building sat on 160 acres of land. Willis Moore, the son of Riley, and his wife, Lillian, bought the old Coalville Post Office to make it their permanent home. (Courtesy of Shelba Nivens.)

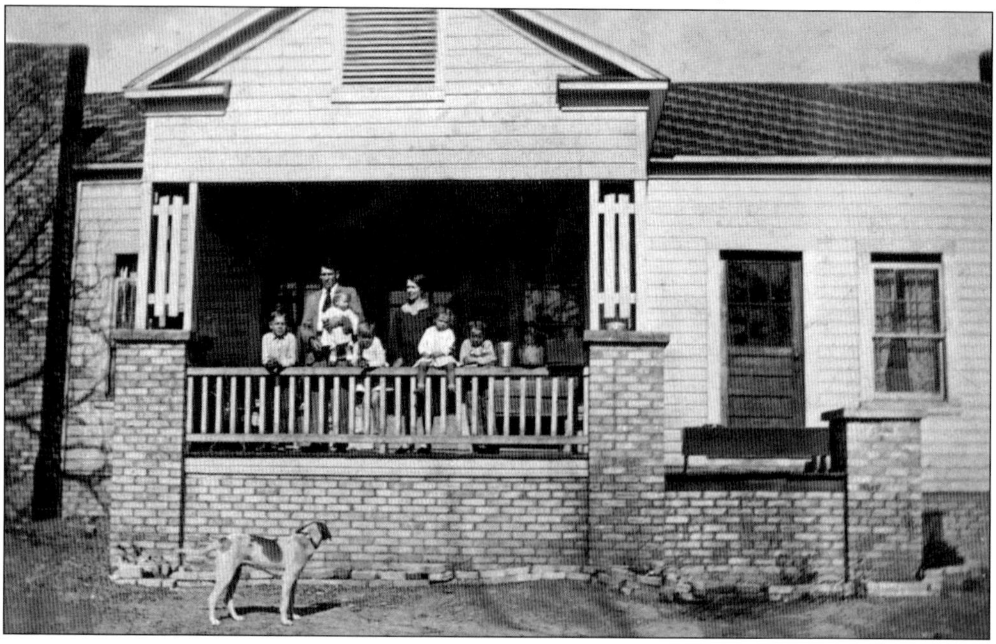

Willis and Lillian Moore's Home, 1933. Expansive renovations took place to make this building livable and comfortable. It became the permanent home for the Willis Moore family and was where their children grew up in Chelsea. (Courtesy of Shelba Nivens and SCHS.)

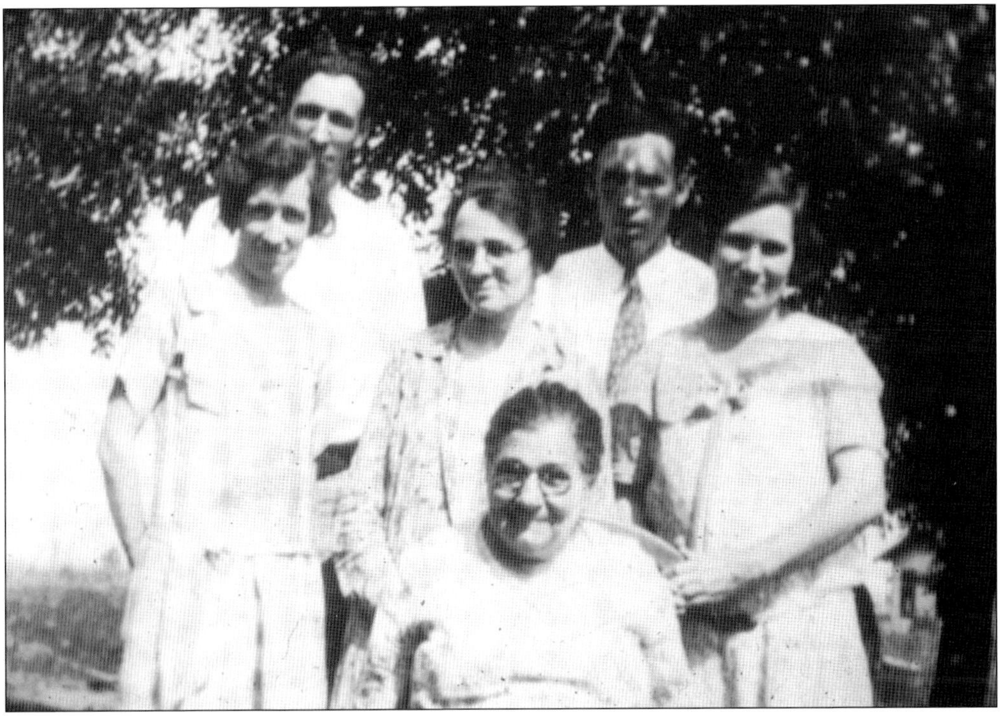

Fannie and Adult Children. Fannie (Frances) Moore is pictured with some of her adult children in the 1920s or 1930s. The children of Riley and Fannie Moore were J.R., Beatrice, W. Blanton, Bertie, Tabitha, Elizabeth, Eva, Willis D., Forest, and Winfred A. (Courtesy of Shelba Nivens.)

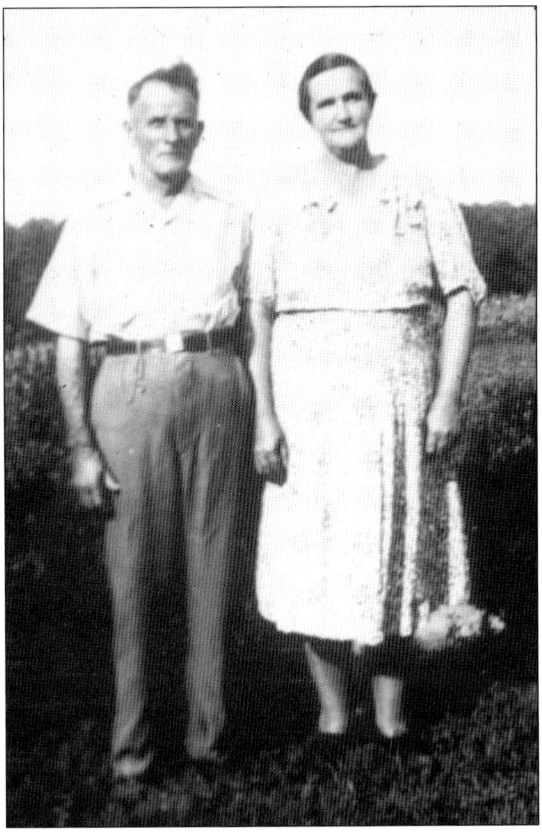

W. Blanton Moore and Josie Gamble Moore. W. Blanton Moore and Josie Gamble Moore are pictured here. They had nine children: Harold, Joe, Melvin, Anna, Bruce, Max, Claude, Pauline, and Sterling. (Courtesy of Shelba Nivens.)

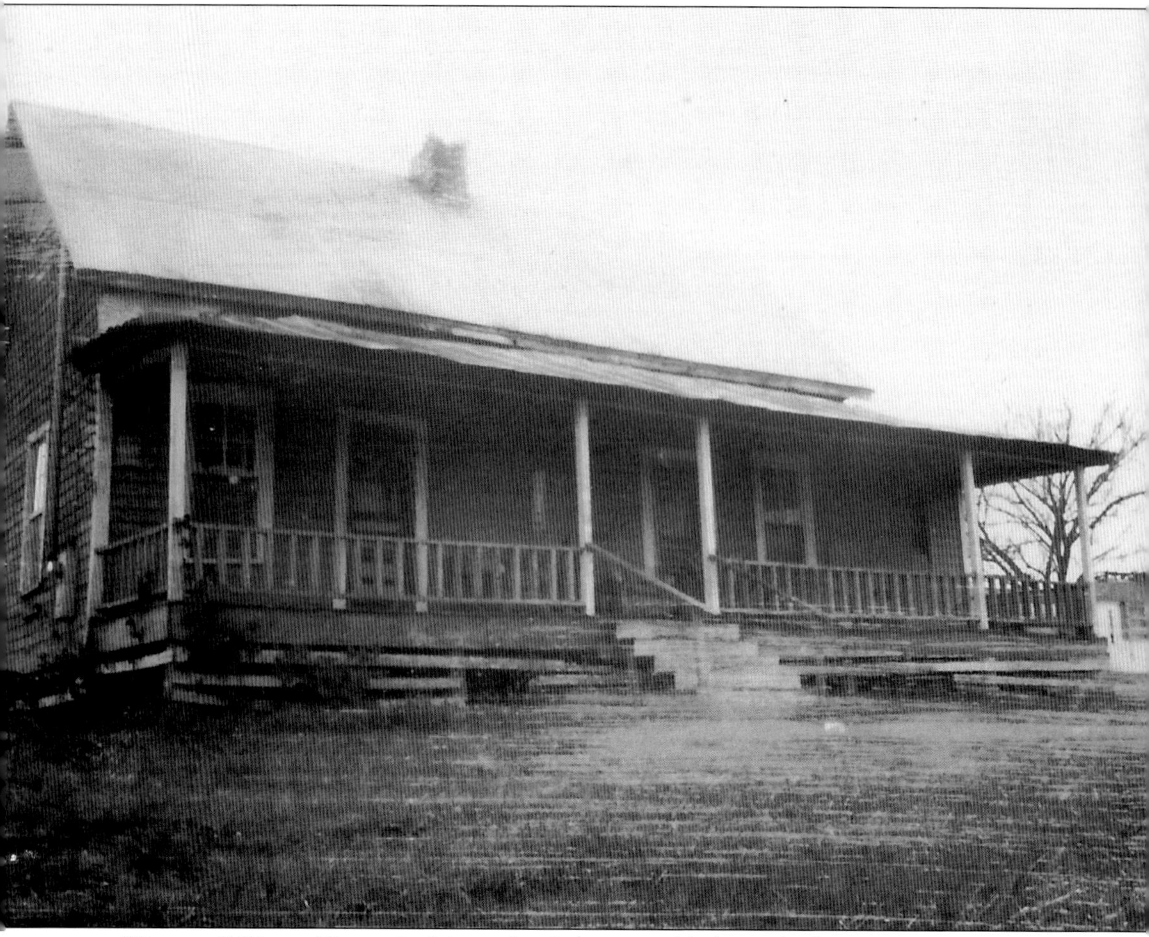

"Blantie" Home. This is the Moore family home in Chelsea, which was in the family for many years. Remnants of the home still exist today. (Courtesy of Shelba Nivens.)

Two

The Railroad and Businesses

As families began to settle in the hills of Melrose, they were starting not only homes but also opportunities for growth with businesses. One of the first businesses in Chelsea was a sawmill. There was later a barbershop, general store, post office, planing mill, gristmill, blacksmith shop, and cotton gin. The presence of the railroad, which came through Chelsea in 1908, allowed for expansion as more pioneers settled near the tracks. The railroad renamed the area Chelsea. One of the notable businesses that encouraged growth was started by local resident G.W. Weldon. He opened a general store around 1915. Frank Chesser opened Chesser Grocery as well. Chesser's son Lloyd later owned Rex's Tavern and then transformed it to the popular Lloyd's Restaurant, which is still in business.

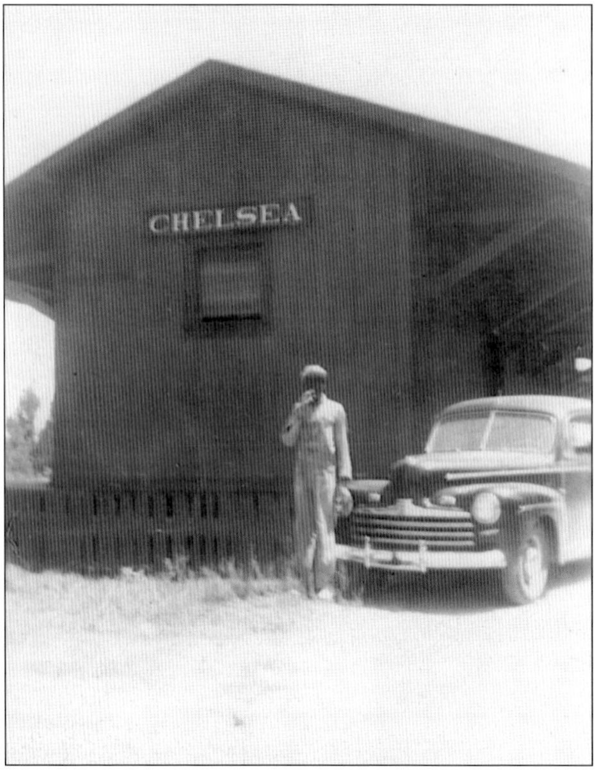

The Train Depot. This is the only existing photograph of the train depot that once served Chelsea. It was located near Highways 47 and 39. When the railroad came through town in 1908, it changed everything for Chelsea. The train allowed for commercial business as well as passengers to travel by means of the railway. (Courtesy of Chelsea City Hall Museum.)

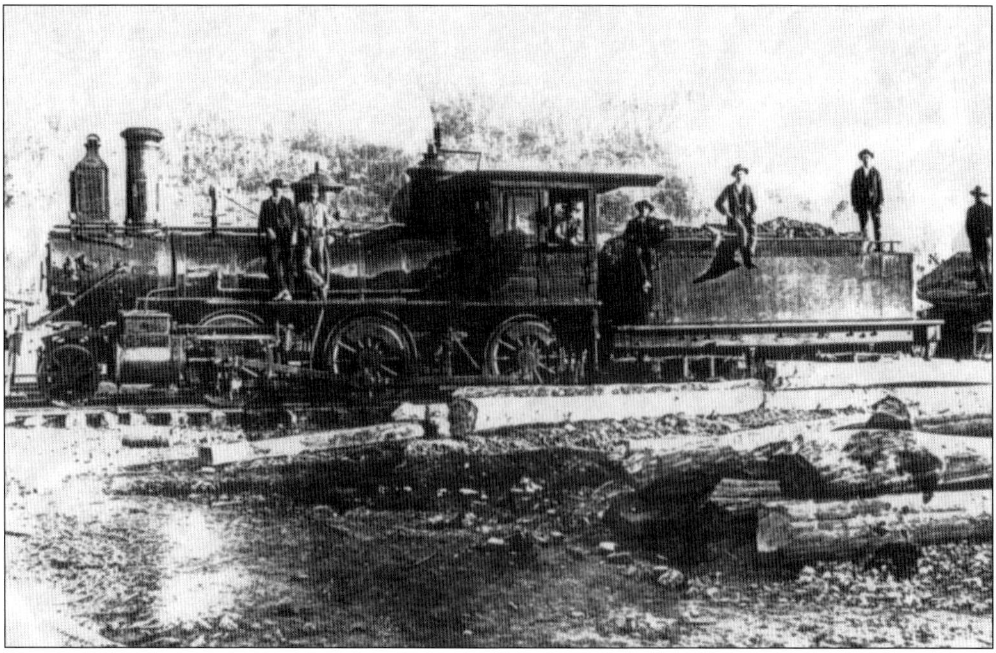

Railroad and Growth. This is a staged early-to-mid-1900s photograph of an engine with railcar. The Atlanta, Birmingham & Atlantic Railway was consolidated with others in 1967 and became part of the CSX Railway System that runs through Chelsea today. (Courtesy of Shelba Nivens.)

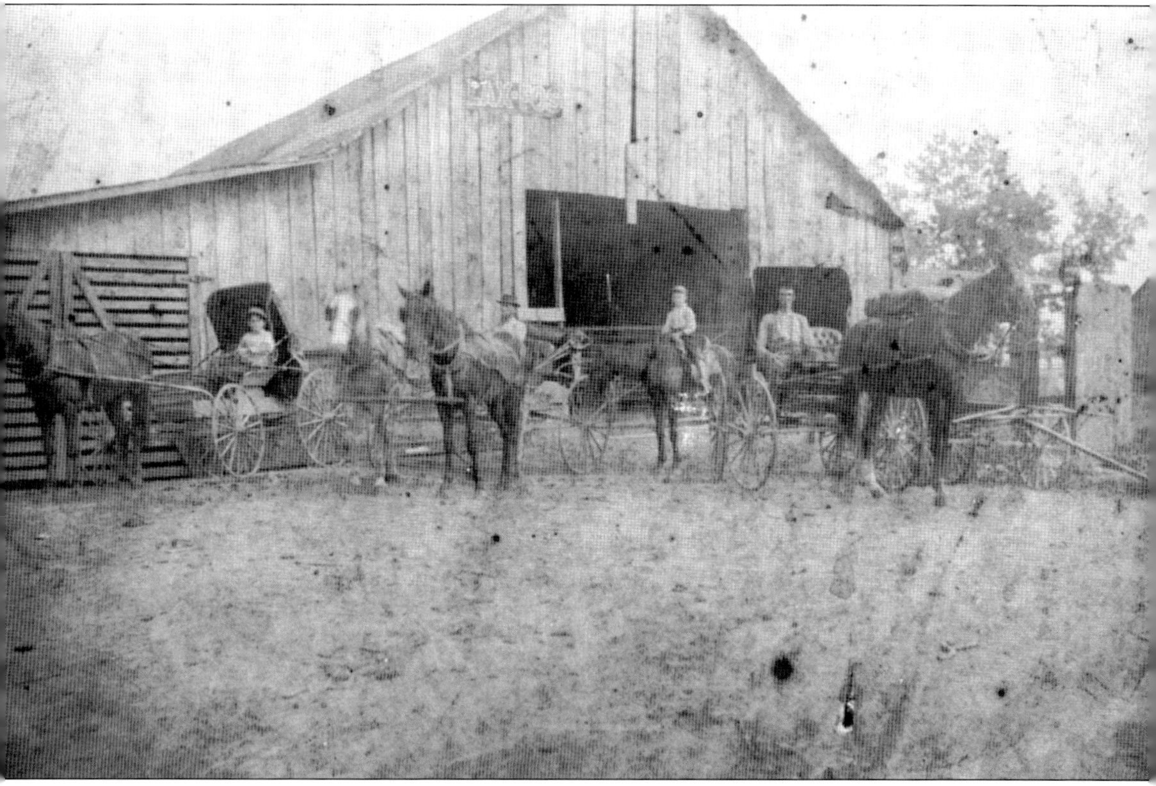

The First Sawmill. This c. 1900 photograph shows the first sawmill in Chelsea. (Courtesy of SCHS.)

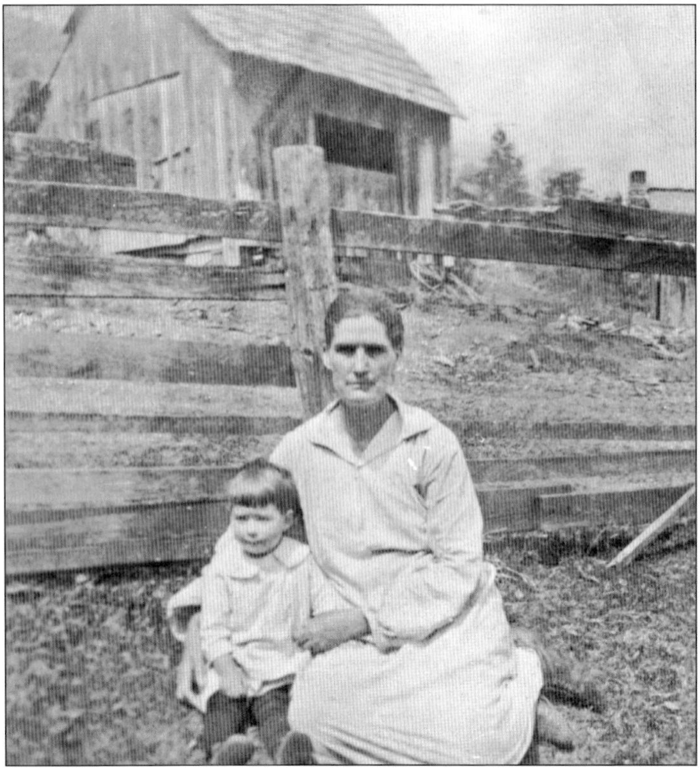

Midwife. This is Rosetta Simmons in 1926. She and this young child are at the Simmons home located in the Narrows. Rosetta was a midwife and traveled a large area to provide services for families. (Courtesy of SCHS.)

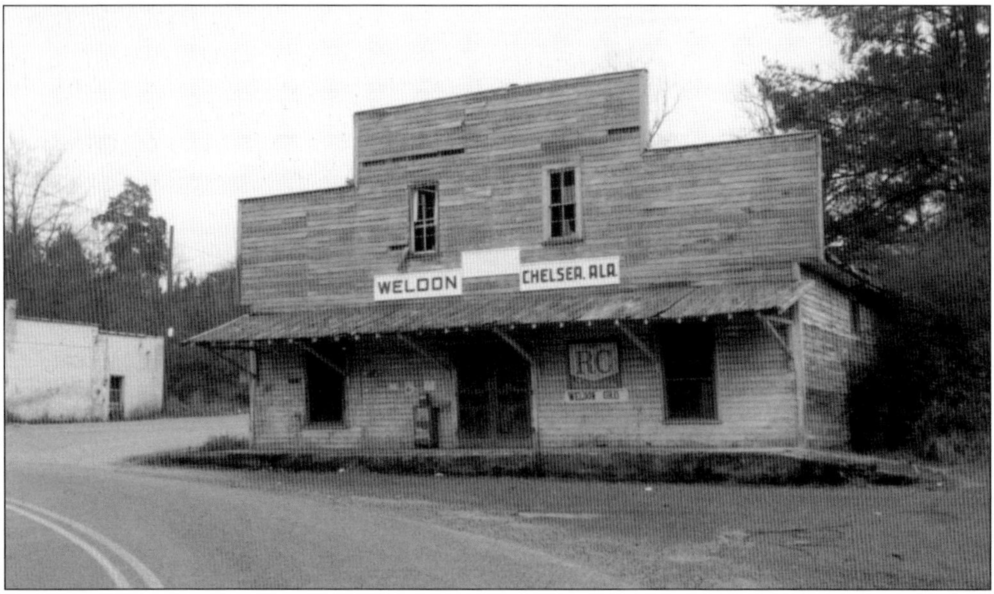

The Weldon Store. One of the first mercantile businesses after the railroad came through Chelsea was the Weldon Store. The store carried all types of goods for locals. G.W. Weldon even sold caskets that were stored on the top floor of the building. The caskets made for some fun times, with curious children playing and hiding in them. The original store was built in 1915. It burned and had to be rebuilt. The Weldon Store still stands today as a reminder of the past. The future of the store, however, is unknown as progress may call for it to be removed. (Courtesy of SCHS.)

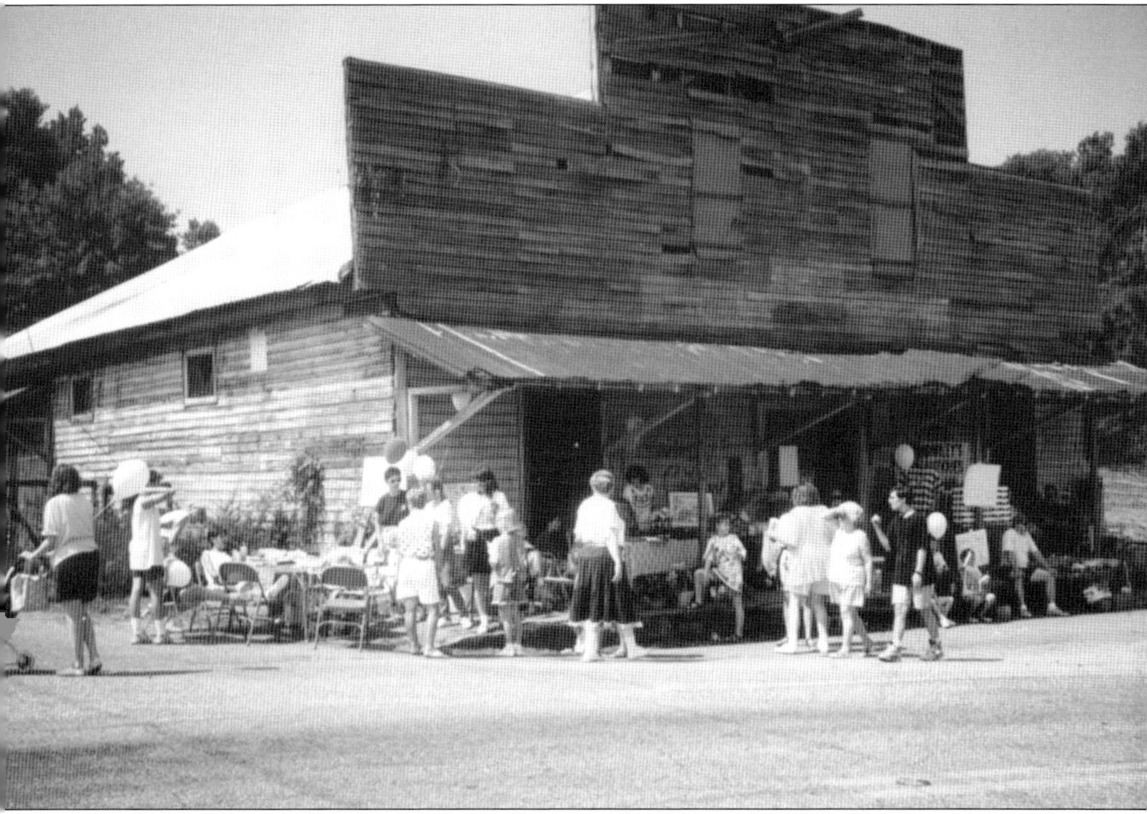

A Gathering Spot. Even after the Weldon Store closed for business, it was still a popular gathering spot for community events and announcements. Today, a large American flag is draped over the front of the old boards of the store, and a banner reads "God Bless America." Chesser Grocery was opened by Frank P. Chesser next door to the Weldon Store. Chesser later sold the business to local resident James Bailey. It was then called Chelsea Feed & Seed. (Courtesy of SCHS.)

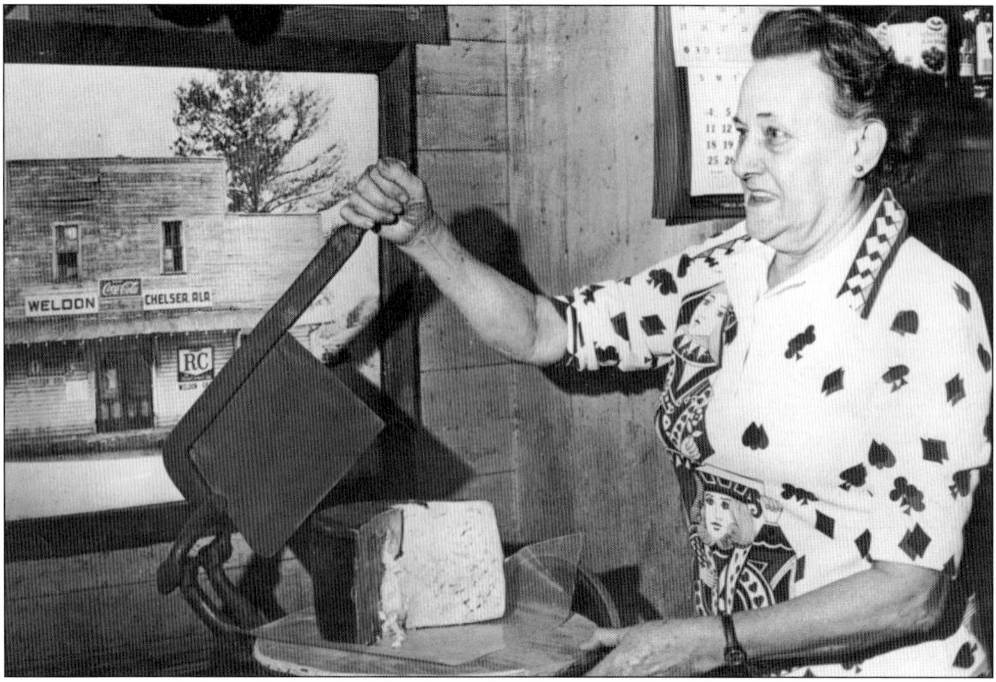

Velarie Running the Store. This is G.W. Weldon's daughter Velarie working in her father's store. Velarie took over the store from her father, managing it until 1979, when it was closed. She was known to have started the trend of trading ice-cream lids for a photograph of a famous face that she had hanging in the store: 10 ice-cream lids earned a child a celebrity photograph! (Courtesy of Olean Kenny.)

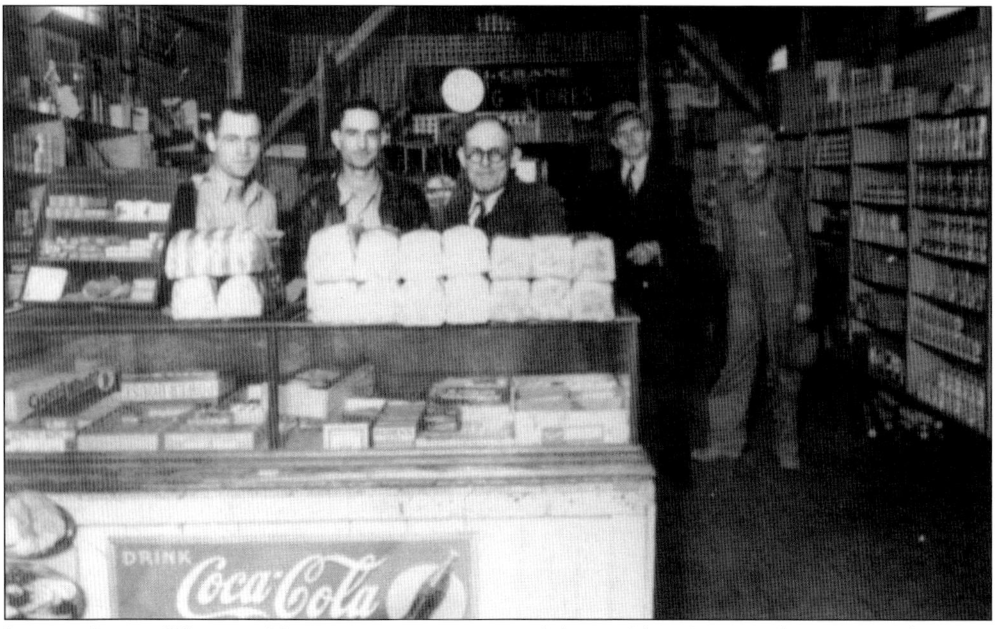

Locals Inside Weldon. Here is an interior view of the Weldon Store with patrons. The store carried all kinds of goods, including overalls for men. Over the years, the Weldon building has often been the center of attention for artists and photographers. (Courtesy of SCHS.)

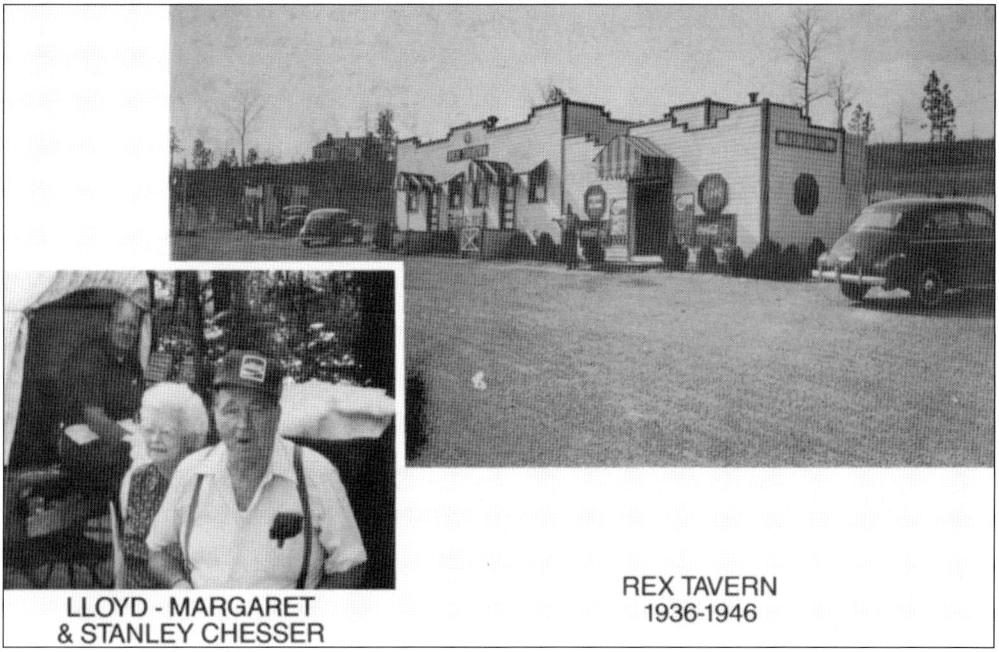

Margaret and Lloyd Chesser. Margaret and Lloyd Chesser are seen with son Stanley, sitting in the wagon. Lloyd opened Lloyd's Restaurant (first called Rex's Tavern) in 1936. It gained popularity and quickly became known for items like its onion rings. (Courtesy of Olean Kenny.)

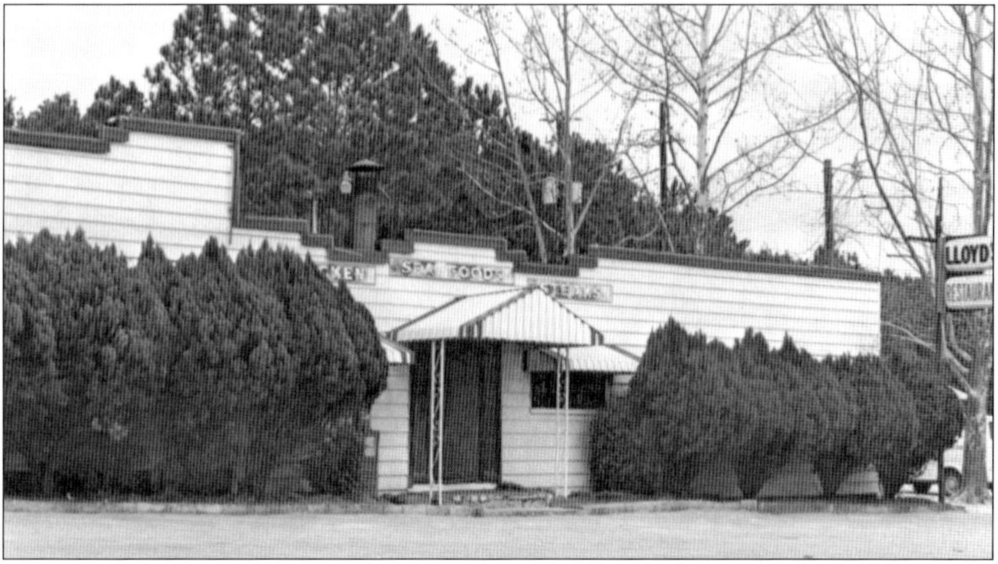

Lloyd's Restaurant. Pictured before it was moved to its existing location on Highway 280 near Greystone is Lloyd's Restaurant in Chelsea. In the early 1970s, Eli Stevens, who sold bread to the restaurant, bought it when the Chessers were ready to get out of the restaurant business. At the time, the business was located on old Highway 280. Soon after Stevens bought it, the new Highway 280 was built, bypassing the old highway and restaurant. Stevens needed to relocate. He had a choice to move it east toward Harpersville or west, closer to Birmingham. He chose toward Birmingham, and the restaurant is located today in North Shelby County near Highway 119. Just as in the past, it is well known for its barbecue and onion rings. (Courtesy of Shelba Nivens.)

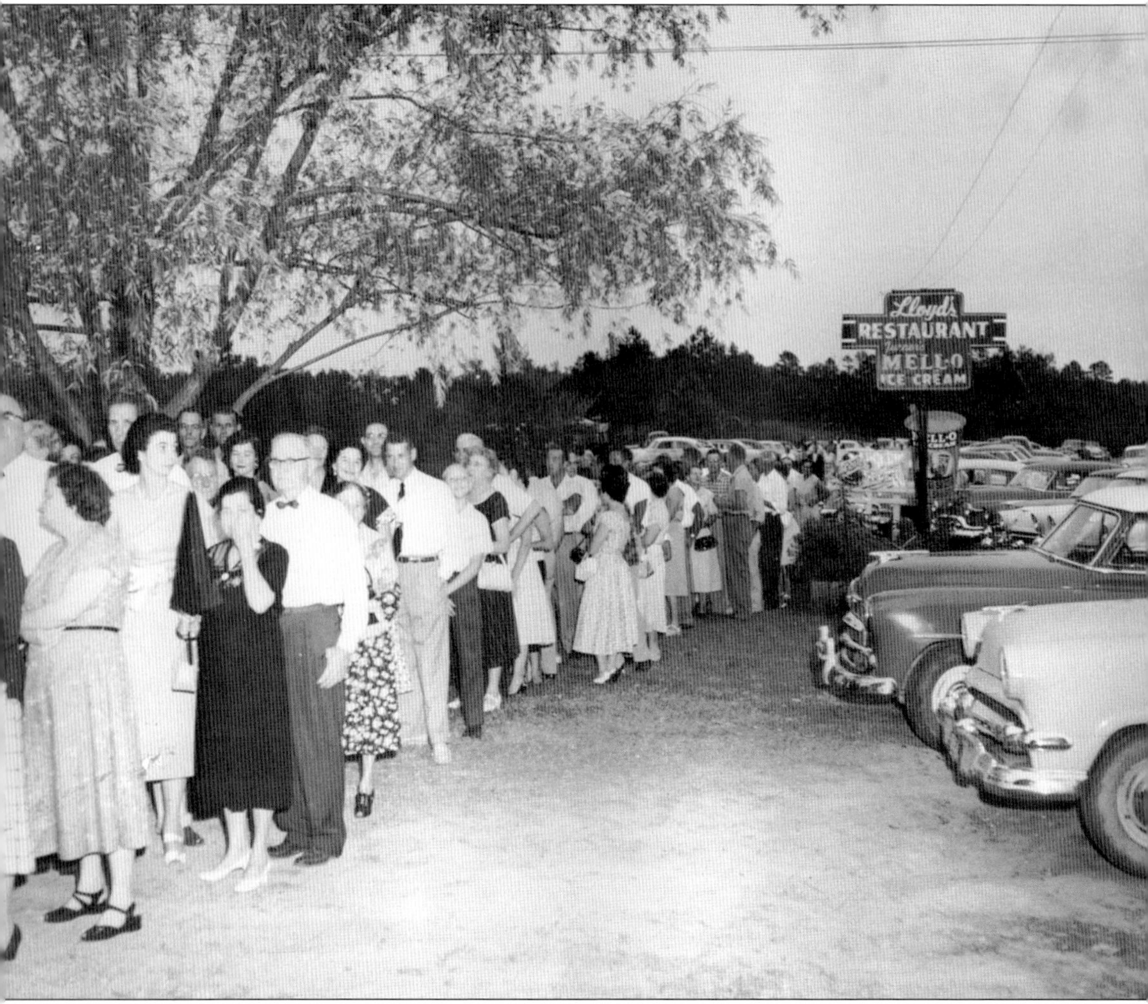

A Line at Lloyd's. A line is pictured here outside of Lloyd's restaurant. Mayor Earl Niven recalls that not only was business good, but also that a telephone booth had just been installed, and many people were anxious to learn how to use it. (Courtesy of Olean Kenny.)

Three

Church Bells

A theme of humble beginnings continues in the story of Chelsea's churches. Several churches date back more than 100 years. The roots of Liberty Baptist Church can be traced back to the early 1840s. The first pastor was Rev. T.P. Holcombe, who was buried at the church's cemetery. By 1852, Liberty Baptist was one of 10 constituting churches of the Shelby Baptist Association.

K Springs Church of God was formed in 1903. It first consisted of a group of believers meeting in each other's homes. A building was erected in 1908 near Yellowleaf Creek, and the congregation met there for the next 20 years. By 1927, they were holding services in the old K Springs schoolhouse. That building was torn down in 1931, and the present-day white building was established. Today, that building is leased to a ministry. It was not until 1978 that the congregation built its present-day church on Highway 39. Today, the church is called "the Connection." Recently, the discovery was made that more than 30 veterans are buried in the K Springs Cemetery. There was a drive to raise money to erect a veteran's memorial in their honor.

Mount Calvary Baptist Church's history goes back more than 150 years. It is located four miles from Chelsea on Highway 74. The church was constituted by four families, the Mooneys, Stones, Minors, and Shaws, in September 1859. At one time, the church was a hub of activity for citizens of the area. There was a school affiliated with the church, and located nearby were a pony express and several businesses, such as a sawmill and post office. After World War I, the church had an interim where families took care of it. Then, a church in neighboring Columbiana sponsored it as a mission church. The people who began attending were longtime members who had moved away. The church is not active today, but is cared for and attended to by descendants of former congregation members. They maintain the building through donations.

Pleasant Valley Church and Cemetery is a long-standing church that is well over 100 years old. Some of its first members were Jud and Carrie Kendrick. Many longtime Chelsea residents are buried at Pleasant Valley Cemetery.

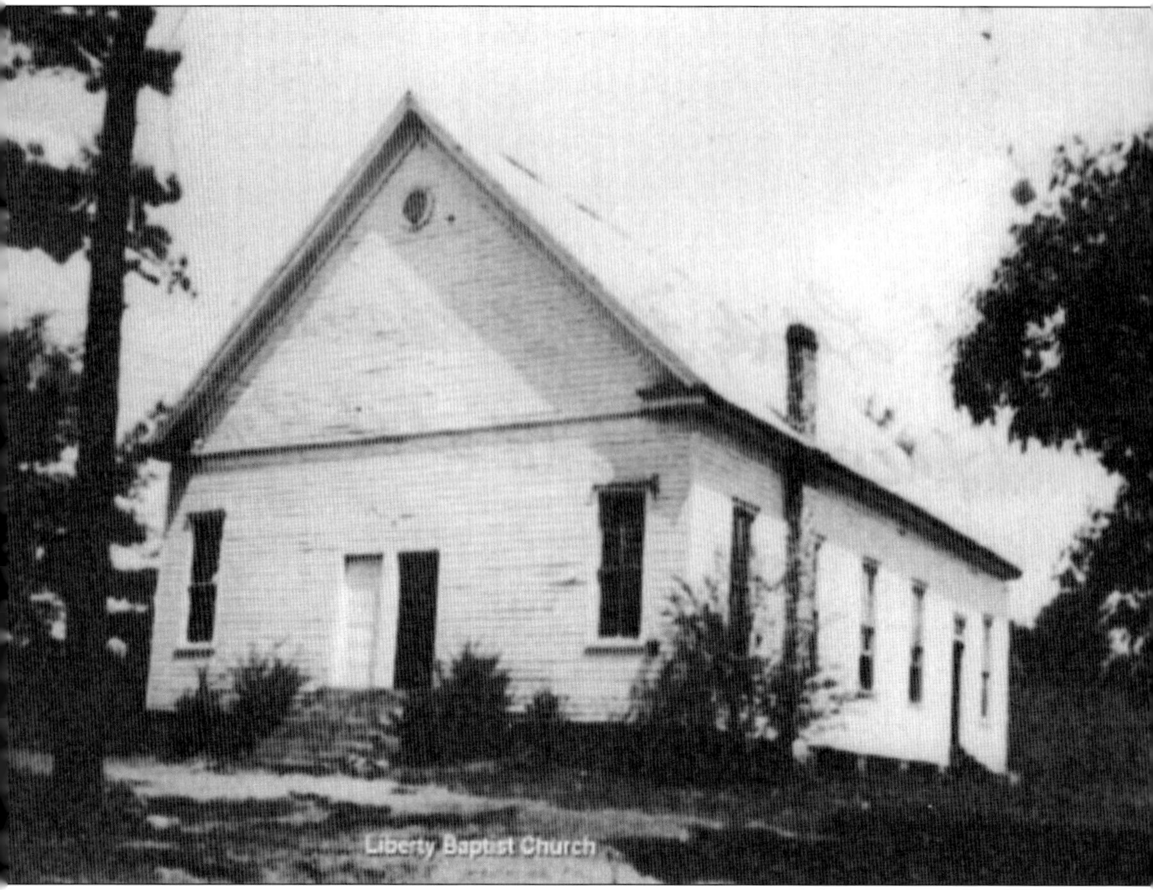

LIBERTY BAPTIST CHURCH. Dating back to around 1843, Liberty Baptist Church was among the first 10 original churches of the Shelby Baptist Association. Its first pastor was T.P. Holcombe. In 1961, the building that stands today was renovated and turned around to face Highway 47. Much of the original building is enclosed in what is Liberty Baptist's Chapel. A newspaper article from 1977 details quite an interesting find related to the church. A hunter near the property came upon a trash pile in the woods. In the rubble was an old church ledger ranging from 1910 to 1930. Also, the original deed was found; it was handwritten and dated 1857. The paperwork detailed three acres of land bought by the church for $5. There was also a list of members who split from the church to form Mount Signal Baptist. The salary of the minister was noted as $93 per year in 1913. (Courtesy of Chelsea Historical Museum.)

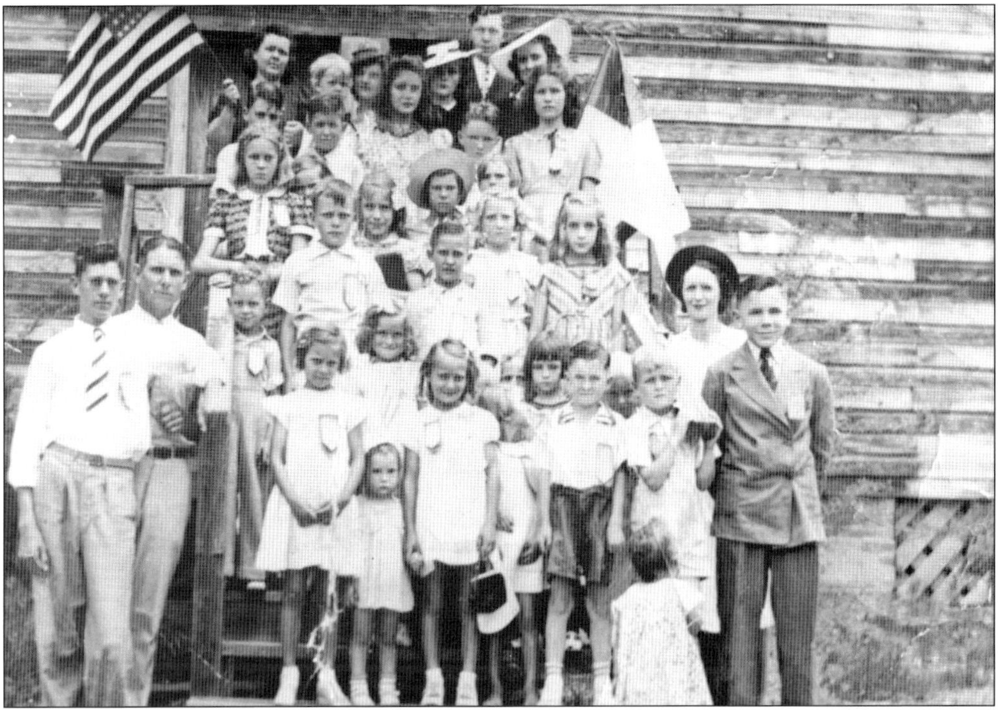

First Vacation Bible School Class, Liberty Baptist Church, 1940. Pictured in front of Liberty Baptist Church is its first vacation Bible school class in 1940.

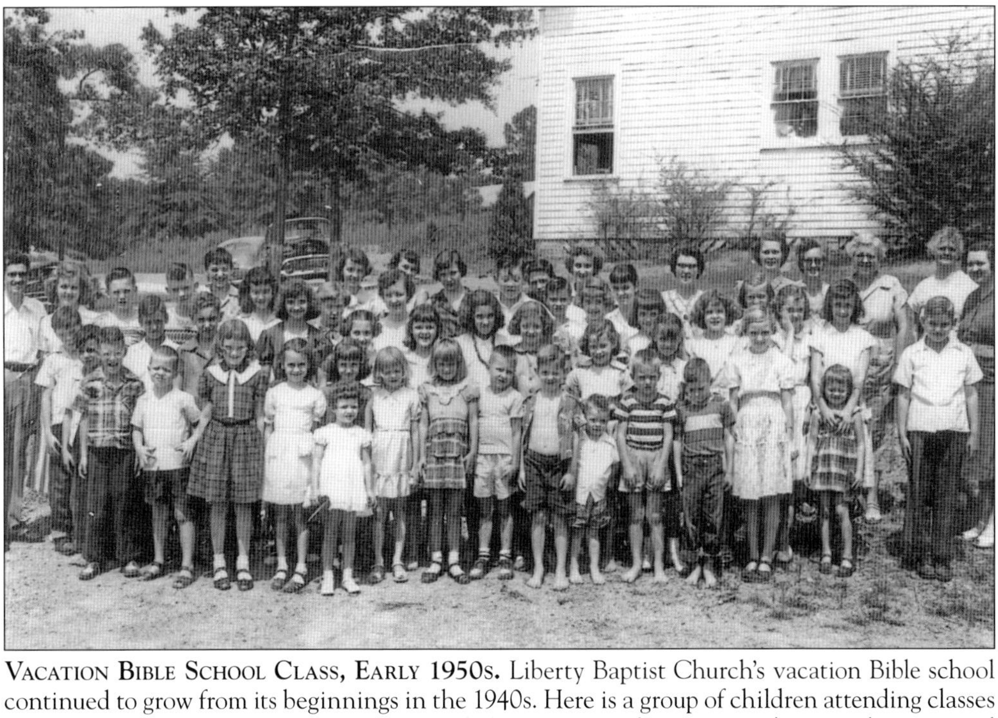

Vacation Bible School Class, Early 1950s. Liberty Baptist Church's vacation Bible school continued to grow from its beginnings in the 1940s. Here is a group of children attending classes at Liberty Baptist in the early 1950s. Future Chelsea mayor Earl Niven is in the second row, second from the left. (Courtesy of Olean Kenny.)

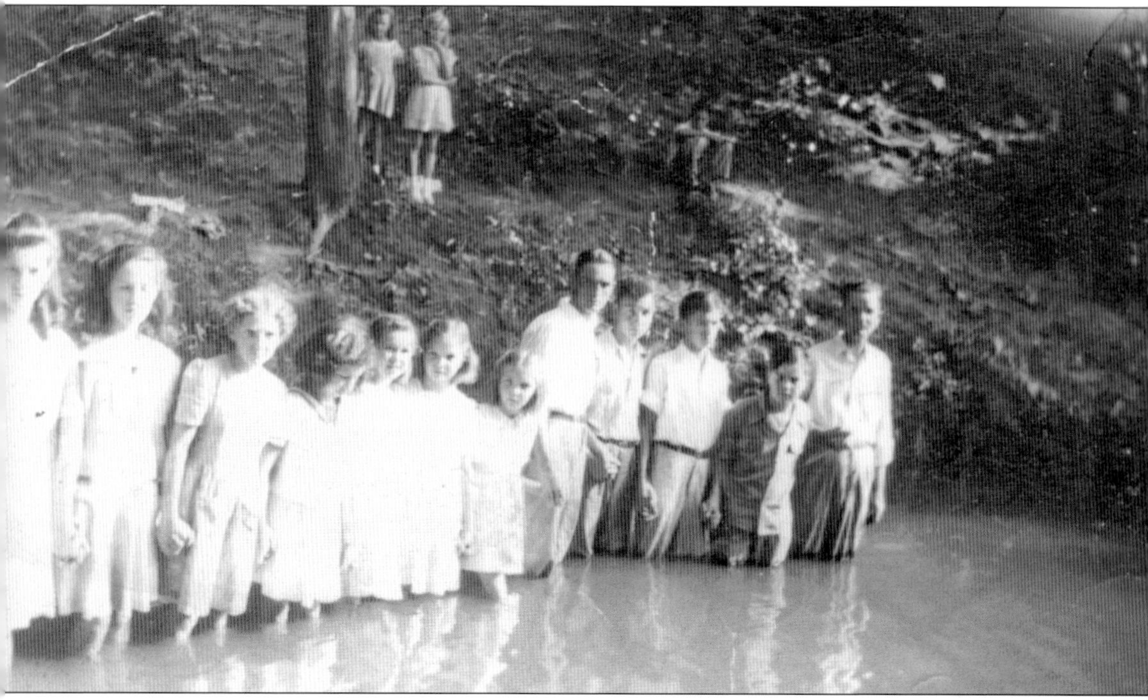

Baptism in Yellowleaf Creek. A Liberty Baptist Church baptism is taking place in Yellowleaf Creek around 1942. From left to right are Doris Williamson, Charlene Quarles, Mary Ellen Holcombe, Nita Williamson, Geraline Ellison, Jo Holcombe, Katy Ray Blackerby (her father, Lewis, was the principal of Chelsea School in the 1940s), Leroy Taylor, unidentified, C.J. Ellison, unidentified, and E.E. Wells, the preacher. Standing on the hillside are Juanita Weldon and Marilyn Weldon. The baptism took place under the bridge before the train tracks where Highway 47 is located. (Courtesy of Mrs. Jo Moore.)

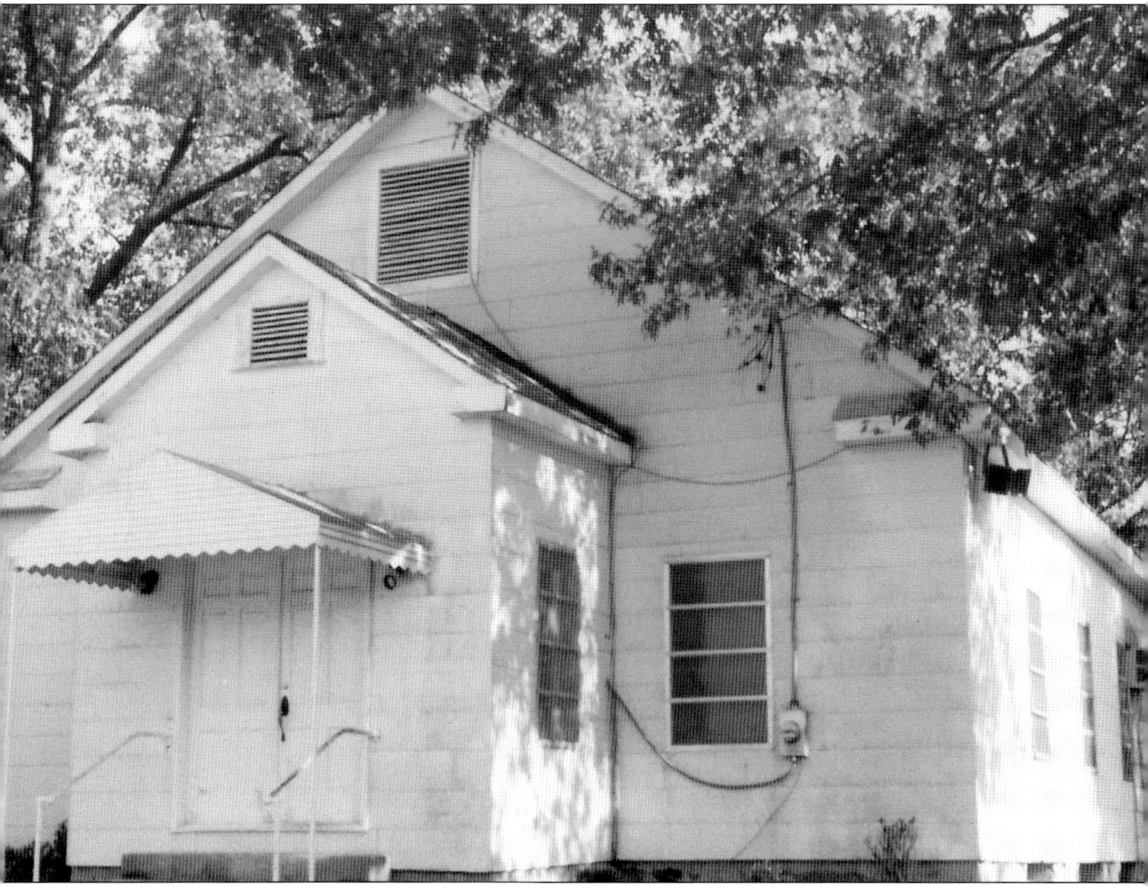

K Springs Church Founding. K Springs Church of God was born around 1903. A small group began meeting in homes and later moved to the old Morris schoolhouse in East Saginaw, not far from Chelsea. Around 1927, services were held in the old K Springs schoolhouse and would remain there for the next 20 years. In 1931, that building was torn down, and a small white building was erected that remains today off of Highway 39. (Courtesy of SCHS.)

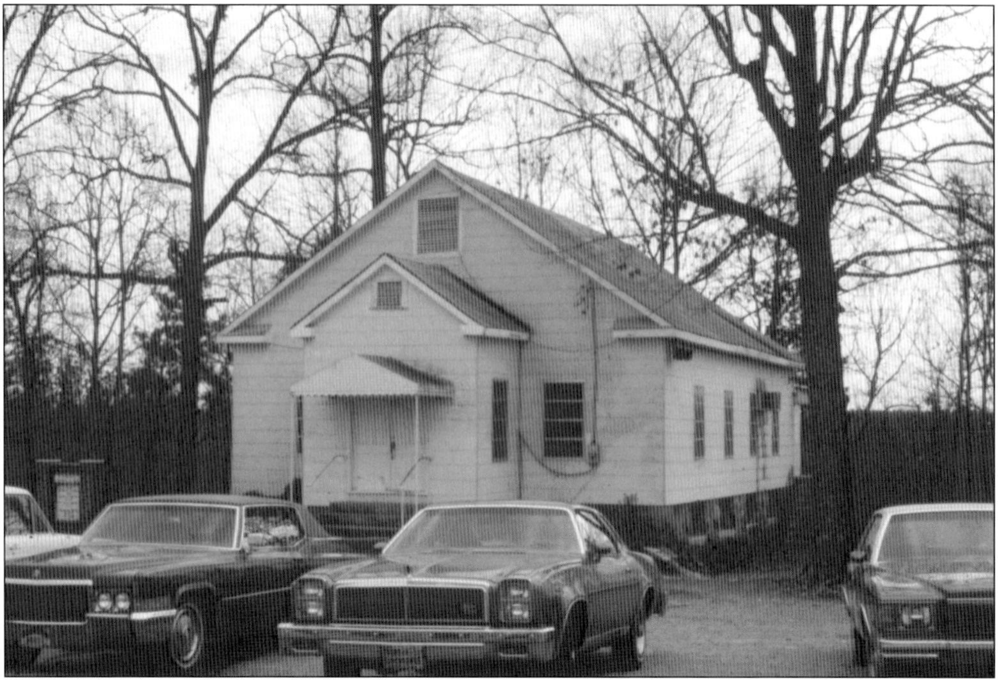

K SPRINGS CHURCH. The small, white building that first housed K Springs Church of God is leased today and used for other ministries. In 1977–1978, the brick building was built across from the original structure. The church has been renamed "the Connection." (Courtesy of Shelba Nivens.)

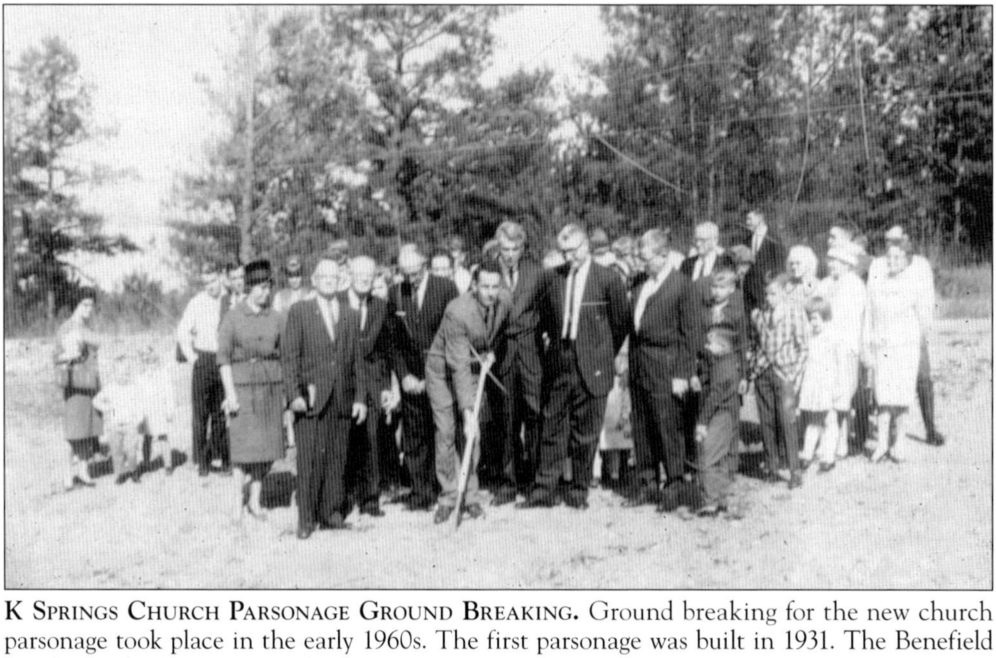

K SPRINGS CHURCH PARSONAGE GROUND BREAKING. Ground breaking for the new church parsonage took place in the early 1960s. The first parsonage was built in 1931. The Benefield family was the first to live in this parsonage as well as the first to live in the brick parsonage built in the 1960s. The area's springs served as sources of water for the surrounding homes for years. (Courtesy of Shelba Nivens.)

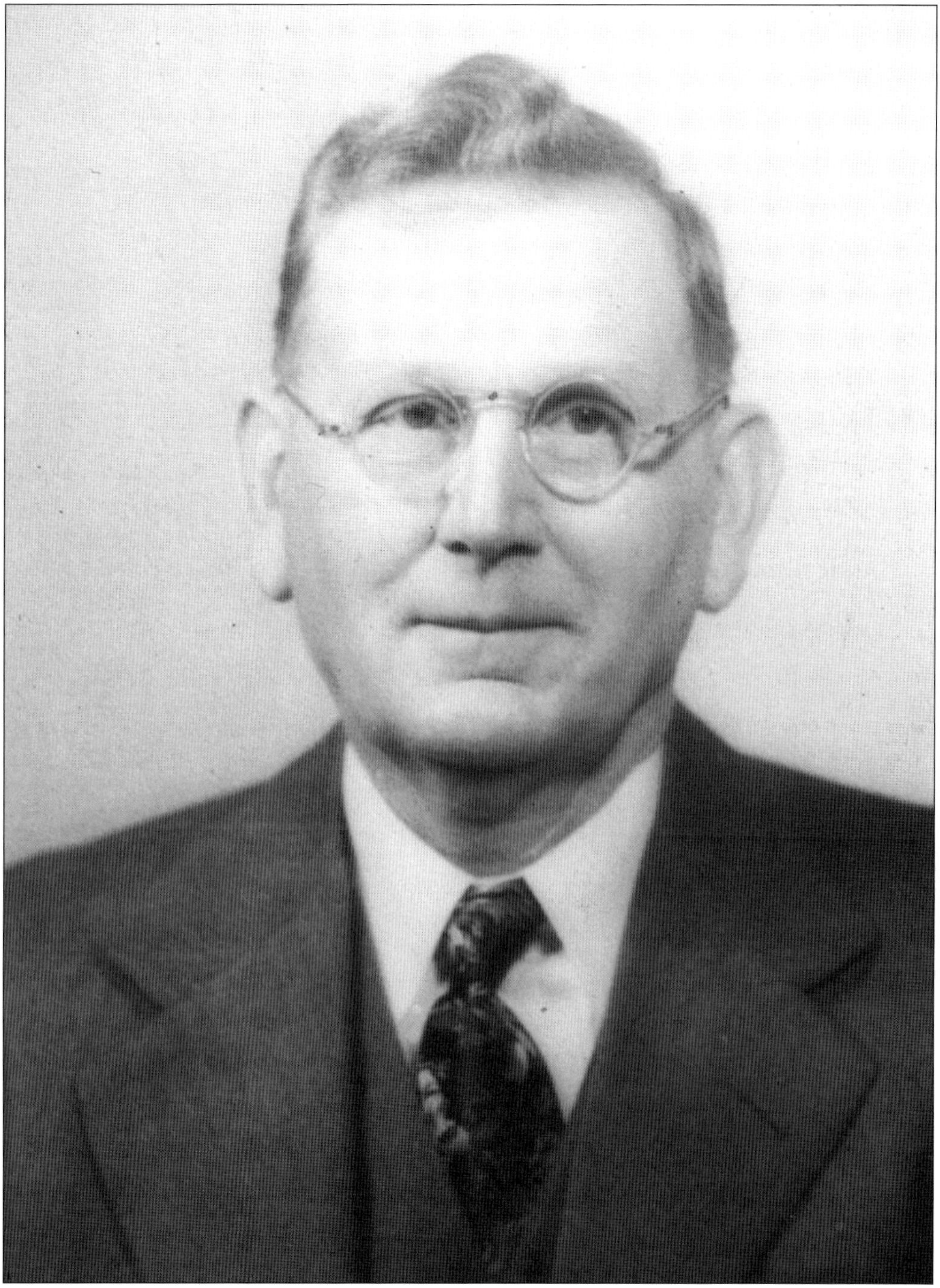

Reverend Benefield. The first full-time pastor of K Springs Church of God was Rev. A.W. Benefield in 1932. Before the church had a full-time pastor, ministers came from various places to preach. It is noted that sometimes they had to take the log train or even handcars that were propelled manually down the train track. Reverend Benefield served the church for 25 years and retired in the community. He died in 1972 and is buried at K Springs Cemetery. (Courtesy of Shelba Nivens.)

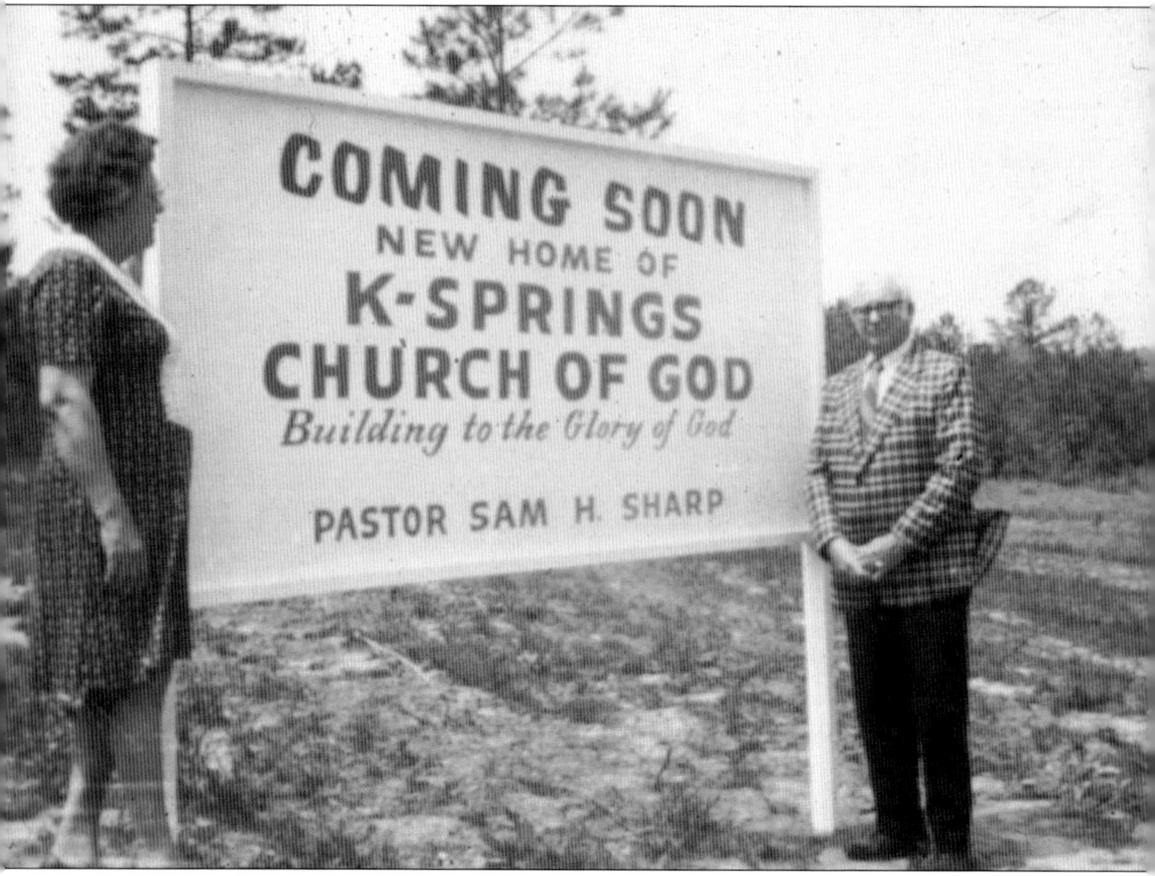

K Springs Coming Soon. In 1976, the congregation of K Springs voted to bring in Pastor Sam Sharp from South Carolina to lead them in building and ministering their new church. It was completed by 1978 and seated more than 300 people. Reverend Sharp and his family returned to South Carolina after the project, and Rev. Norman Pirkey took over. (Courtesy of Shelby Nivens.)

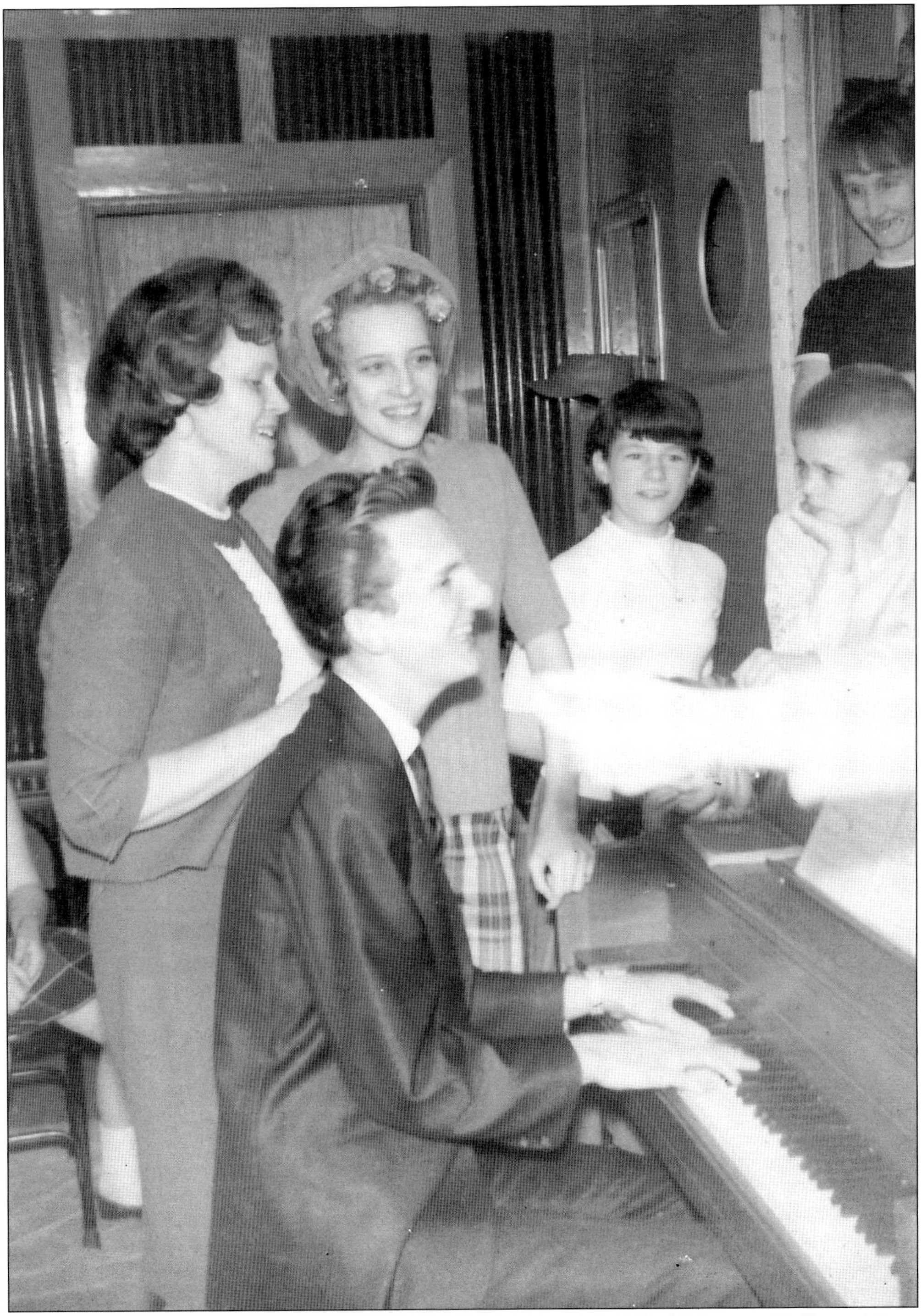

Billy and Suzy Minor's Home. This is a 1950s photograph inside the home of Billy and Suzy Minor. Pictured are James Wayne Lee at the piano, along with Shelba Nivens, Toney Nivens, and Debra Minor King. Shelba Nivens recalled that James Wayne Lee would go around to different churches singing hymns. (Courtesy of Shelba Nivens.)

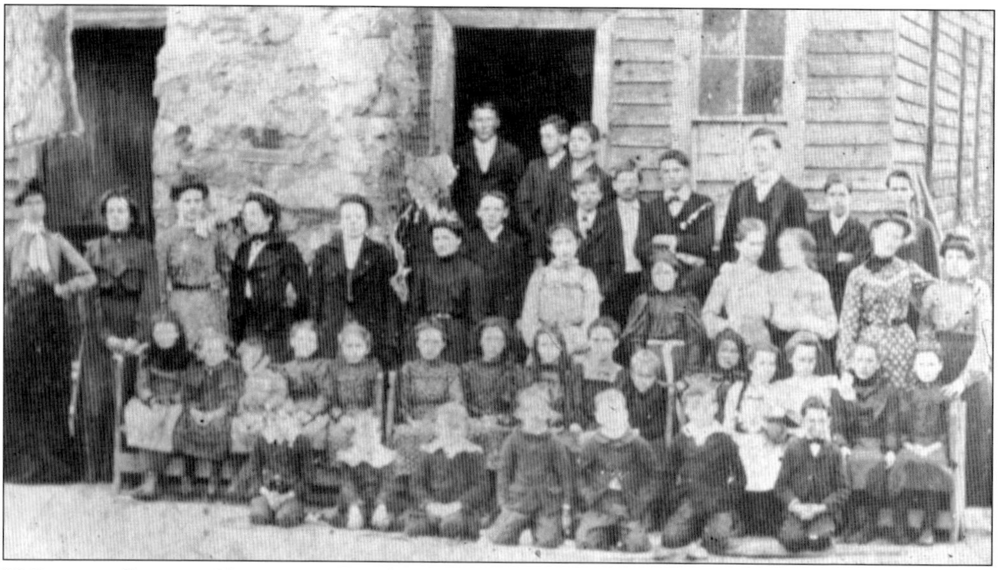

K Springs School, Early 1900s. This group of students is standing in front of Old K Springs School. Many of those pictured are from the Kendrick family. Teacher Nellie Kidd is on the far left. (Courtesy of Shelba Nivens.)

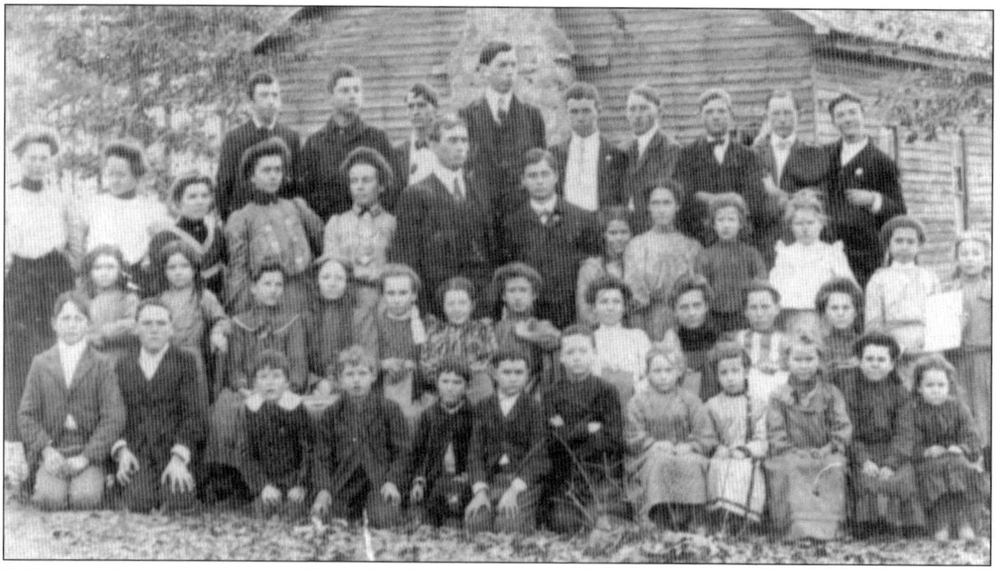

K Springs Schoolchildren, 1903. This 1903 photograph shows a group of K Springs schoolchildren. Clifton Kendrick is kneeling at far left in the first row. His father, Luther, donated land around 1896 for a school building. It was built where the old K Springs Church is today. From left to right are (first row) Clifton Kendrick, Louie Davis, Arnold Farrell, Hutson Davis, Gurny Brasher, Irving Crane, Forrest Davis, Era Kendrick, Zenia Gilbert, Annie Hathaway, Elmer Crane, and Dorothy Crane; (second row) Flossie Brasher, Lossie Brasher, Mand Davis, Delpher Brasher, Ressie Rick, Ruby Kendrick, Clara Smith, Dovie Crane, Pearl Gilbert, Hattie Kendrick, and Audry Farrell; (third row) Mary Gilbert, Birdie Kendrick, Ada G. Crane, Rosie Gilbert, Clara Moore, teacher Henry Gilbert, Walter Kendrick, the Patmon sisters, Vonie Smith, Stella Farrell, Myrtle Gilbert, and Stella Vick; (fourth row) B. Gilbert, General Patmon, Walter Gilbert, Arthur Davis, Martis Kendrick, Walter Davis, Lawrence Kendrick, and Ernest Brasher. (Courtesy of Shelba Nivens.)

CHELSEA "SCHOOL BUS." School consolidation made transportation a necessity in the 1920s. The county did not have funds to purchase an adequate number of buses to transport students. This left the job open for locals to contract with the county board to use trucks as buses to transport students. The inside of the truck was gutted and wooden boards laid down for seating. The pay was $100 dollars per month to haul the students. Members of the community often used the bus to go grocery shopping or to attend a church function. When the school year ended, the bus was used to haul lumber. (Courtesy of Shelba Nivens.)

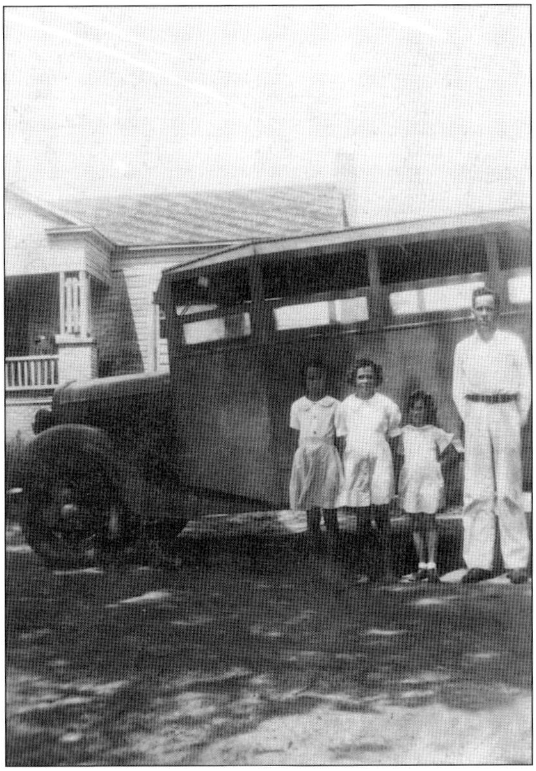

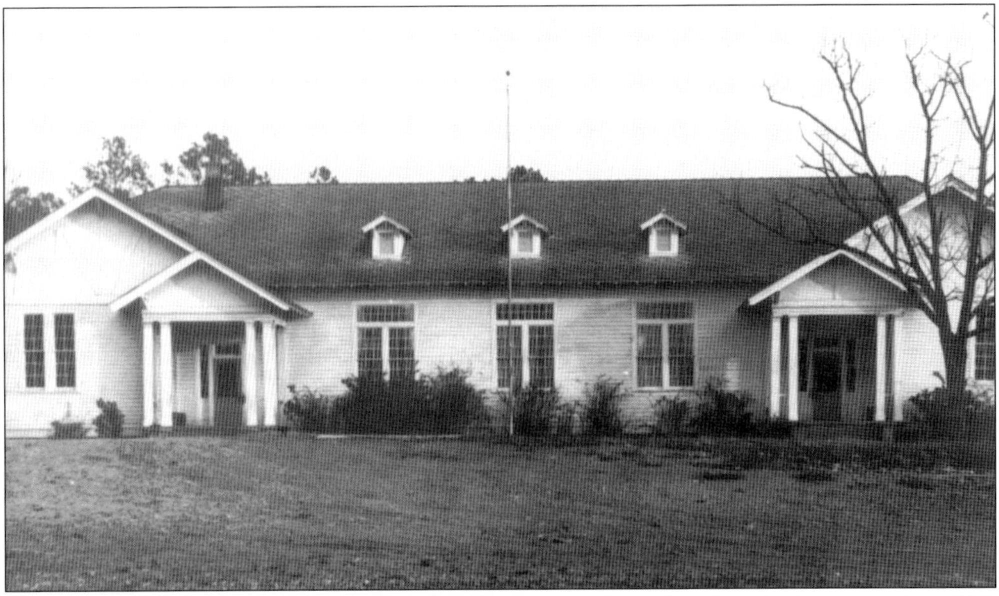

CHELSEA SCHOOLHOUSE. Chelsea had a schoolhouse near the railroad tracks that burned in 1913. After the fire, construction on a new building began where Chelsea Intermediate School is today. In 1927, construction on what would become today's Chelsea Middle School was started after consolidation took place. The present-day high school was erected in 1964, and the elementary school was built in 1972. When the schools first merged, the facilities in Chelsea totaled four rooms and an auditorium. (Courtesy of Norma Jean Harper.)

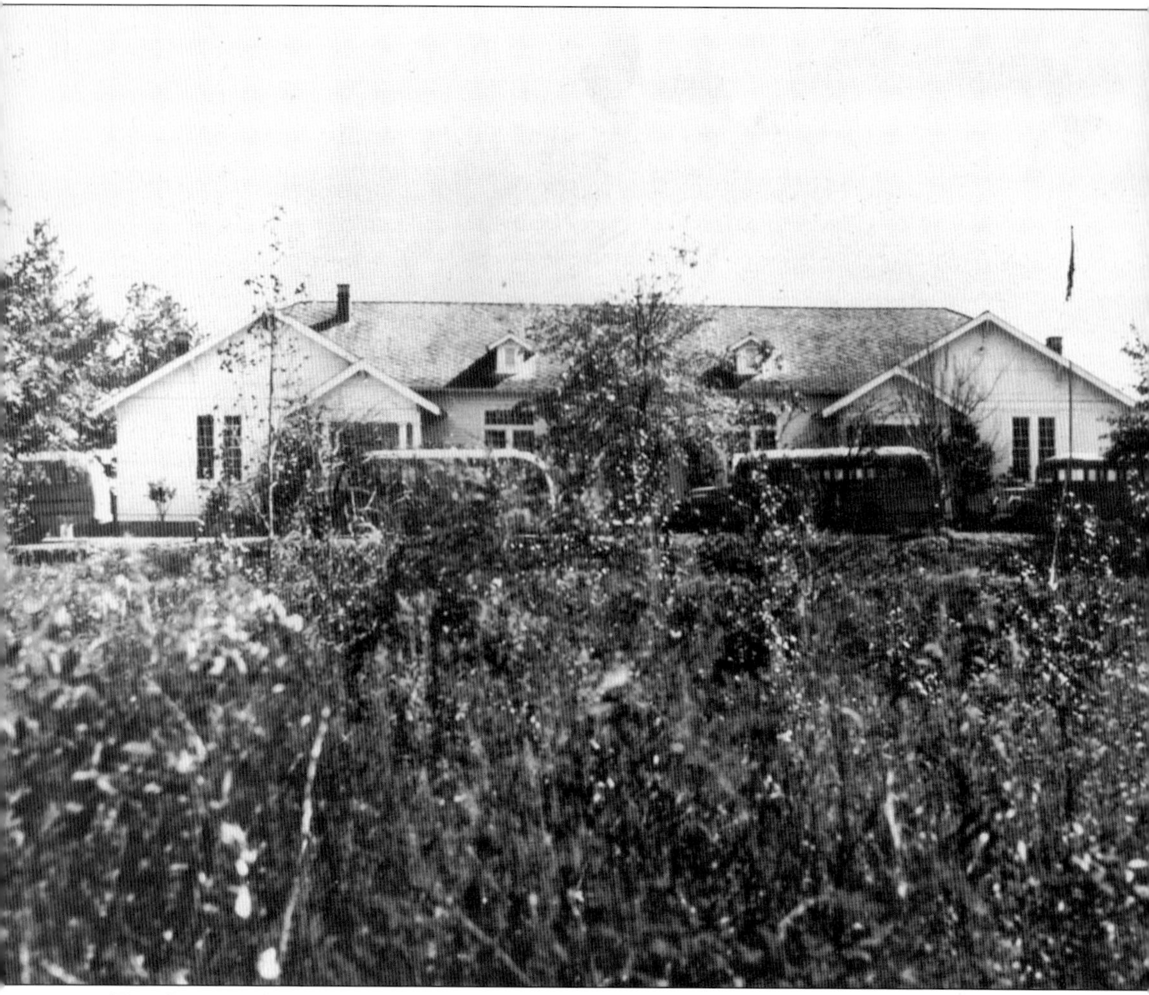

THE CHELSEA SCHOOL BUILDING WITH A NEW ADDITION. Using building materials taken from schools that were closing and spending another $500, an addition was built onto the school; it was used to house the teachers. The building is still standing today. Note the school buses in this photograph. (Courtesy of Norma Jean Harper.)

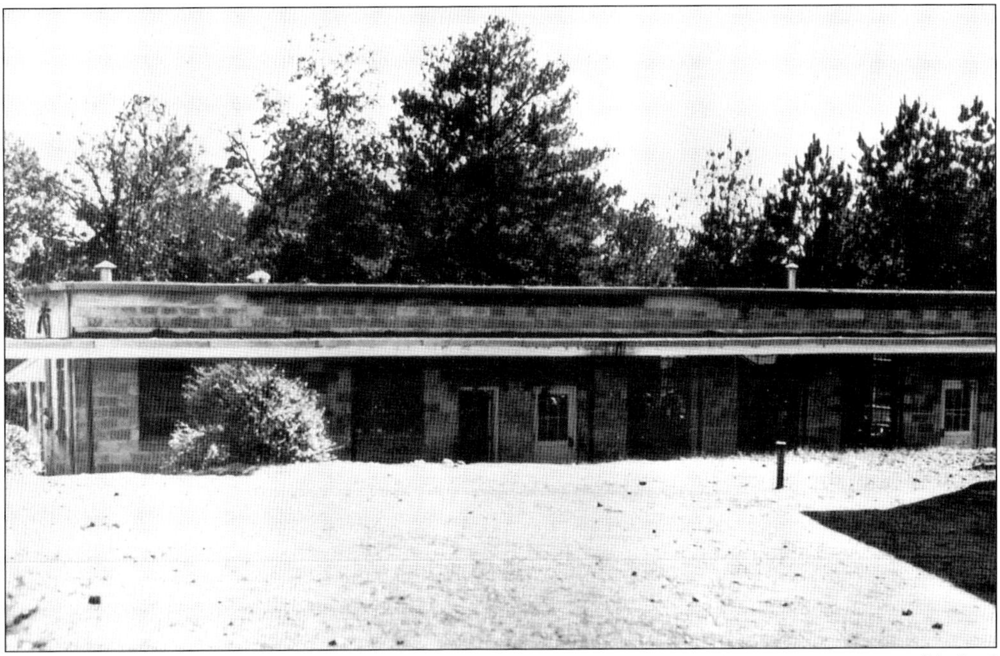

The First Lunchroom in the County. The first lunchroom in Shelby County was established as an experiment in Chelsea. Parents volunteered to help the first and only lunchroom worker. The school reportedly bought milk from farmers who lived in the area, one of them being Luther Kendrick. (Courtesy of Olean Kenny.)

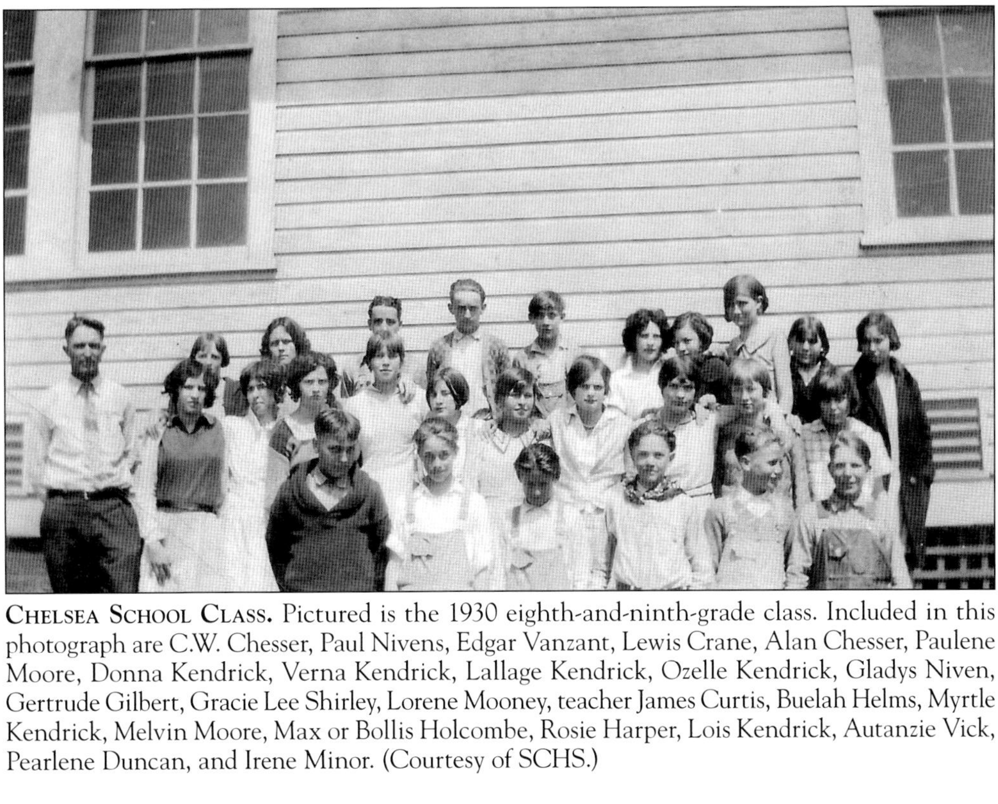

Chelsea School Class. Pictured is the 1930 eighth-and-ninth-grade class. Included in this photograph are C.W. Chesser, Paul Nivens, Edgar Vanzant, Lewis Crane, Alan Chesser, Paulene Moore, Donna Kendrick, Verna Kendrick, Lallage Kendrick, Ozelle Kendrick, Gladys Niven, Gertrude Gilbert, Gracie Lee Shirley, Lorene Mooney, teacher James Curtis, Buelah Helms, Myrtle Kendrick, Melvin Moore, Max or Bollis Holcombe, Rosie Harper, Lois Kendrick, Autanzie Vick, Pearlene Duncan, and Irene Minor. (Courtesy of SCHS.)

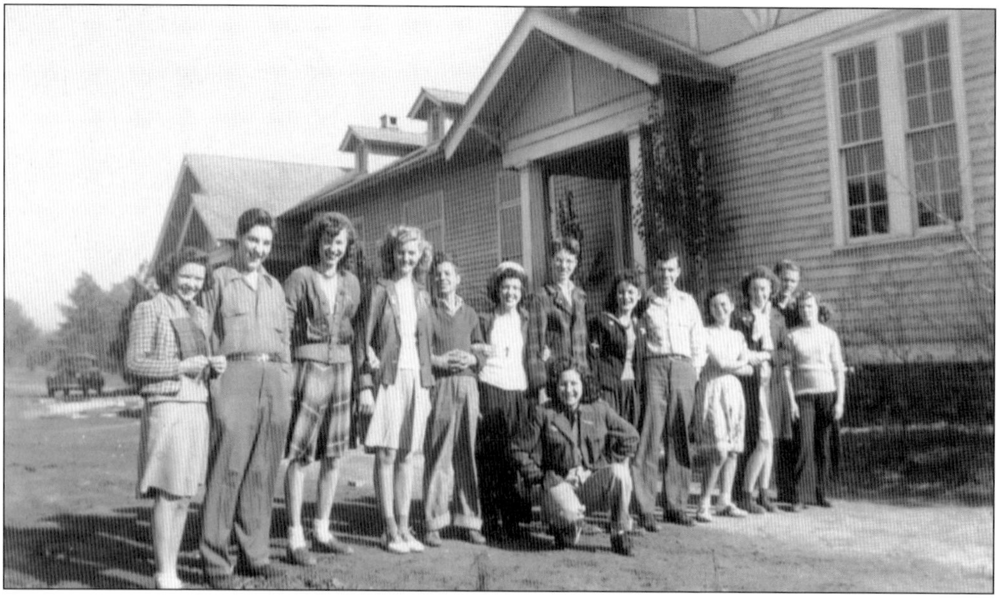

Chelsea Ninth Grade. This is a picture of a graduating class of ninth graders in 1946. For years, Chelsea schooling did not go past the ninth grade. If students wanted to attend high school, they would have to go somewhere else, like Vincent or Columbiana. However, most young adults joined the workforce after the ninth grade. (Courtesy of Shelba Nivens.)

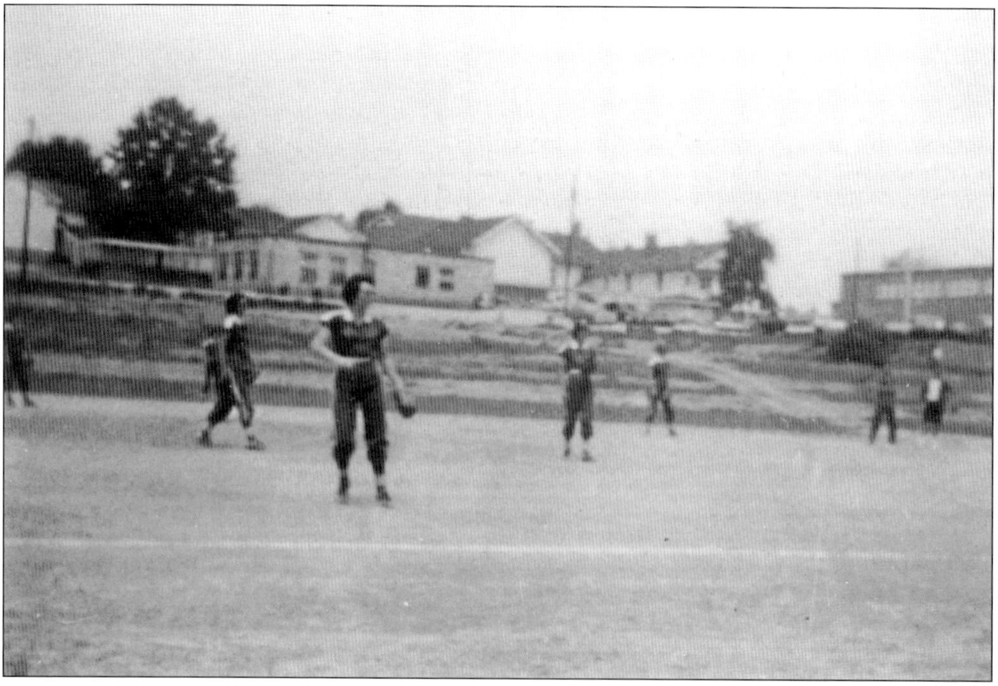

Chelsea Softball Game. A group of Chelsea students has gathered in the back of the school to play softball. Local resident Olean Kenny recalls that there were no organized school sports, so students organized games themselves. Often, they played their Wilsonville neighbors. (Courtesy of Olean Kenny.)

Five

"My, How You've Grown"

Chelsea has been called the fastest-growing city in the fastest-growing county in Alabama. The city was incorporated in 1996. Earl Niven took an early leave from Alabama Power and still serves as the city's first and only mayor. The population stands at more than 11,000, a nearly 300-percent increase since the year 2000. The community boasts several quality schools to accommodate the growth rate: Chelsea Park Elementary, Chelsea Middle School, Chelsea High School, Mount Laurel Elementary, and the newly built Forest Oaks Elementary. A large recreation park sits off of Highway 39. The park houses a playground, softball fields, picnic tables, and walking trails. Chelsea Youth Fields complex off of Highway 47 offers fall and spring sports for the community. The retail district is ever growing, with specialty shops, boutiques, and salons. Some of the largest developments are Walgreens, Walmart, and a Publix shopping center at Chelsea Crossroads. Fast-food chains and locally owned eateries line Highway 280. The city is also recognizing its latest improvement, a senior community center on Highway 47 across from Liberty Baptist Church. A lesser known fact about the town is that Chelsea was named a Tree City by the National Arbor Day Foundation and has its own tree commission. The commitment to community forestry has earned the city national recognition. Chelsea has been involved in the Tree City USA program for 16 years.

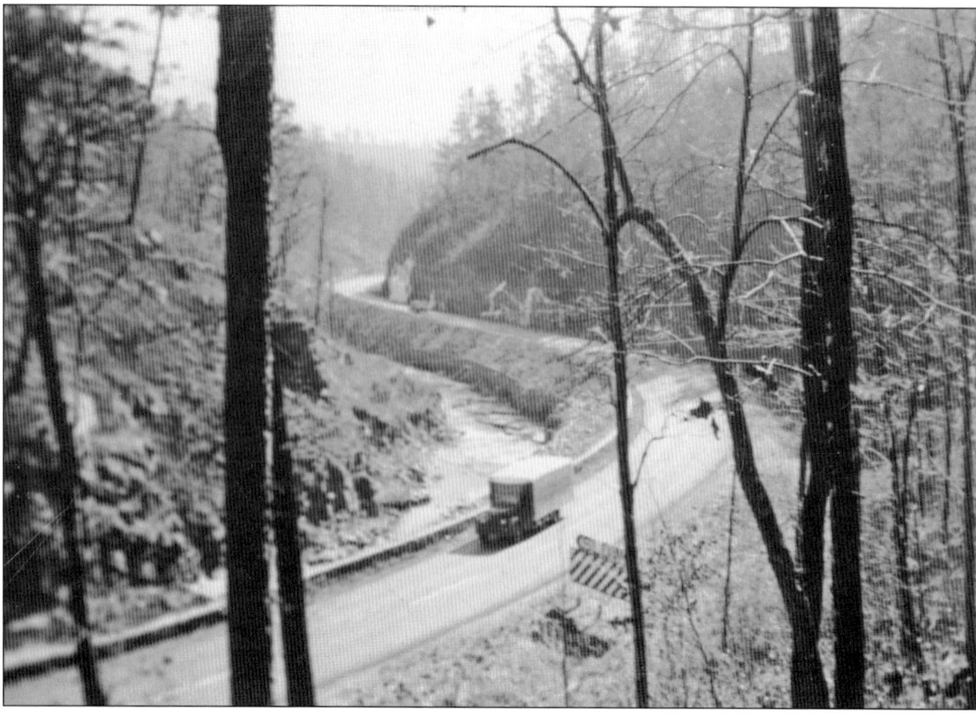

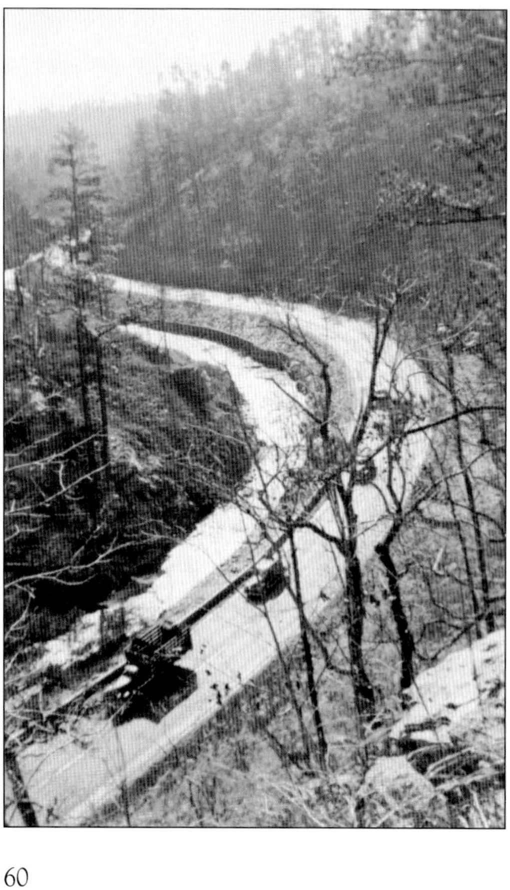

The Narrows. Red roses once adorned the roadside of what is called the Narrows. For years, Highway 91 was called the Florida Short Route. These photographs were taken during the construction of the road in the 1930s. It was built by prisoners on work release and by Works Progress Administration (WPA) workers. The WPA was an ambitious part of the New Deal agency. The program employed millions of unemployed, typically unskilled, men to carry out the public works projects, including road construction. (Both, courtesy of SCHS.)

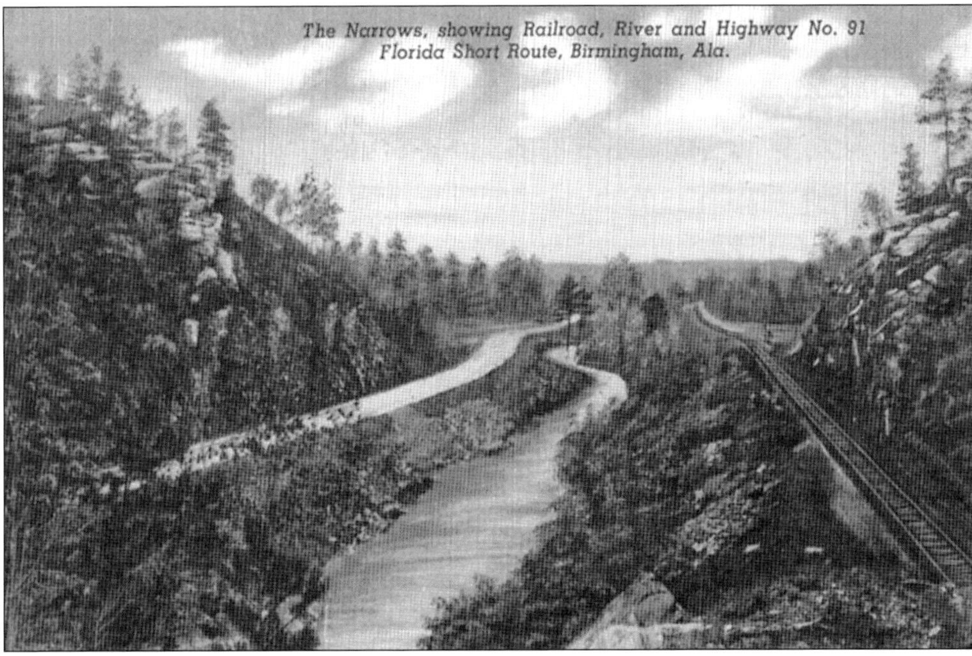

THE NARROWS POSTCARD. This vintage postcard shows progress on the Narrows. Extensive blasting took place to get through the rock in the area. This new road was significant since it allowed travelers to go straight to Birmingham without having to go through Pelham. (Courtesy of Martin Evers.)

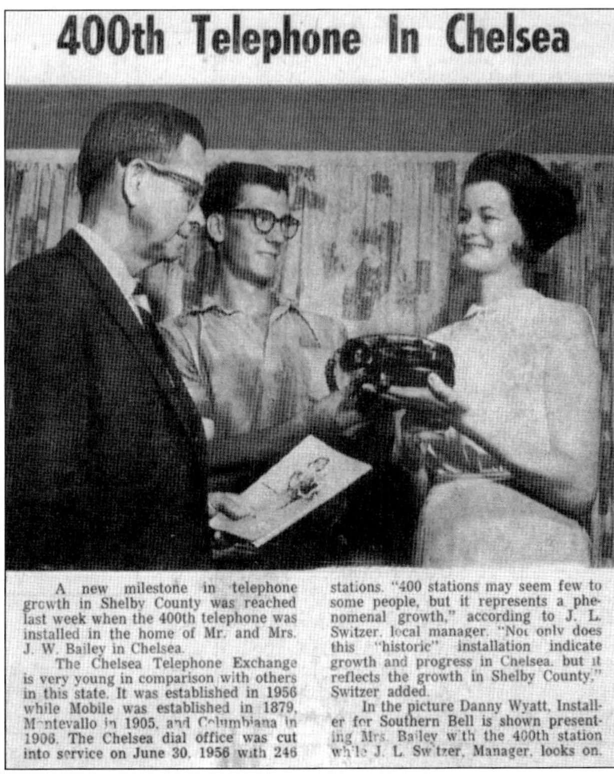

400th Telephone In Chelsea

A new milestone in telephone growth in Shelby County was reached last week when the 400th telephone was installed in the home of Mr. and Mrs. J. W. Bailey in Chelsea.

The Chelsea Telephone Exchange is very young in comparison with others in this state. It was established in 1956 while Mobile was established in 1879, Montevallo in 1905, and Columbiana in 1906. The Chelsea dial office was cut into service on June 30, 1956 with 246 stations. "400 stations may seem few to some people, but it represents a phenomenal growth," according to J. L. Switzer, local manager. "Not only does this "historic" installation indicate growth and progress in Chelsea, but it reflects the growth in Shelby County," Switzer added.

In the picture Danny Wyatt, Installer for Southern Bell is shown presenting Mrs. Bailey with the 400th station while J. L. Switzer, Manager, looks on.

THE TELEPHONE. The 400th telephone installment in Chelsea was captured in this newspaper article from the 1960s. The installments were considered a significant advancement at the time. The telephone was set up in the home of James and Judy Bailey. Service began in Chelsea in 1956. Judy Bailey accepted the phone from a Southern Bell associate. (Courtesy of Olean Kenny.)

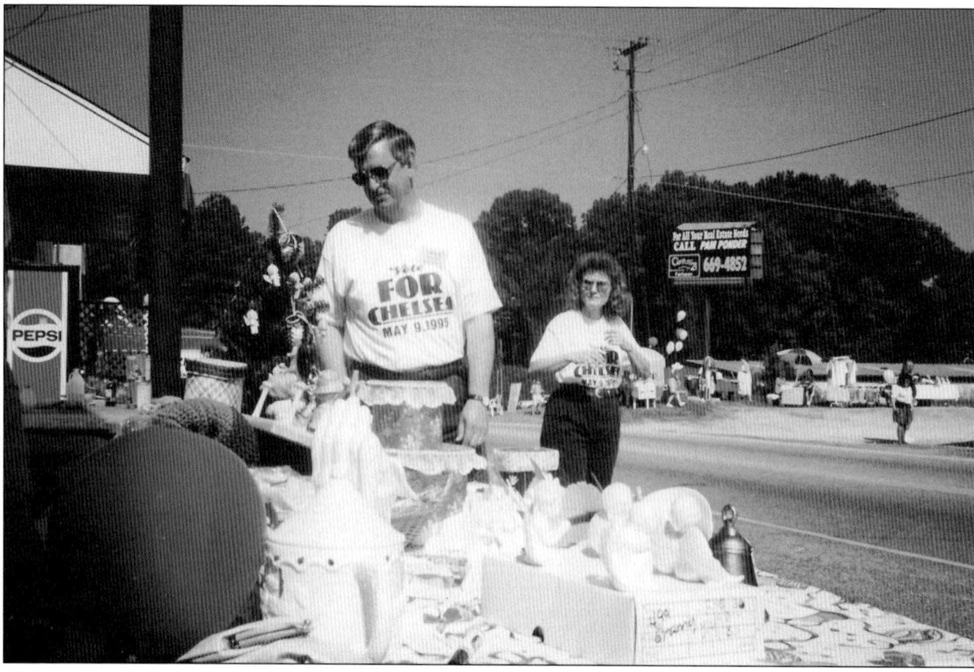

CHELSEA'S INCORPORATION AND ELECTION. Chelsea elected Earl Niven mayor in 1996 when the city was incorporated. He has been the mayor since and has seen firsthand the growth and expansion of this booming city. At the time of incorporation, the population was around 900. Today, that population reaches past 11,000. Mayor Niven was the first math teacher at Chelsea High School before a 28-year career at Alabama Power. (Courtesy of Shelba Nivens.)

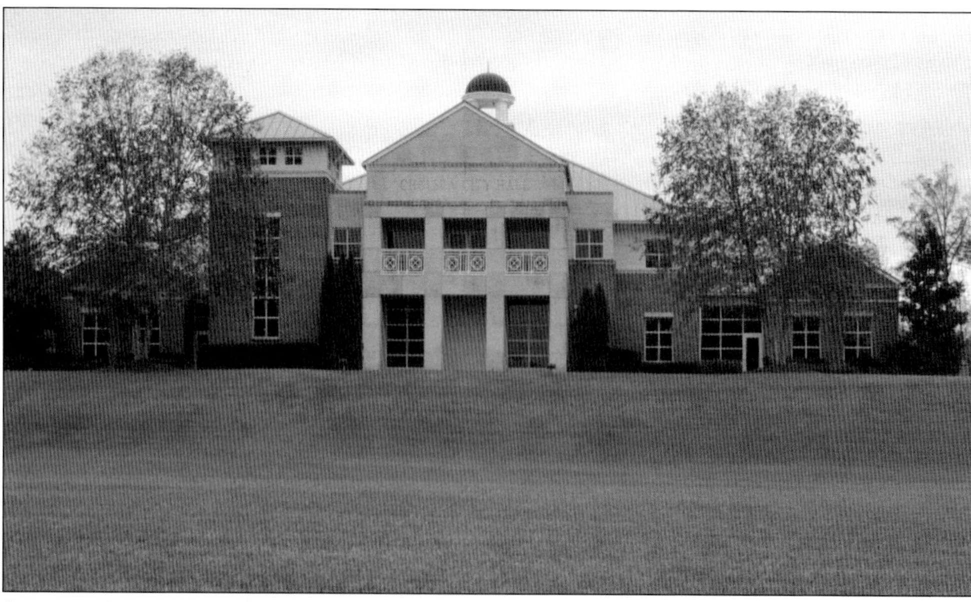

CHELSEA CITY HALL. Chelsea City Hall is perched on a hill just past the train tracks that started it all for the small town. Today's city hall was constructed in 2004. City council members are Juanita Champion, David Ingram, Alison Moore Nichols, Tony Pickelsimer, and Dale Neuendorf. (Courtesy of Chelsea City Hall.)

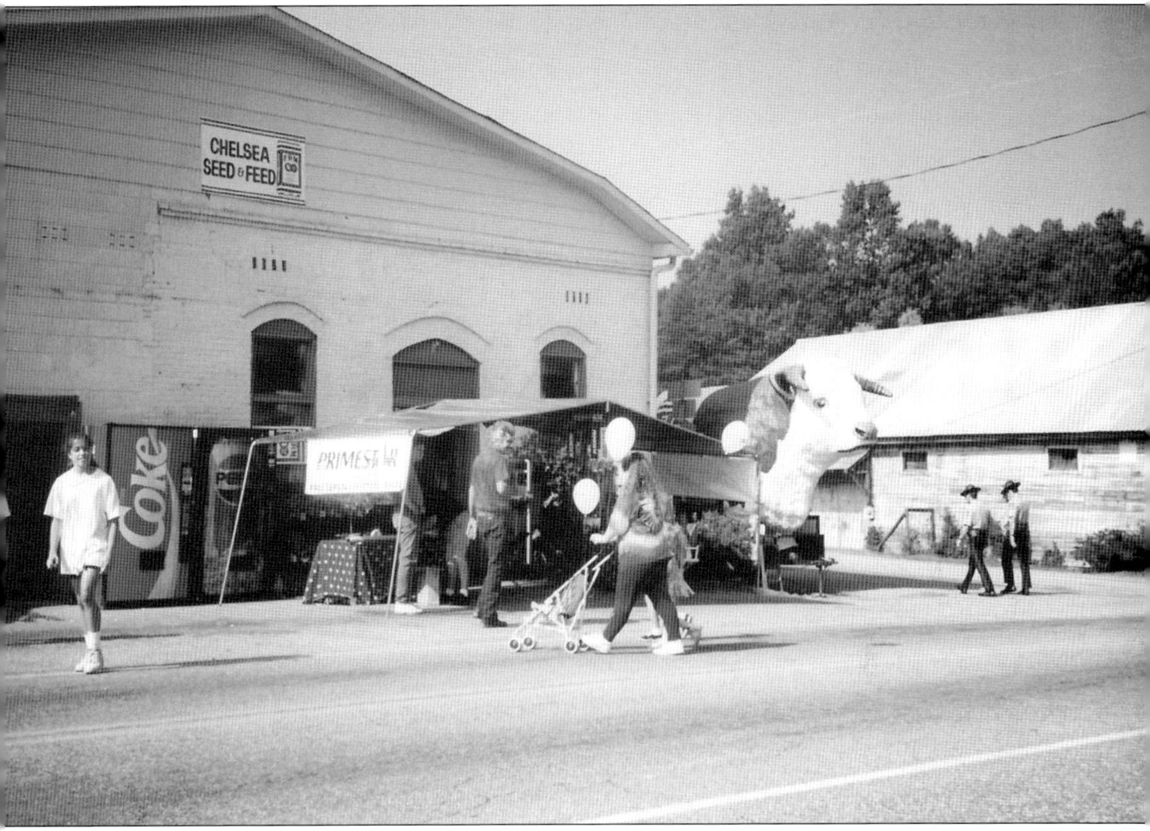

Chelsea Feed & Seed and Chelsea Day Tradition. "Chelsea Day" is a tradition that was informally started by local resident Jim Bailey and his daughter Sherry. For years, Jim Bailey owned Chelsea Feed & Seed. He recalls patrons coming in the store, running into each other, and taking the time to visit and catch up with one another. One day, with some help, he slowed traffic in front of his store on the corner of Highways 39 and 47. Bailey says his goal was for people of the town to talk to each other. And so they did, essentially kick-starting "Chelsea Day," a tradition that continues in the community on the lawn in front of city hall. Today, Chelsea Day draws attention to the Chelsea High School Band.

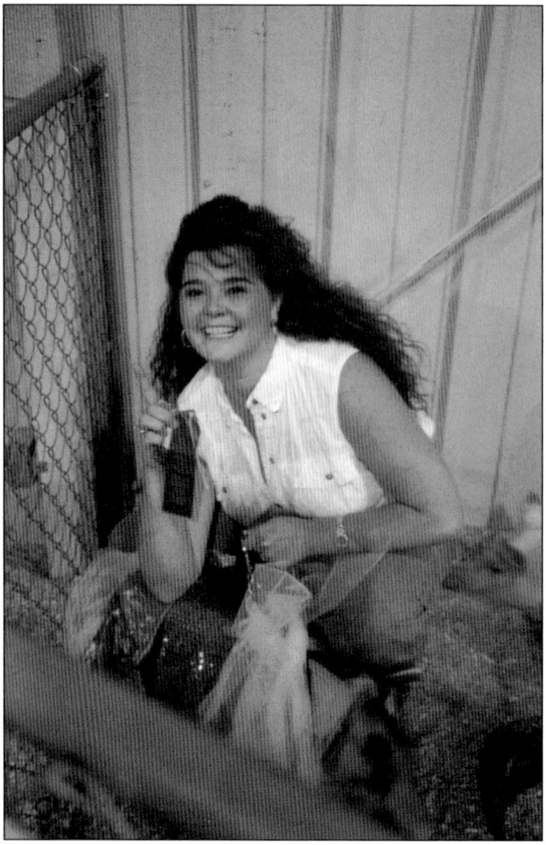

CHELSEA DAY, SHERRY BAILEY'S PIG. Sherry Bailey Reynolds poses in the mid-1990s during what has become Chelsea Day. She won first place for the best dressed pig. Sherry was a descendant of the Kendrick family. She owned Sherry's Hair Design in Chelsea for many years. She passed away in June 2014. After her death, her father encouraged Sherry's Hair Design to remain in business in her honor.

ANOTHER VIEW OF CHELSEA DAY. Pictured is another 1990s Chelsea Day with a view of Sherry Bailey's Hair Design business. The building once housed Chelsea's post office in what was considered the downtown area of the city. The building remains standing today but is vacant. (Courtesy of Shelba Nivens.)

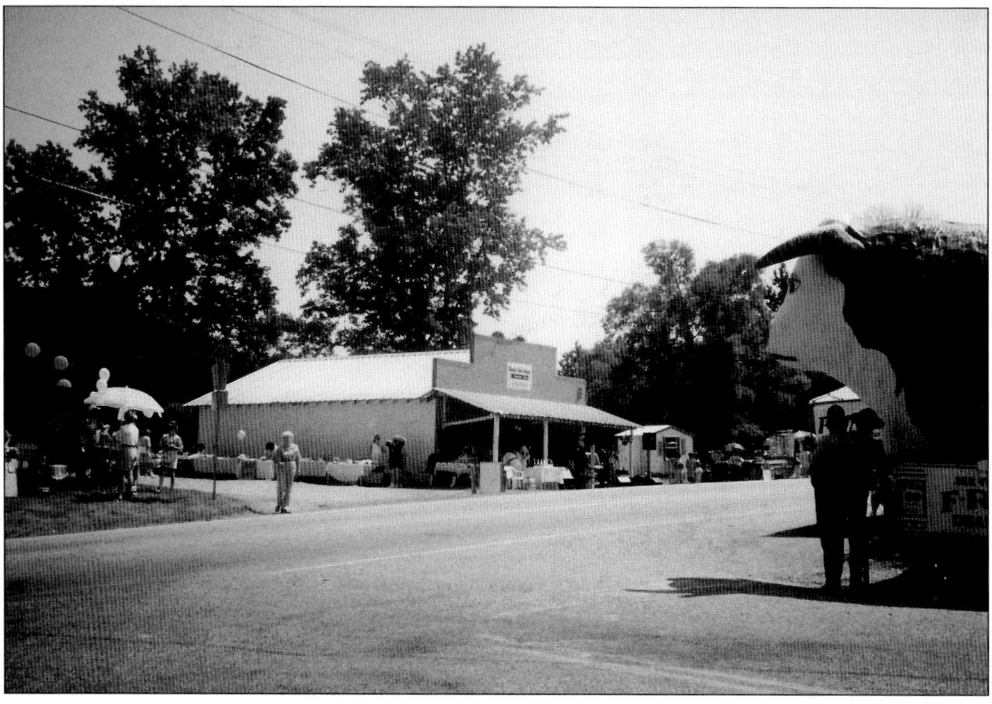

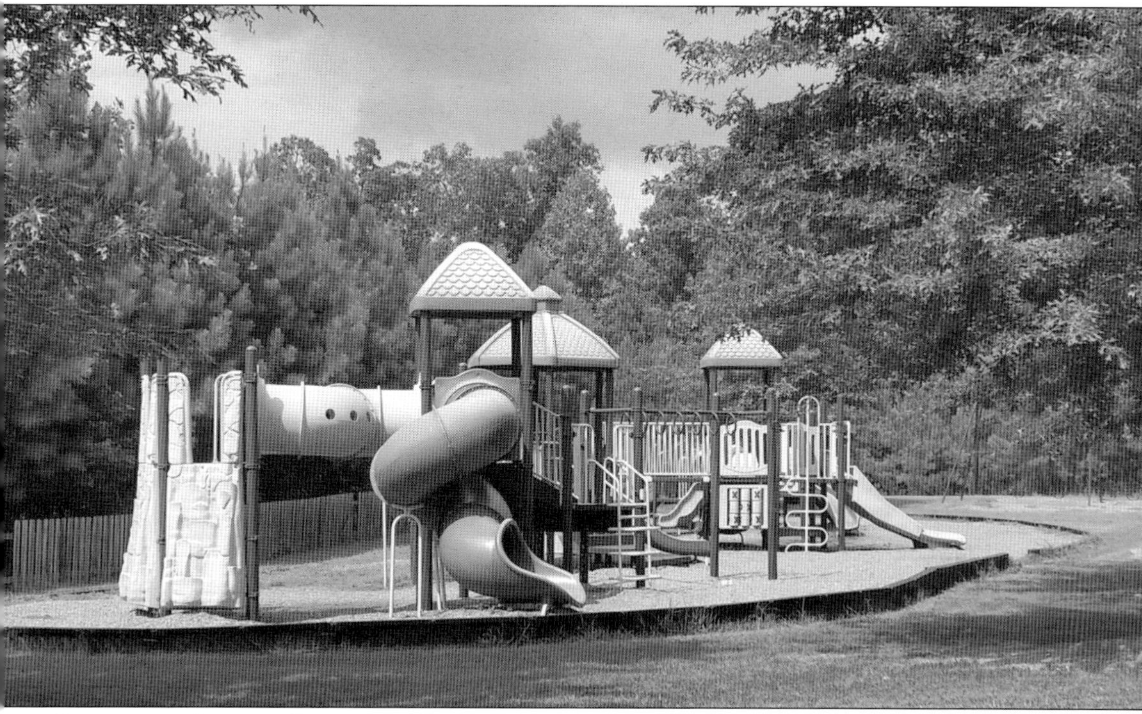

COMMUNITY GROWTH, RECREATION PARK. Chelsea Recreation Park is located along Highway 39. The park boasts a walking trail encompassing a children's playground and picnic tables. Several fields for baseball, softball, and football are located there. (Courtesy of Chelsea City Hall.)

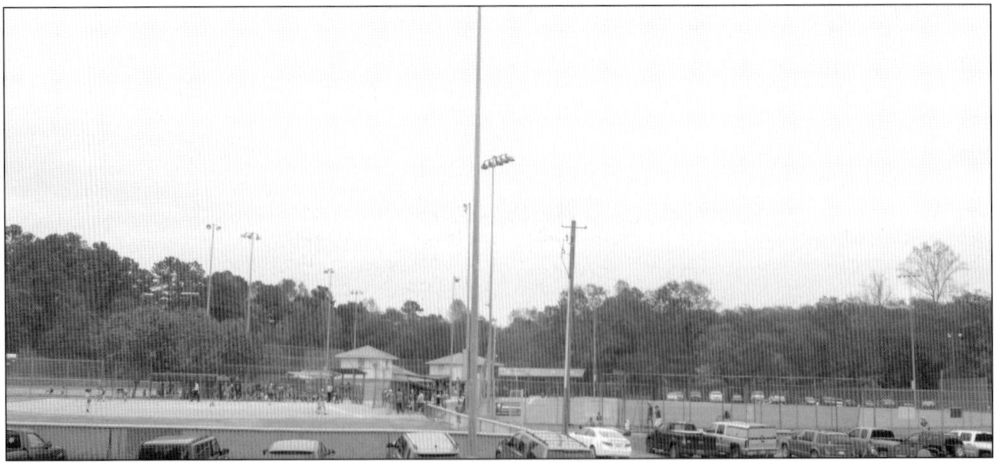

The Chelsea Ballpark. The Chelsea Youth Club is a growing opportunity for youth in the city to get involved in baseball and softball. Practices and games are held at the Chelsea Youth Fields next to Liberty Baptist Church. Spring and fall ball are offered during the year. The spring league is open to ages 4 through 14, while the fall league is open to ages 4 through 12. The CYC program has grown to more than 450 children in the spring program and more than 200 in the fall program. (Both, courtesy of Chelsea City Hall.)

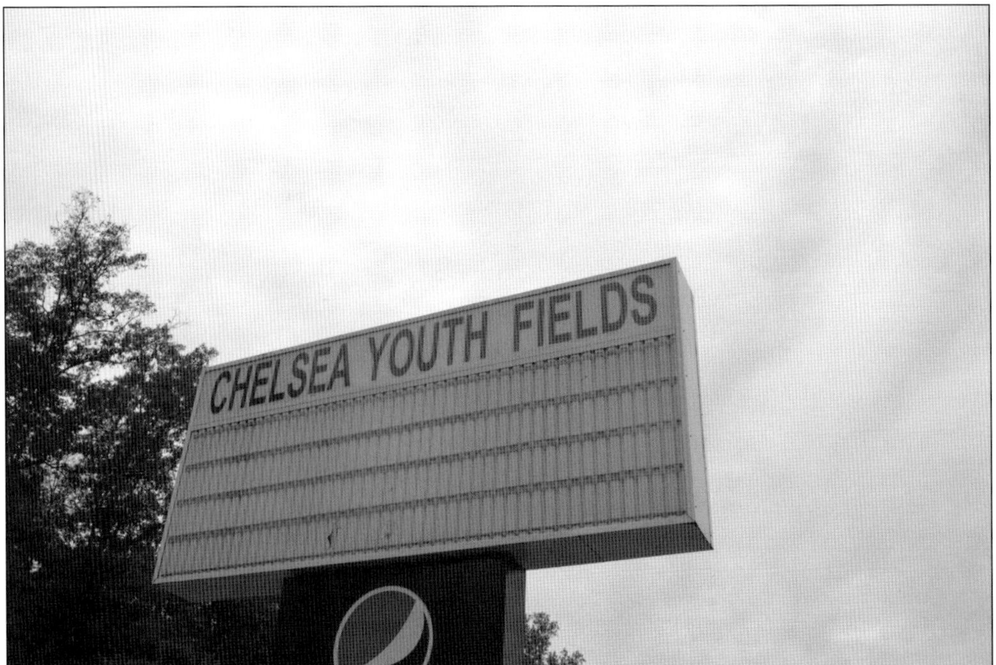

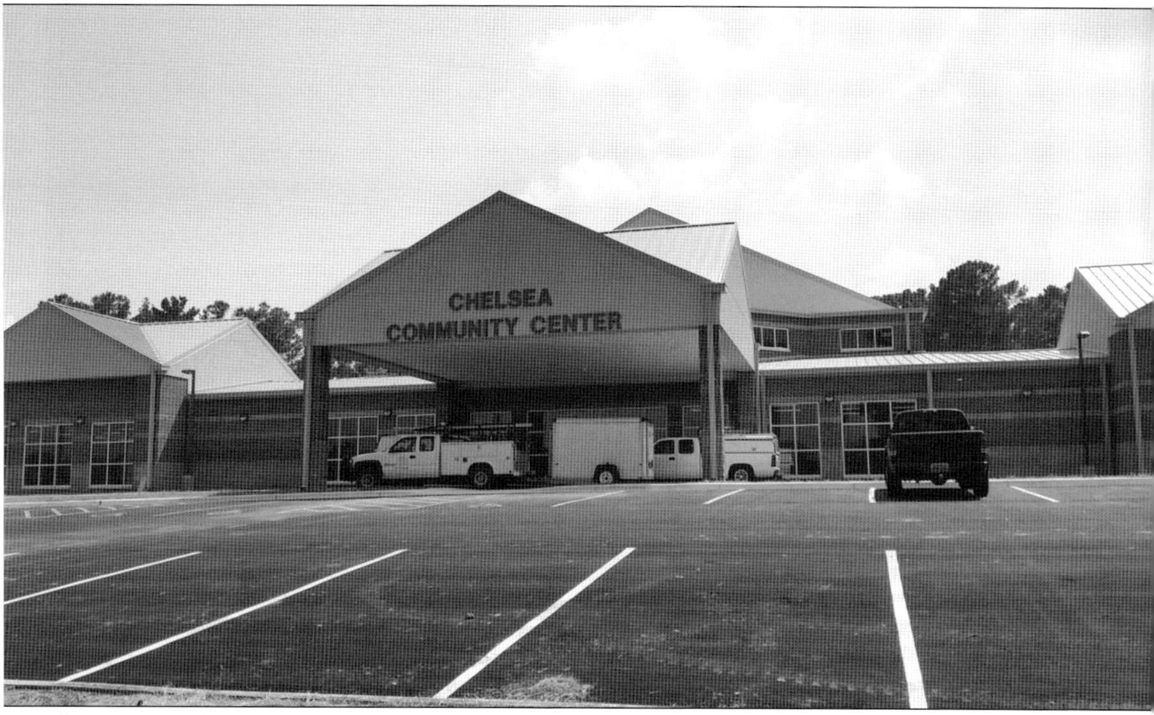

Community Growth, Community Center. The Chelsea Community Center opened in 2015. The nearly 30,000-square-foot building is situated on 37 acres of land off of Highway 47, across from Liberty Baptist Church. There is a gymnasium and walking track, among other amenities. (Courtesy of Chelsea City Hall.)

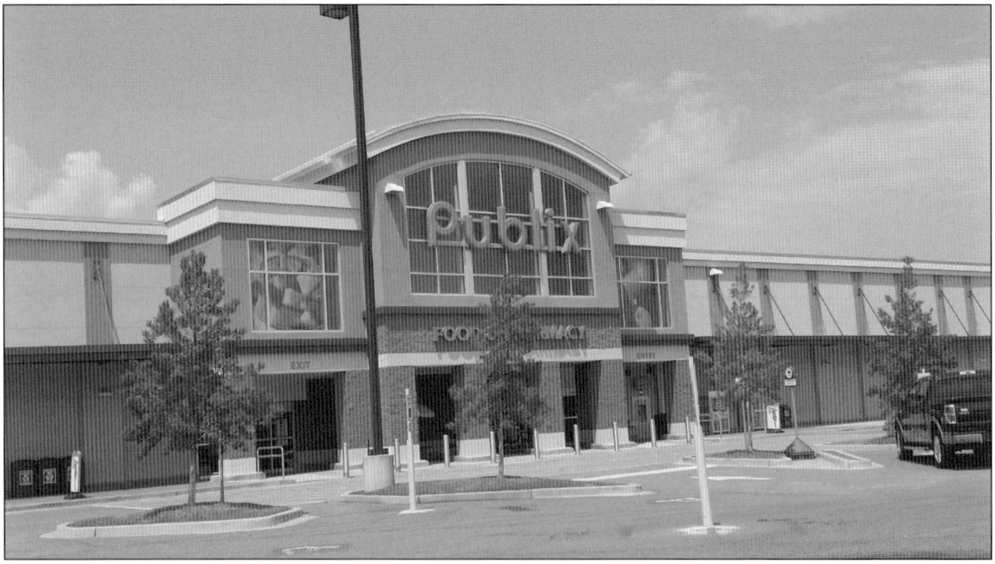

Large Developments, Publix. A significant development in the city is the Publix shopping center. Publix opened in 2011 at Chelsea Crossroads. The grocery store is a 45,000-foot facility with around 100 employees. (Courtesy of Chelsea City Hall.)

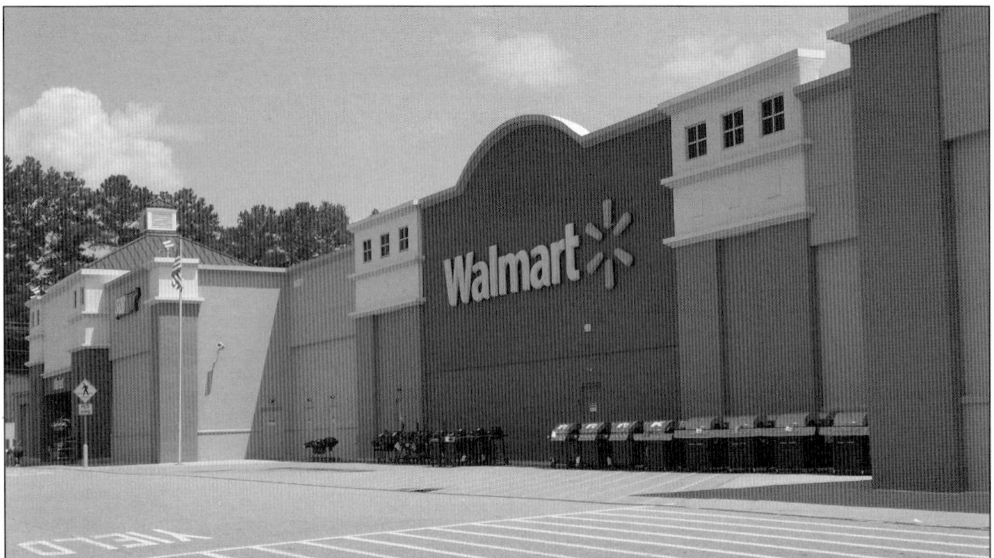

Large Developments, Walmart. Another significant development was the Walmart. The store is a full 24-hour supercenter with a garden shop and auto shop. A gas station was also recently added. (Courtesy of Chelsea City Hall.)

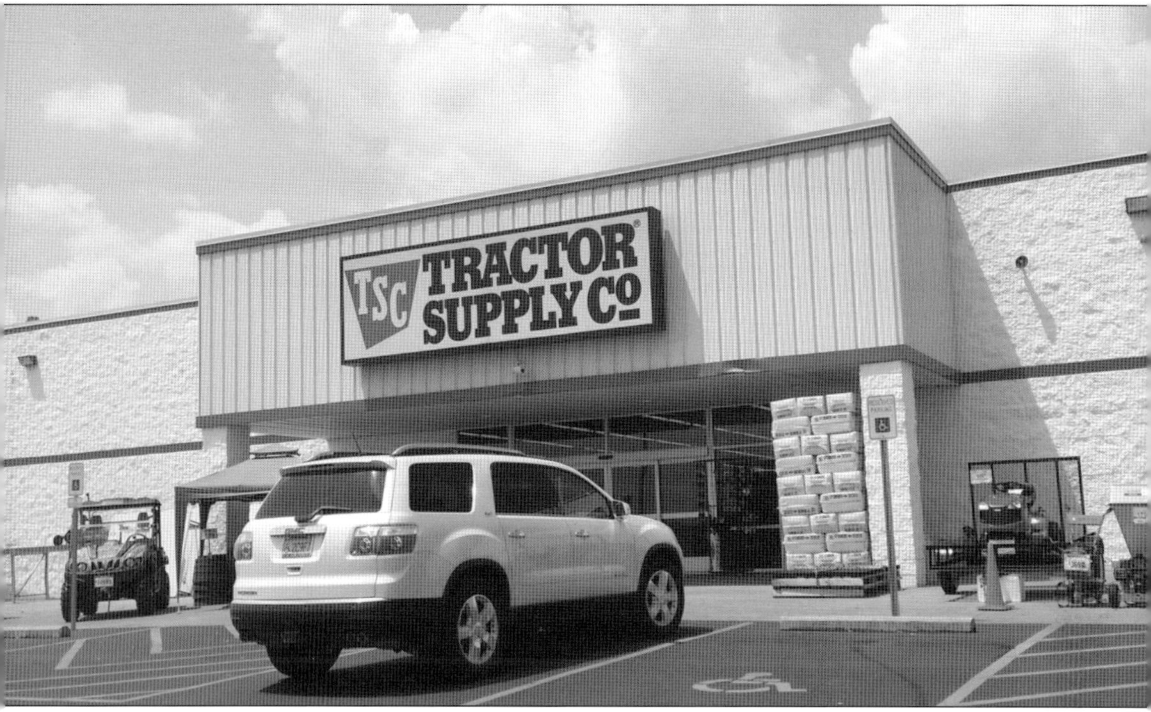

TRACTOR SUPPLY AND FIRE AT THE FOOTHILLS. For the past five years, Tractor Supply has been the scene of the annual Fire at the Foothills, a barbecue and chili cook-off that raises money for the Chelsea Fire and Rescue's fire safety program. It was started when two locals got into a "heated" debate over who had the best chili recipe. The event features Hero the Dalmatian. Fire chief Wayne Shirley believes Hero is the only firehouse Dalmatian that is trained and a certified fire department member in Alabama. Hero performs the "stop, drop, and roll" fire safety procedure for local schoolchildren. Fire at the Foothills attracted around 3,000 people in 2015. (Courtesy of Chelsea City Hall.)

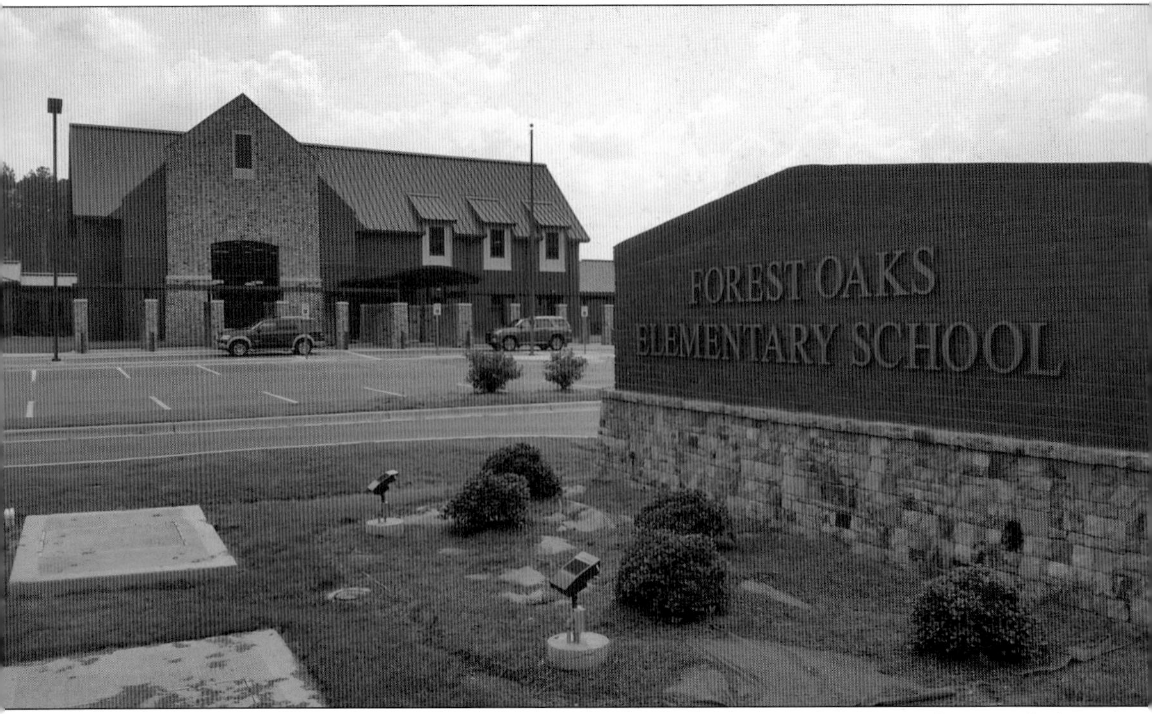

Forest Oaks School. Forest Oaks Elementary opened in January 2014, replacing Chelsea Intermediate School. The building became an extension for Chelsea Middle School. Forest Oaks was established in anticipation of growth in the Chelsea community. The city donated $500,000 to aid in construction of the 7,600-square-foot gymnasium, which is utilized by both the school and the community. (Courtesy of Chelsea City Hall.)

Six

Hargis Retreat

Tucked away in the woods of Chelsea is a beautiful retreat many have explored as children. Often used as a campground and now owned by the YMCA, Hargis Retreat is a well-kept secret, and the story of the family responsible for the retreat is not often shared. The land of Hargis Retreat was first owned by Dr. Estes Hargis and his wife, Florence. In the early 1900s, they owned 1,000 acres of land and created a self-sufficient farm. Dr. Hargis was first assistant to Dr. William J. Mayo, one of the seven doctors who created the Mayo Clinic. Dr. Hargis completed his education at the University of Pennsylvania as well as Minnesota and attended Auburn University from 1915 to 1917. He got an honorary doctorate from Auburn in 1965 and has a building named after him on the campus. Dr. Hargis established the Hargis Clinic in Birmingham in 1928 as well as Hargis Hospital in 1938.

Although quite an achievement, that is not his legacy today. His name resonates in the halls of what is often used as a camp for children and was originally named Hargis Christian Retreat. In the early 1960s, a pastor from First Christian Church on Valleydale Road, Dr. Tom Giltner, embraced a vision of a nondenominational retreat where all were welcome. Dr. Hargis donated 200 acres of his farm, and after much planning and labor, Hargis Retreat is active today. The land was bought in the 1990s by the YMCA. Walter Savage was hired to oversee caretaking of the land and made a life there for himself and his family. His son Walter Savage Jr. followed his father's legacy. He lives on the property today, caretaking and overseeing weddings every weekend on what is called Daffodil Hill. Blooming daffodils grace the property every April.

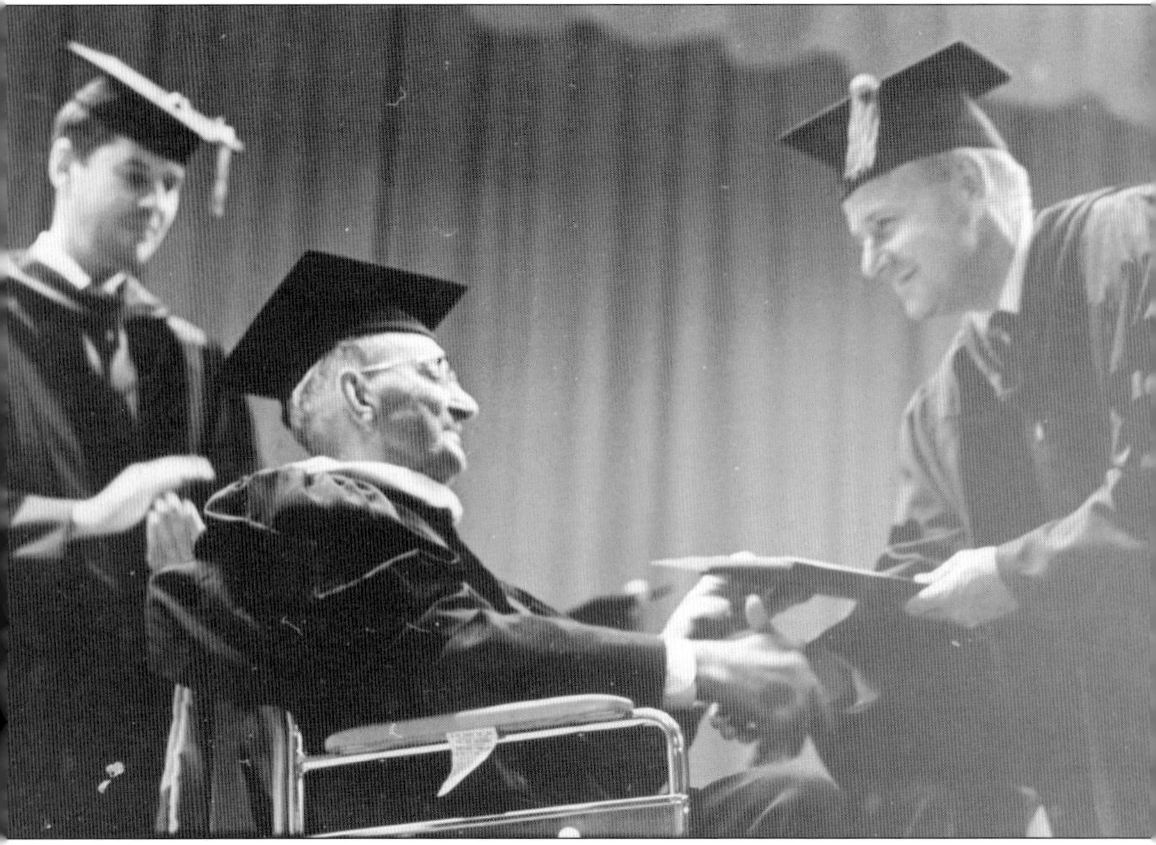

Dr. Hargis Honored. Dr. Estes Hargis received an honorary degree from Auburn University, and a building, Hargis Hall, was named in his honor. Dr. Hargis attended Auburn from 1915 to 1917. He went on to earn a medical degree from the University of Pennsylvania. He was a first assistant in surgery to Dr. W.J. Mayo, one of the seven founders of the famous Mayo Clinic. Dr. Hargis died in 1966 and is buried in Elmwood cemetery. (Courtesy of Walter Savage.)

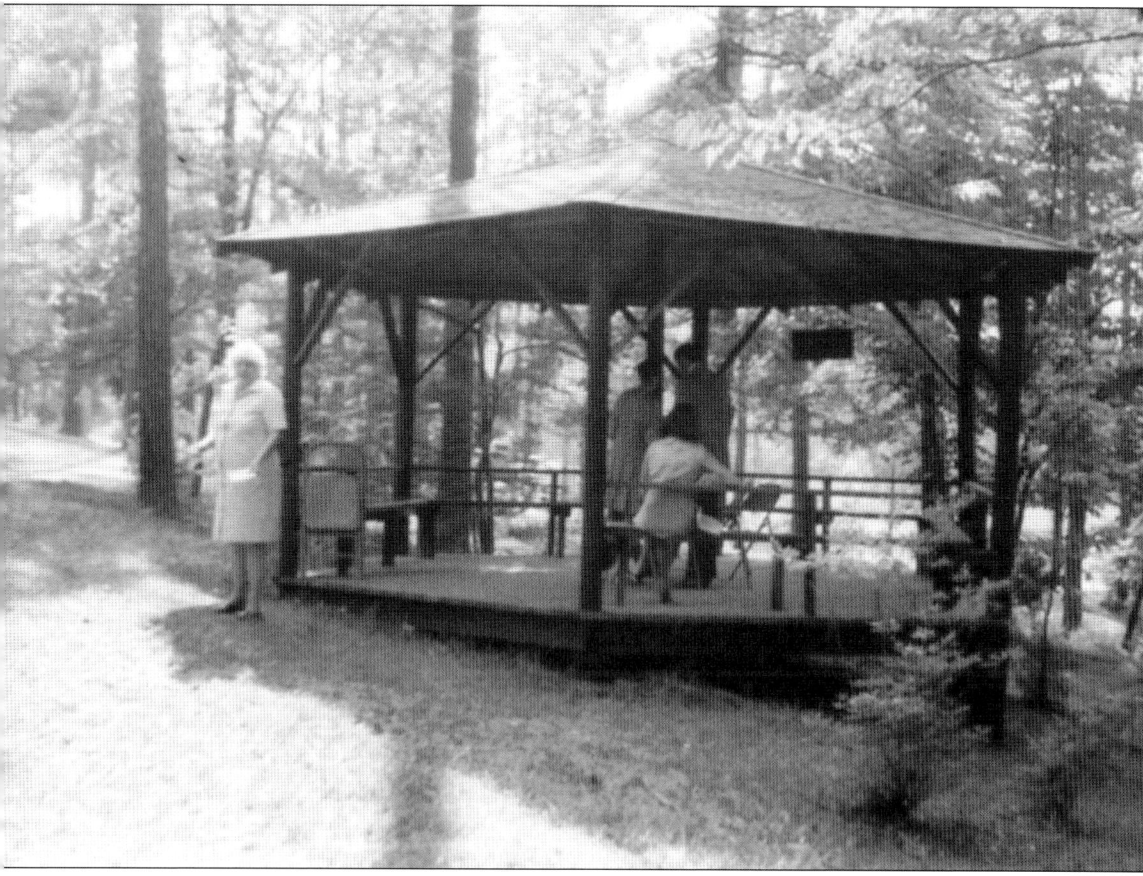

FLORENCE HARGIS. Estes's wife, Florence, shared a love for nature with her husband and the vision of a sanctuary others could enjoy. Florence gave a financial gift in 1970 in her late husband's honor when the Hargis Hall at Auburn University was heavily damaged by fire and in need of renovations. Florence was able to see the completion of Hargis Chapel in 1967. Today, the chapel is used most weekends for weddings. (Courtesy of Walter Savage.)

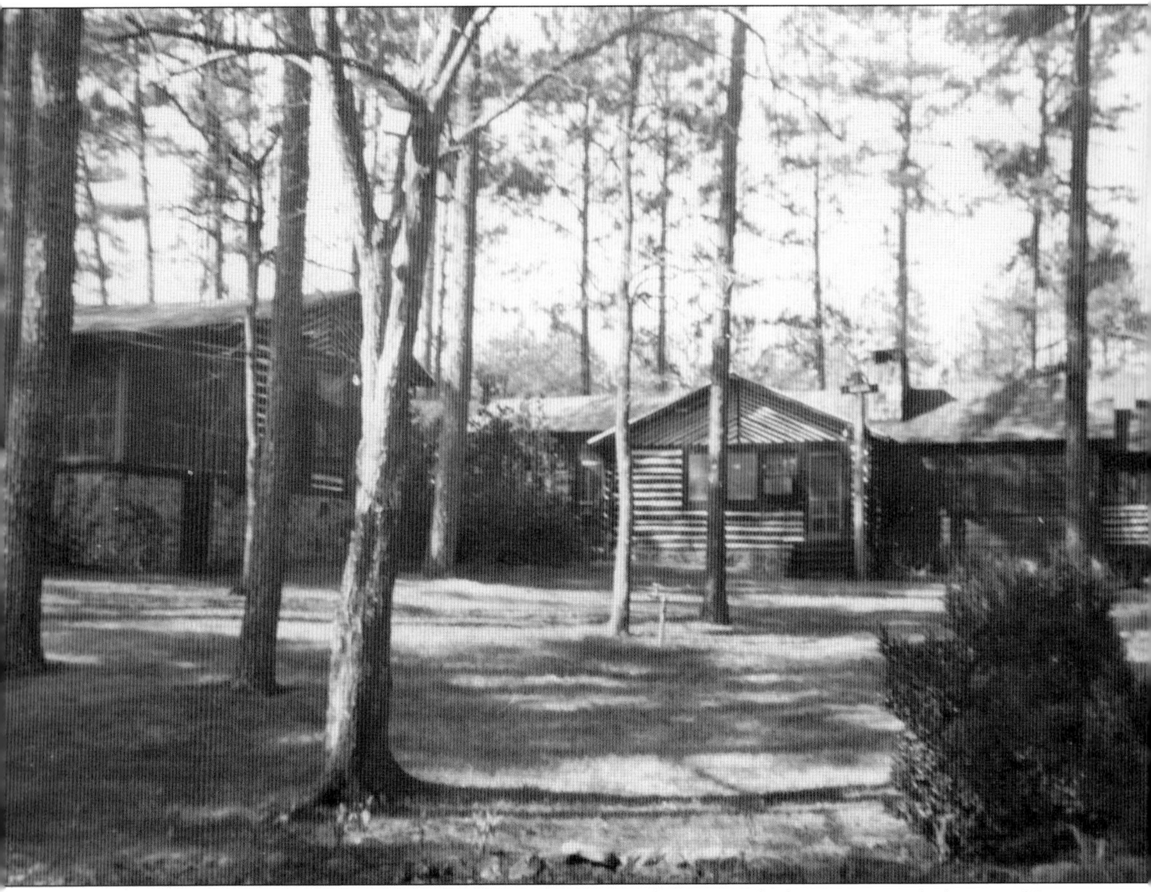

The Hargis Homestead. Here is the beautiful on-site homestead of Dr. Estes and Florence Hargis. The home burned in 1985. Many iron relics from the kitchen were saved and are on display in the museum. (Courtesy of Walter Savage.)

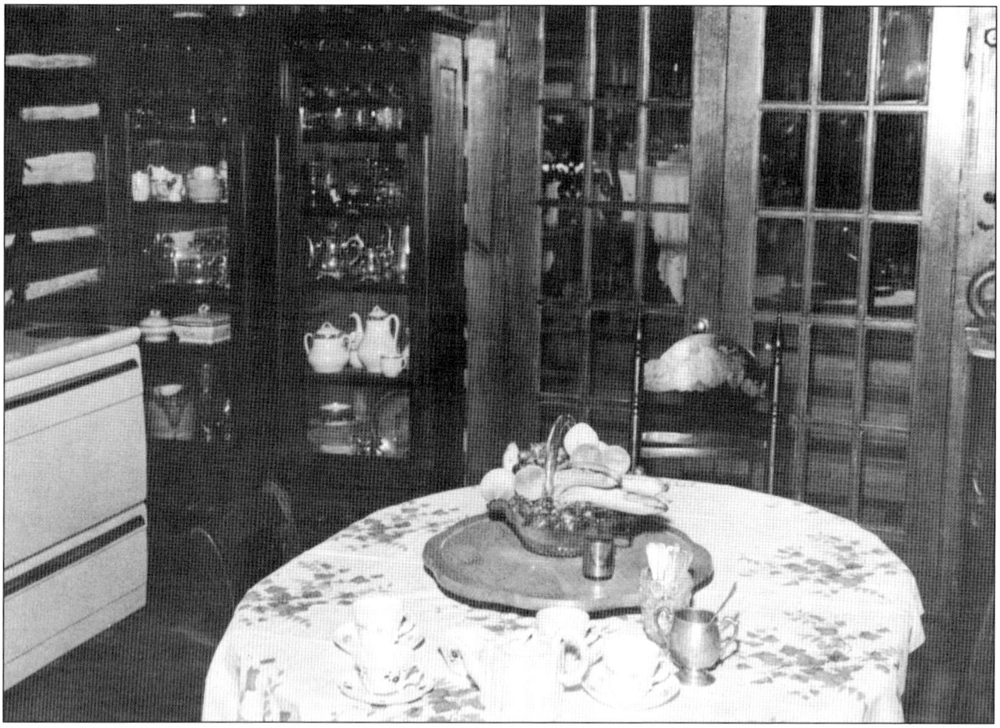

Inside the Hargis Home. These photographs were taken inside the Hargis home. It was once featured in *Southern Living* magazine. Much of the furniture was also saved after the fire in 1985 and is also on display in the museum at Hargis Retreat. (Both, courtesy of Walter Savage.)

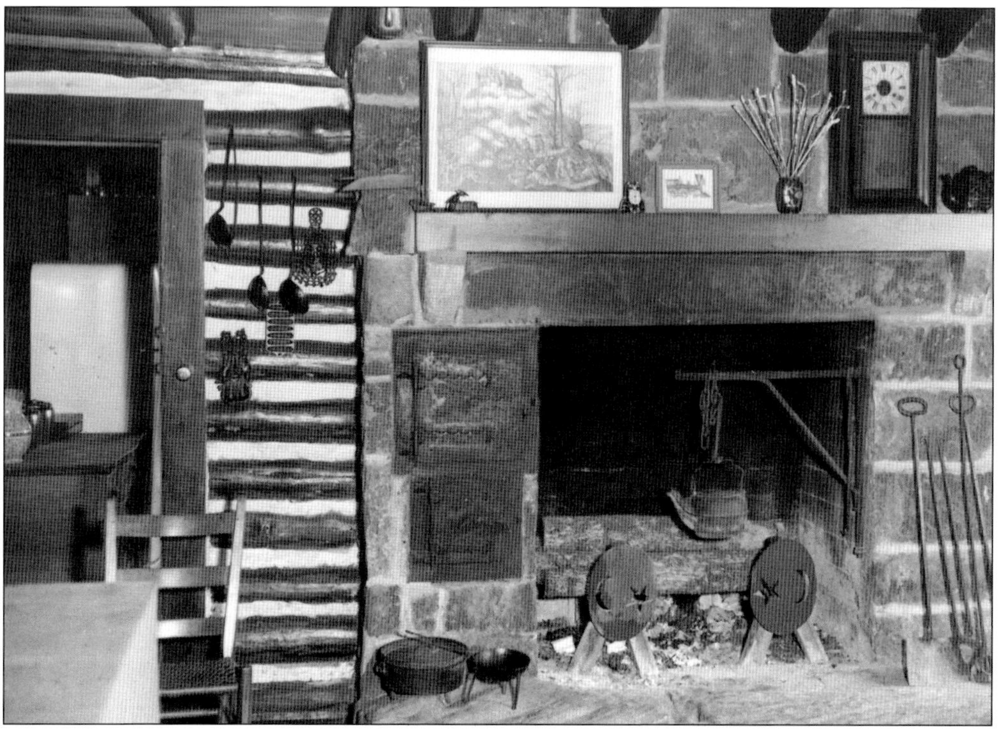

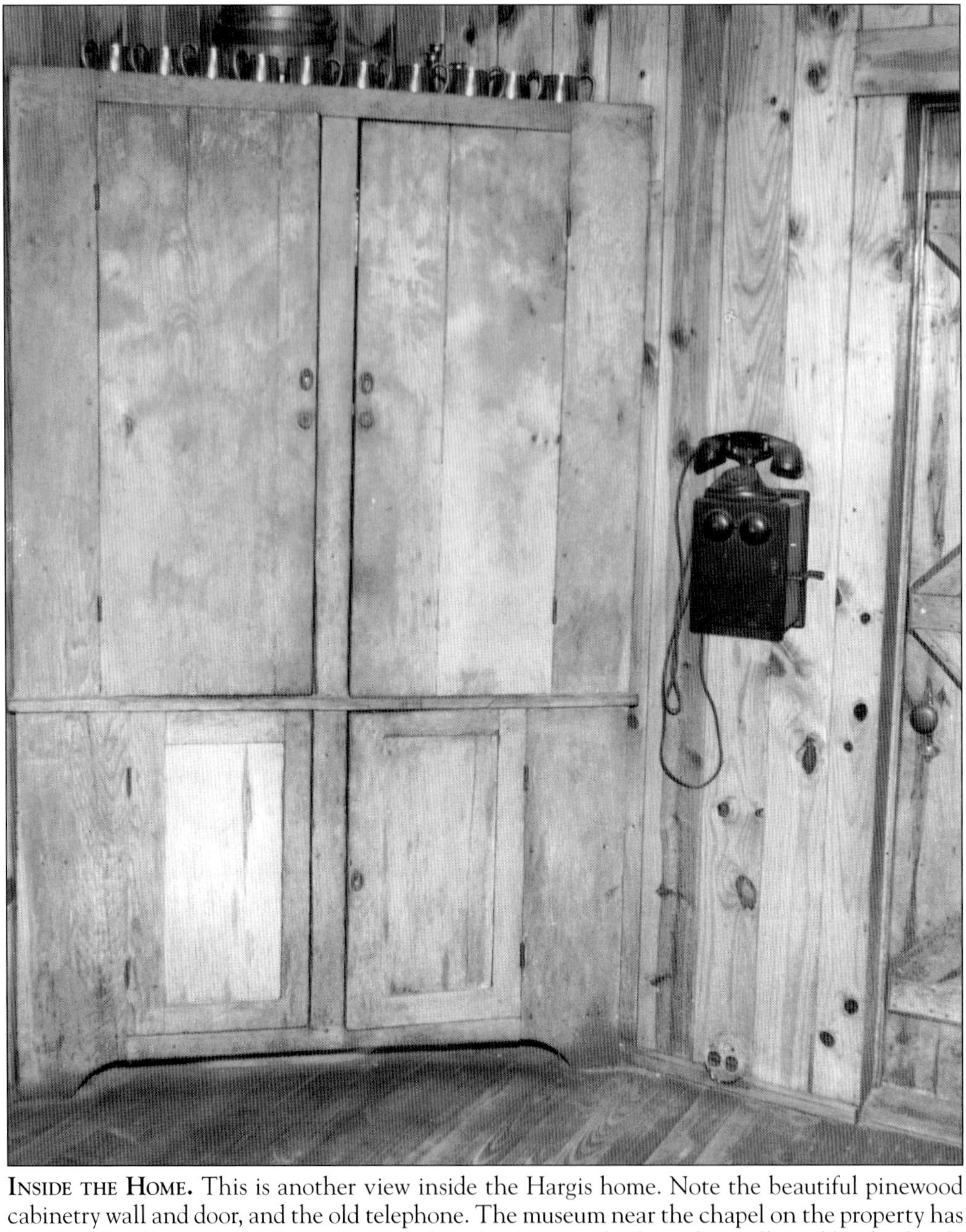

INSIDE THE HOME. This is another view inside the Hargis home. Note the beautiful pinewood cabinetry wall and door, and the old telephone. The museum near the chapel on the property has a multitude of items from the home, including furniture and other relics collected by the family over the years. (Courtesy of Walter Savage.)

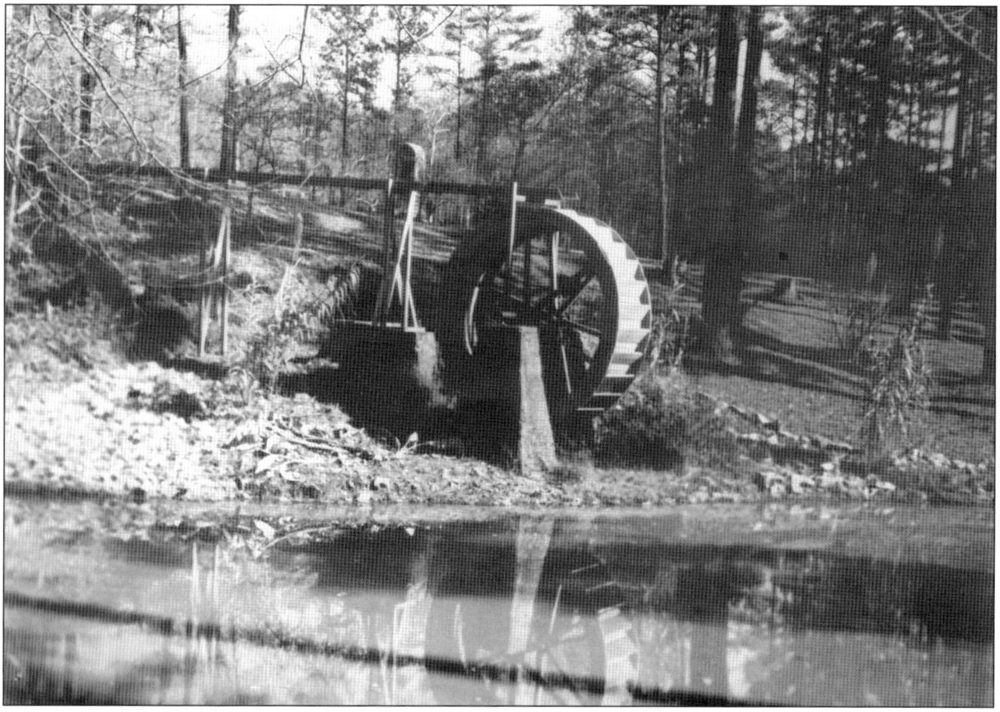

WELL WHEEL. Pictured is an original well wheel on Dr. Estes Hargis's property. An original boathouse, well house, well, and a barn remain on the property today. (Courtesy of Walter Savage.)

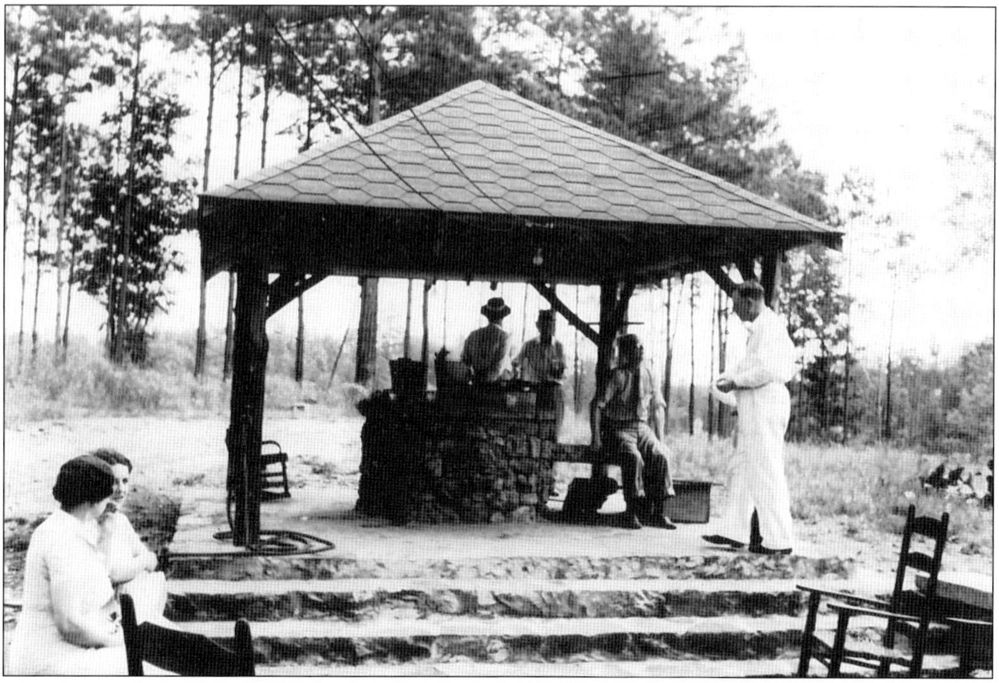

THE WELL. A well on the land of Hargis Retreat is still operational today. The well was used on the original homestead, established in the early 1900s. Dr. Hargis knew that the well and its water were more than sufficient to support his vision for a future retreat. (Courtesy of Walter Savage.)

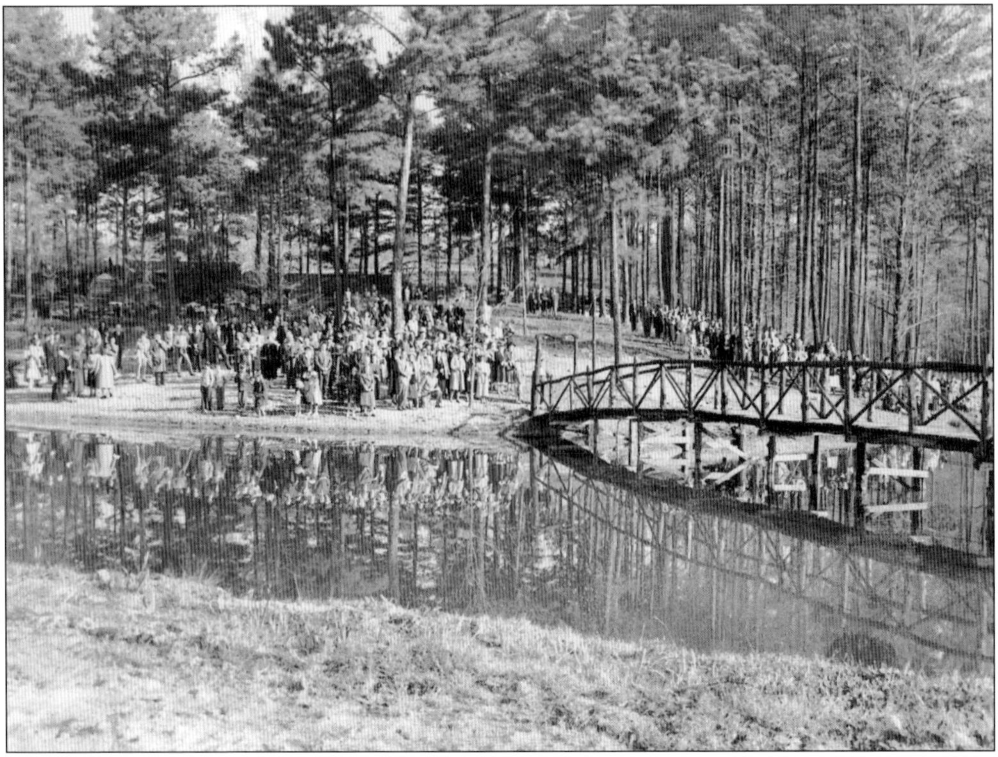

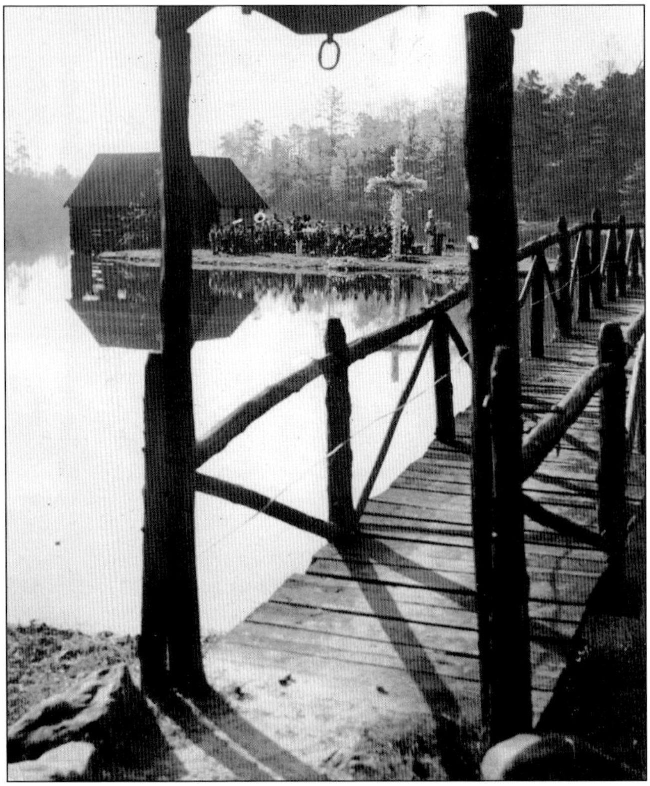

Easter Sunday Service. This 1960s photograph shows an Easter service held on the Hargises' land. First Christian Church on Valleydale Road was the church involved in helping make the dream of sharing the Hargis land with others a reality. Dr. Tom Gilchrist headed the church at the time. (Courtesy of Walter Savage.)

Church Service by the Boathouse. Many church services were held at Hargis Retreat when the project was complete. This service was held by the original boathouse with one of the original wooden bridges on the property in the foreground. (Courtesy of Walter Savage.)

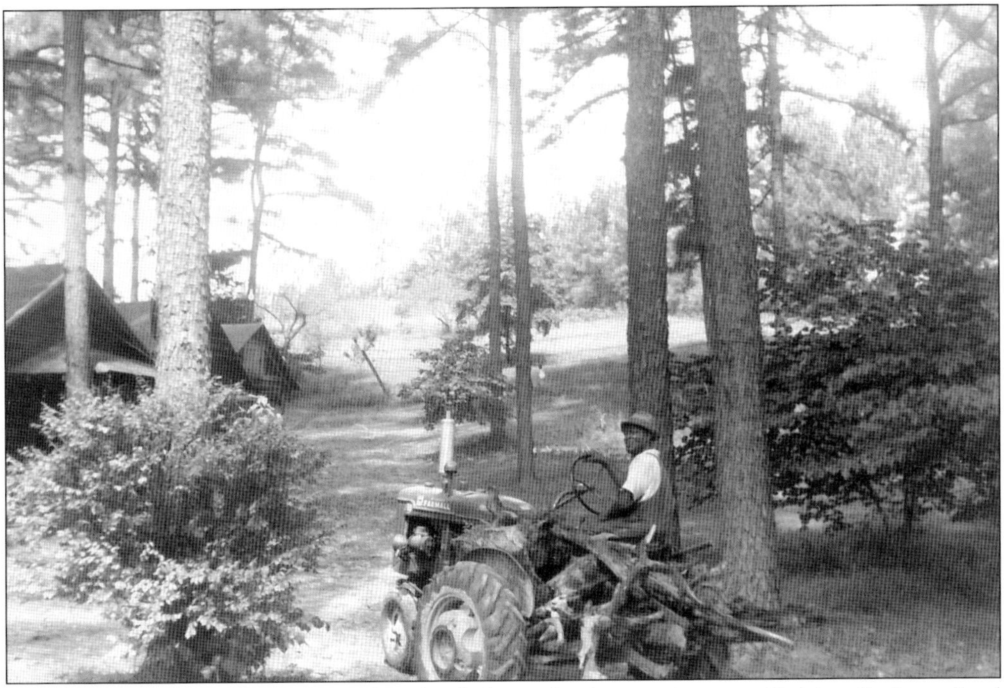

Turner Smith. Turner Smith was hired to help on the farm and retreat. He his wife, Jesse, lived on the land with their children. A chimney from their home remains right outside the museum to honor their work and dedication to the Hargis family. (Courtesy of Walter Savage.)

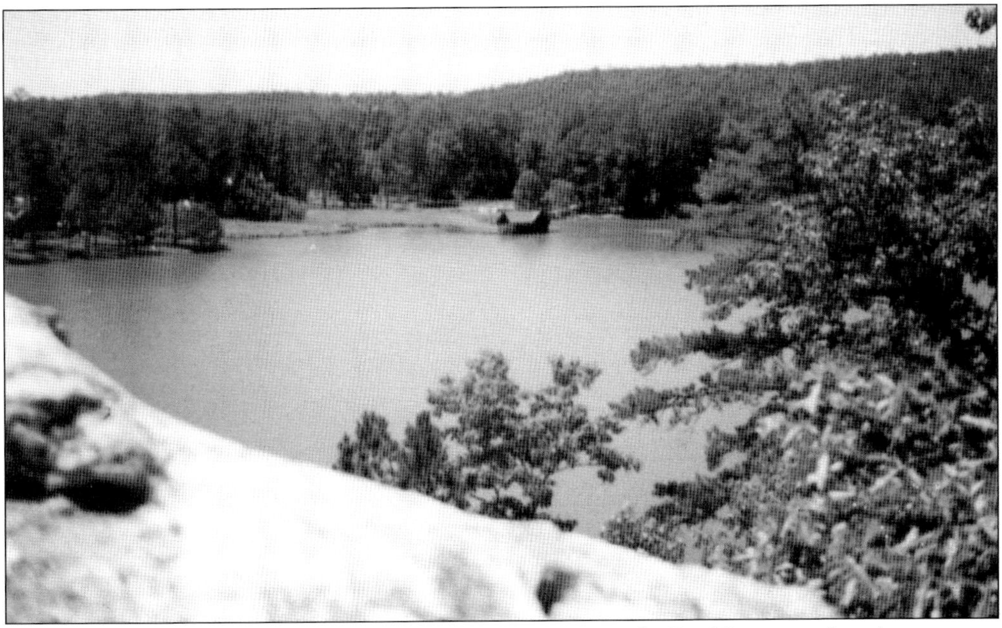

The Lake. The expansive lake at Hargis Retreat is manmade. Dr. Hargis employed many men from the Chelsea area, including George Weldon, who was a friend of his, to construct the lake. The lake holds many great memories for those who have had the chance to enjoy it. It does, however, hold a sobering memory for the family, as Dr. Hargis's mother drowned in the lake after her boat capsized. (Courtesy of Walter Savage.)

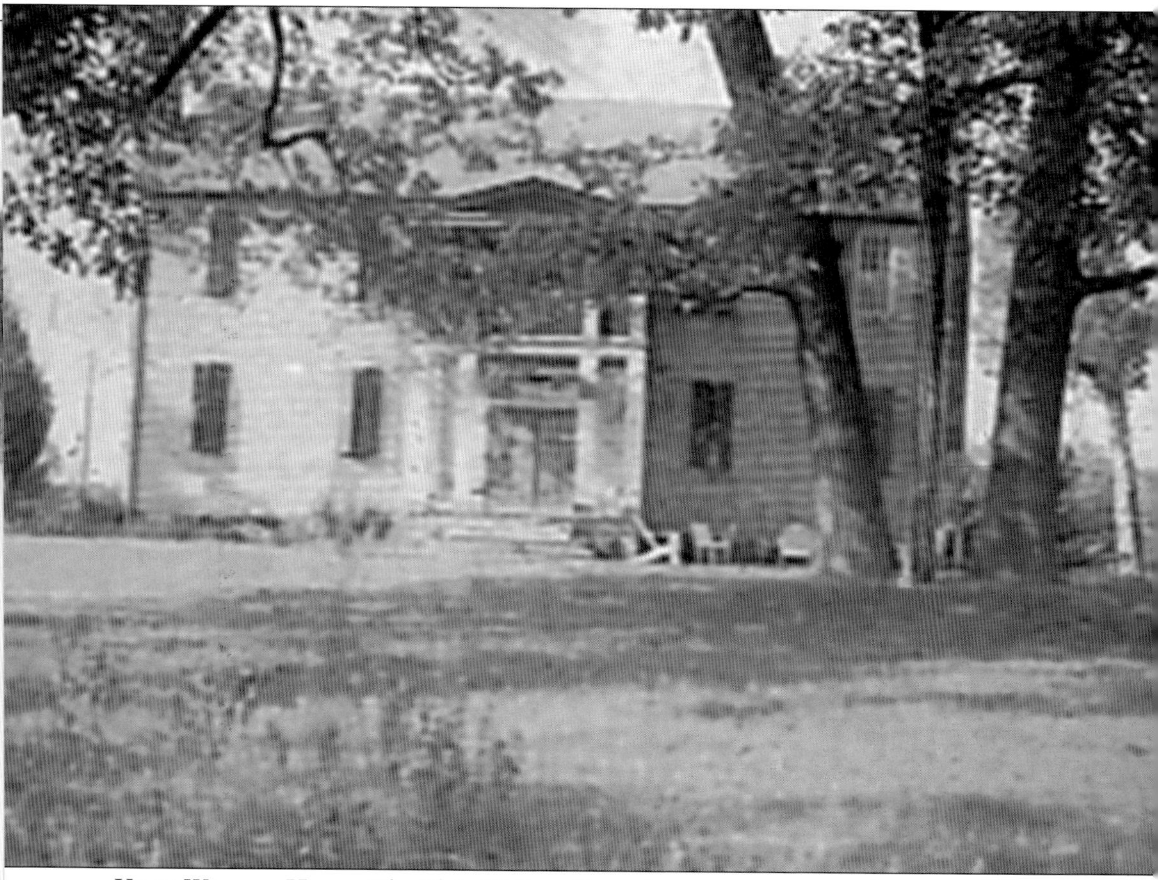

Klein Wallace House. The Klein Wallace House has an interesting and sometimes glamorous story behind it. In the early 1800s, Samuel Wallace of Virginia followed Andrew Jackson to what is present-day Wilsonville. By the 1820s, Wallace returned, bought land, and built a log home in the area. He moved his family and possessions to the new home, a process that took 11 months. Thirty years later, he owned more than 5,000 acres of land and many slaves and was considered a wealthy man. Construction on his plantation home was finished in 1841. It is known today as the Klein Wallace Plantation. The original rocks gathered from nearby still adorn the structure. At one point, Wallace put in a request for a post office and offered three names. The postmaster chose Klein. It has since been known as the Klein Wallace House. Wallace's daughter-in-law is said to have taught both black and white children on the lawn of the home, raising the question of whether this was the first integrated school in Shelby County. It is even said that actor Henry Walthall brought celebrities like Clara Bow and Rudolph Valentino to the plantation as a retreat in between filming. The house has not been occupied since the 1950s after rumors that the family who lived there could not live in it anymore because of ghostly whispers. (Courtesy of SCHS.)

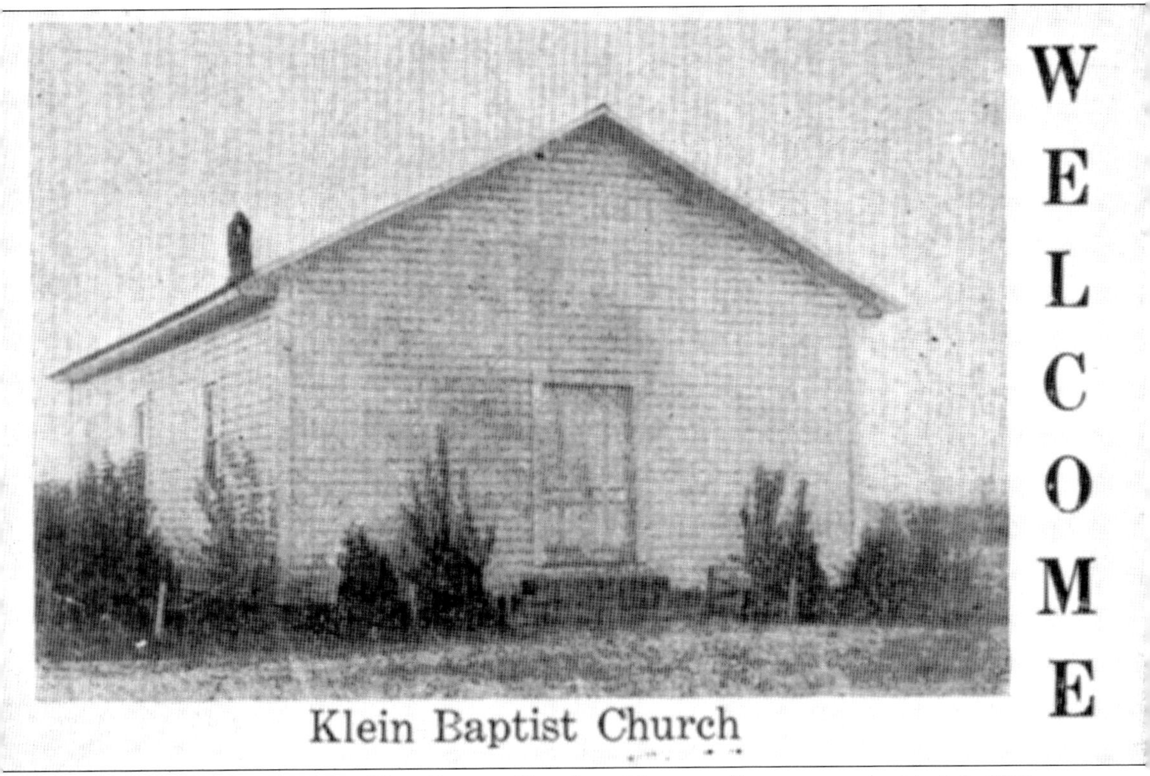

KLEIN BAPTIST CHURCH. The Klein Baptist Church in Harpersville was organized in July 1937. The property the church is on was deeded by the State of Alabama. The building was first used as a one-room school, known as the Wallace School. The building burned and was rebuilt prior to 1937. The year the church was organized, 25 new members were baptized in Yellowleaf Creek. Revs. J.W. Jones, B.F. Hixon, and E.E. Wells were tapped as presbytery. (Courtesy of SCHS.)

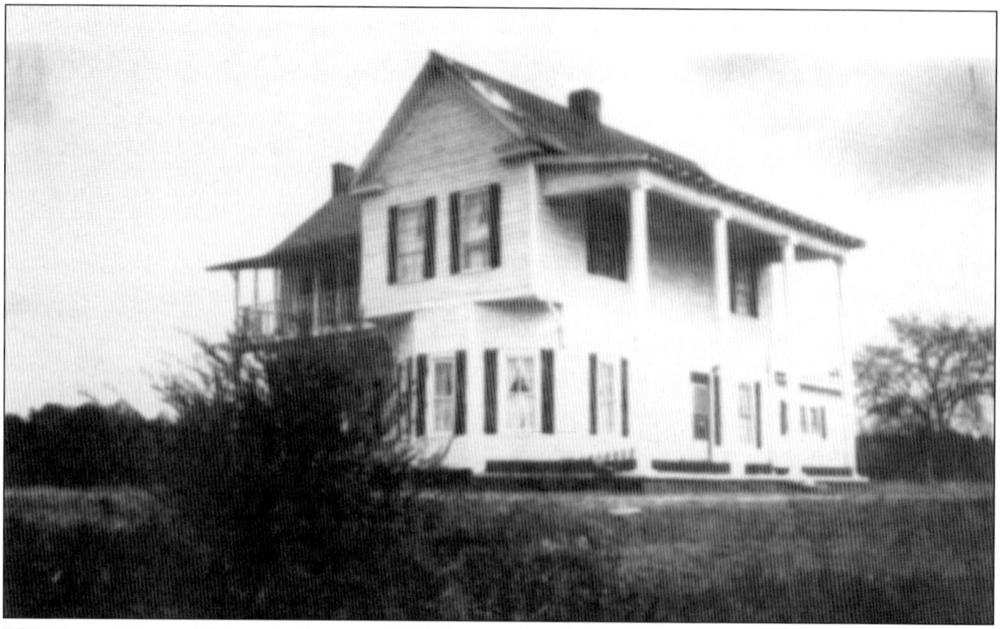

J.W. PITTS HOME. This is the home of J.W. Pitts, a Confederate veteran. Pitts organized Company K, 31st Alabama Infantry, and entered into command as a captain. One year later, he organized Company C, 62nd Alabama infantry, serving again as captain before being selected as a major. In April 1865, Pitts was taken prisoner and held on Ship Island off the coast of Mississippi. After his release at the close of the war, he farmed and represented Shelby County in the legislature for two years. Pitts died in April 1902 and is buried in Harpersville Cemetery. (Both, courtesy of SCHS.)

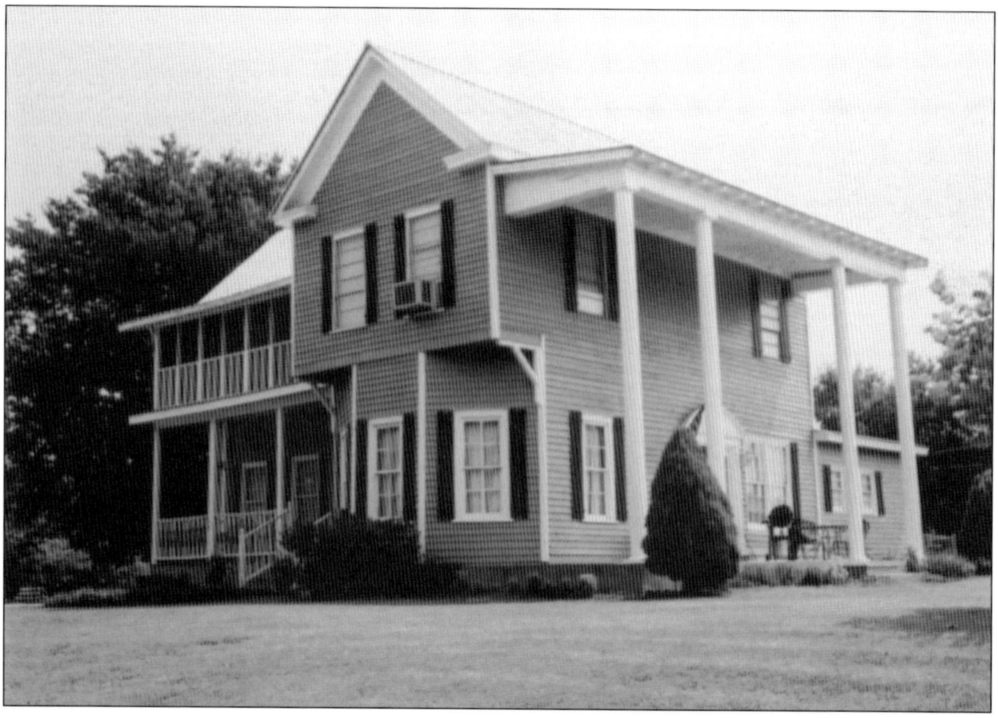

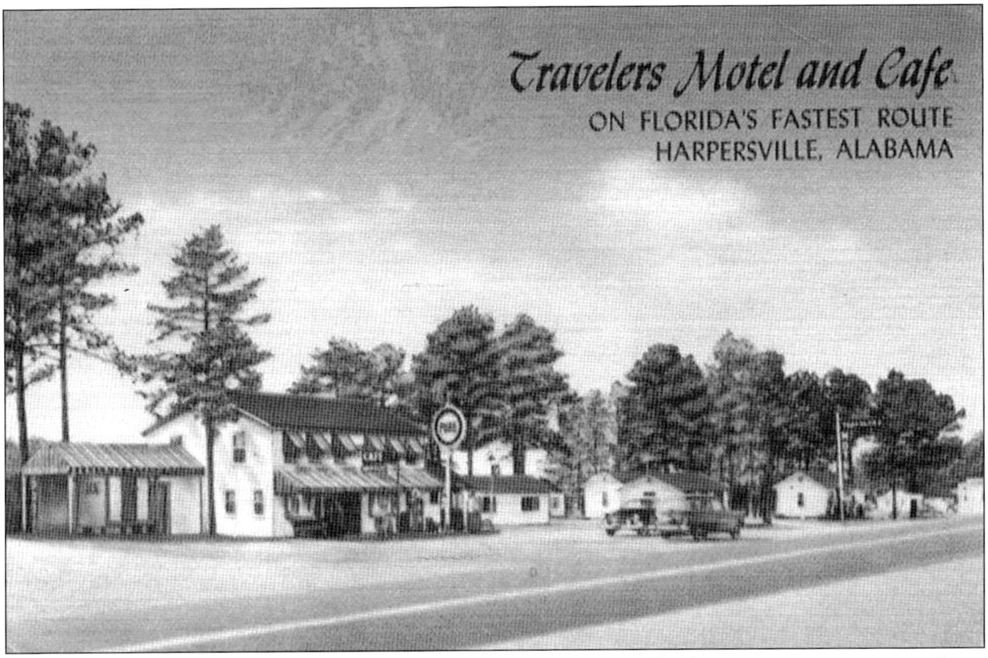

FLORIDA SHORT ROUTE, HIGHWAY 280. This vintage postcard advertises a resting stop along Highway 280, the Florida Short Route. This was a heavily traveled area through Harpersville. (Courtesy of Martin Everse.)

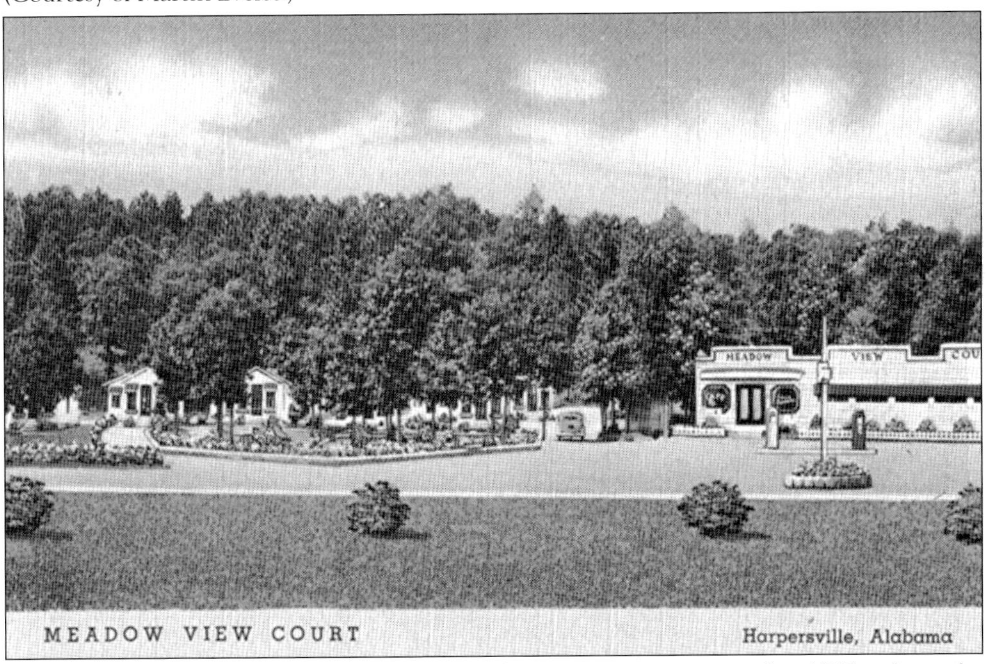

MEADOW VIEW COURT VINTAGE POSTCARD. Highway 280 was constructed in 1925 and was the quickest way to get from Birmingham to the beaches of Florida. It was also the only route to areas such as Chelsea and Columbiana from Birmingham. In the 1970s, expansion took place on Highway 280, which continues today. The new highway detoured around the Narrows. The famous stretch was renamed but is still known to many today as the Florida Short Route. (Courtesy of SCHS.)

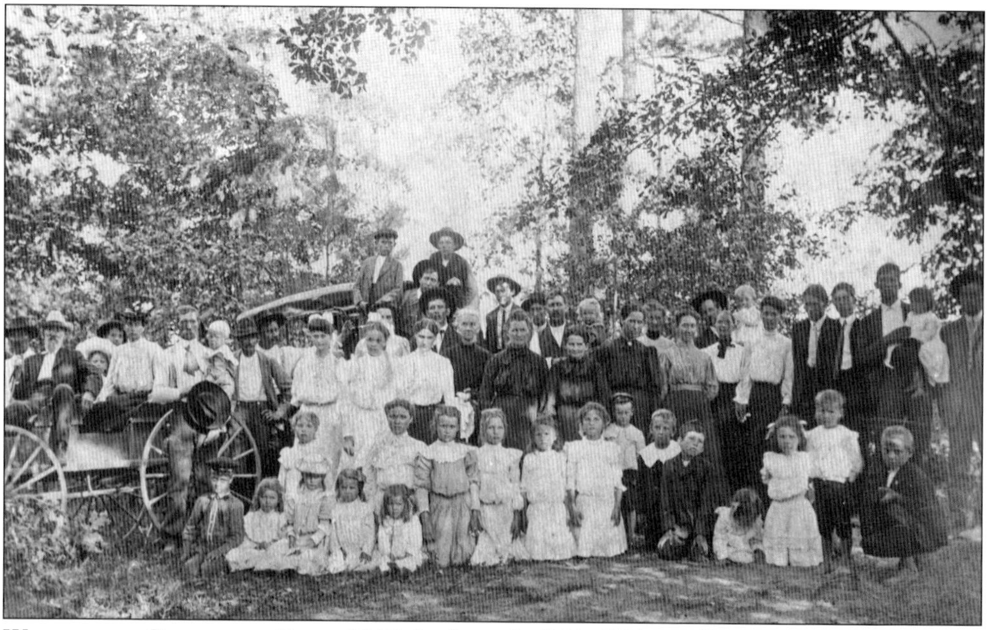

Wilsonville Gathering, Early 1900. In the early 1900s, Wilsonville was a successful, thriving young town. The population was around 1,600 with numerous popular stores. There were physicians, several general stores, a drugstore, saloon, bank, and blacksmith shop, to name a few. Several churches, like the Wilsonville Baptist Church, were forming along with small schoolhouses. (Courtesy of SCHS.)

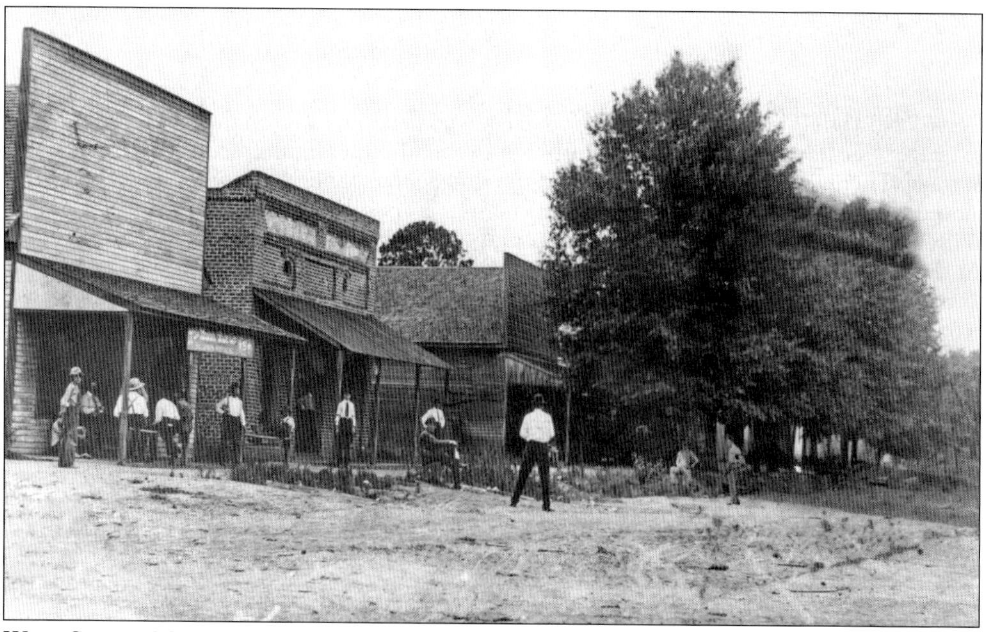

West Side of Main Street. This is a view of Main Street in Wilsonville in 1900. At the time, Wilsonville was the largest town in Shelby County. Beginning in the late 1800s, the town was considered of great importance because of the Southern Railway. It was a stopping point for the old stage route from Montgomery to Huntsville. By the 1930s, the largest mercantile company in the county was established there. (Courtesy of SCHS.)

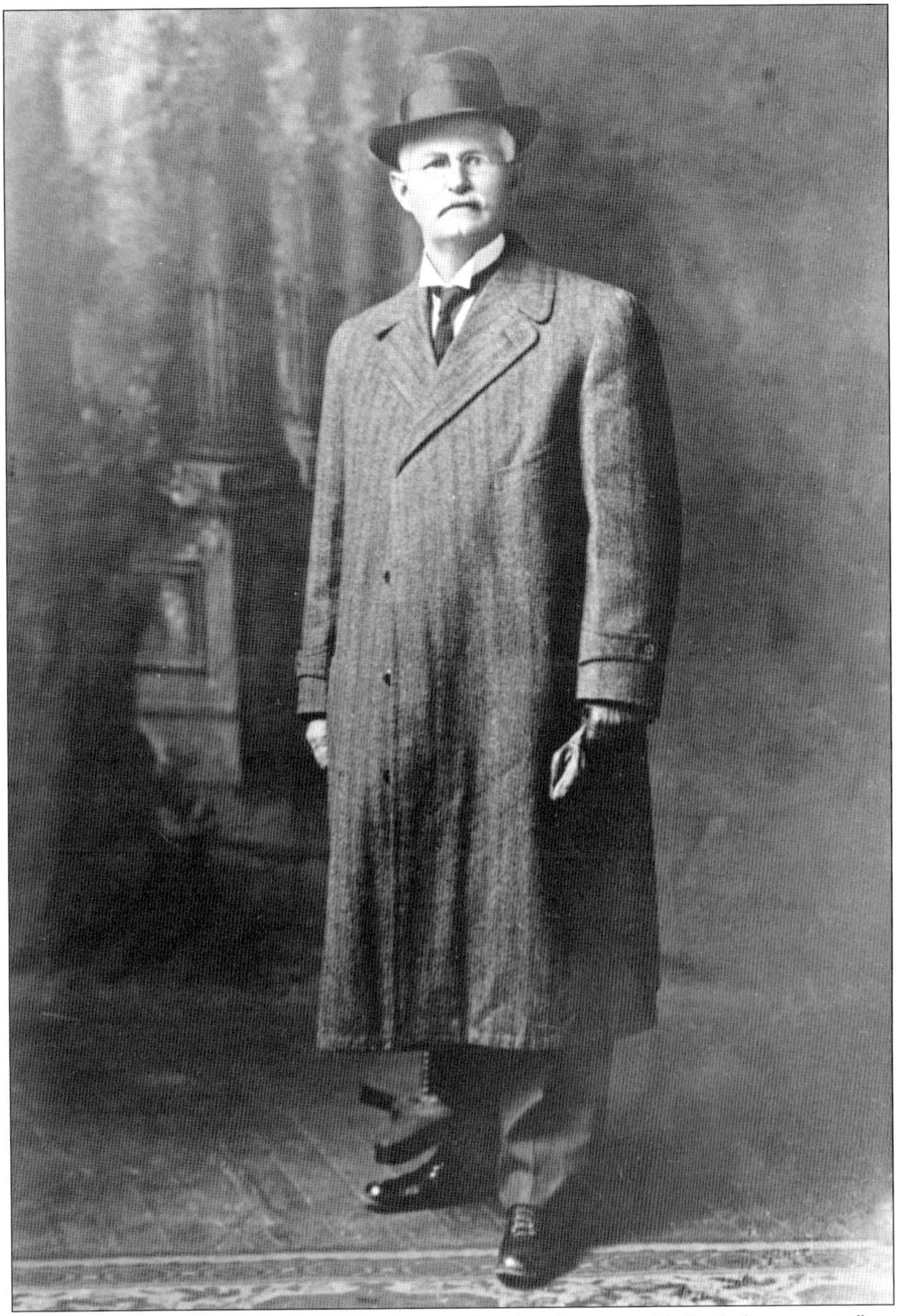

"You Can Get It at Pope's." J.F. Pope is considered to have established the most influential agency for developing and growing trade and community in the history of Wilsonville. In 1878, a young Pope was hired by W.T. Smith to help operate a budding store. Impressed with the young man, Smith sold a half interest of the business to Pope in 1885. Five years later, Smith sold the remaining interest to Pope. Pope is considered to have made mercantile history in Shelby County. The J.F. Pope Store stood for nearly 50 years. The store served residents in East Shelby County and Talladega County. "You can get it at Pope's" became a well-known slogan. (Courtesy of SCHS.)

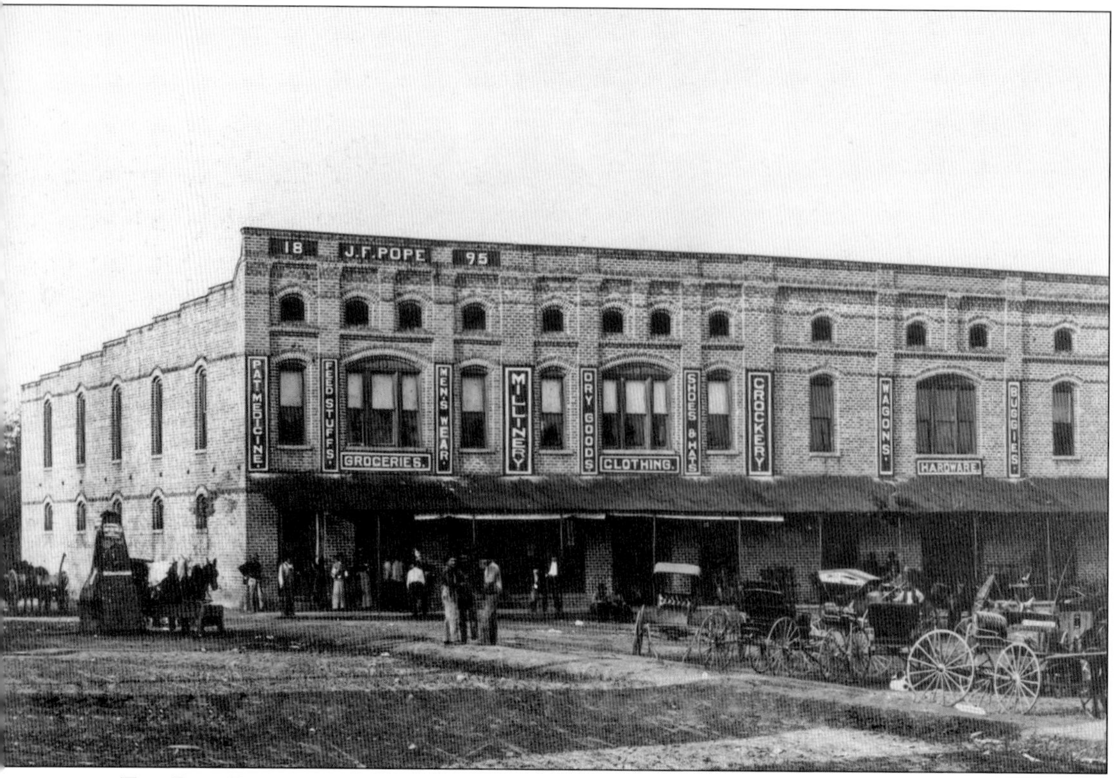

The Pope Building. By 1905, several businesses were operating in the Pope Building. A few were Black and Weldon, druggists; Jos. B. Boyer, physician; Jackson and Sons Sawmill; and a few general merchandise stores. Pope died in 1921, and his heirs tried to carry on the business. There were several owners, many of whom lived a distance from the store. They organized the store into a corporation that folded in 1922. (Courtesy of SCHS.)

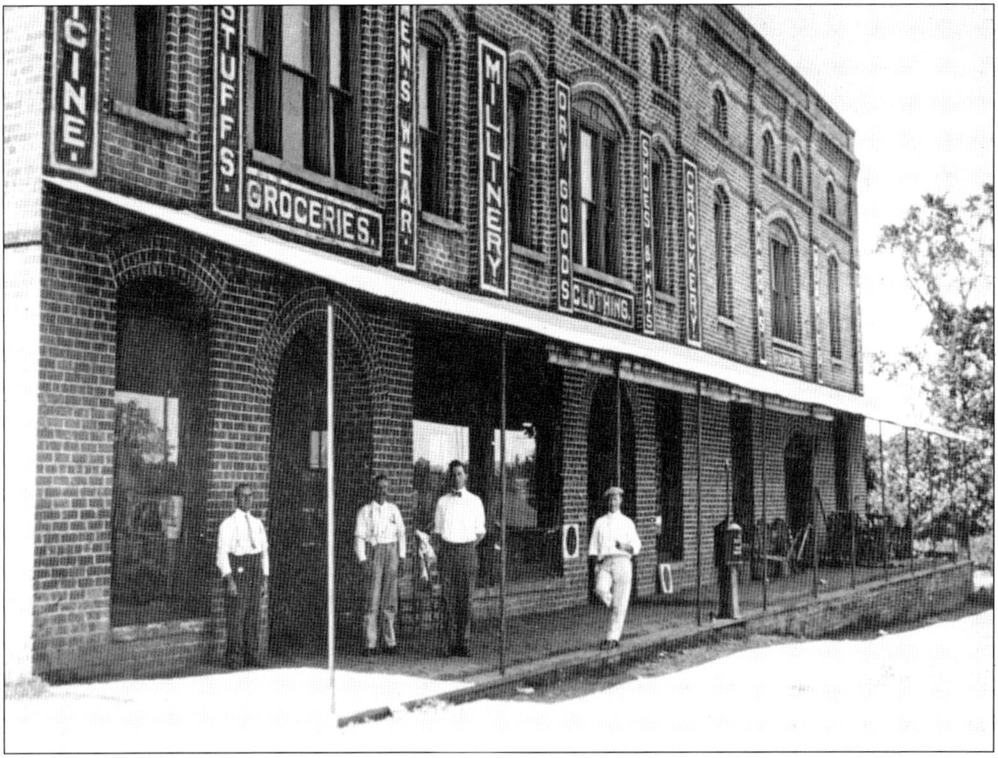

Men at the Pope Store. Pictured in 1913 are, from left to right, Ed Deramus, W.A. Daniel, Otis Strickland, and Leon C. Pope, J.F. Pope's son. (Courtesy of SCHS.)

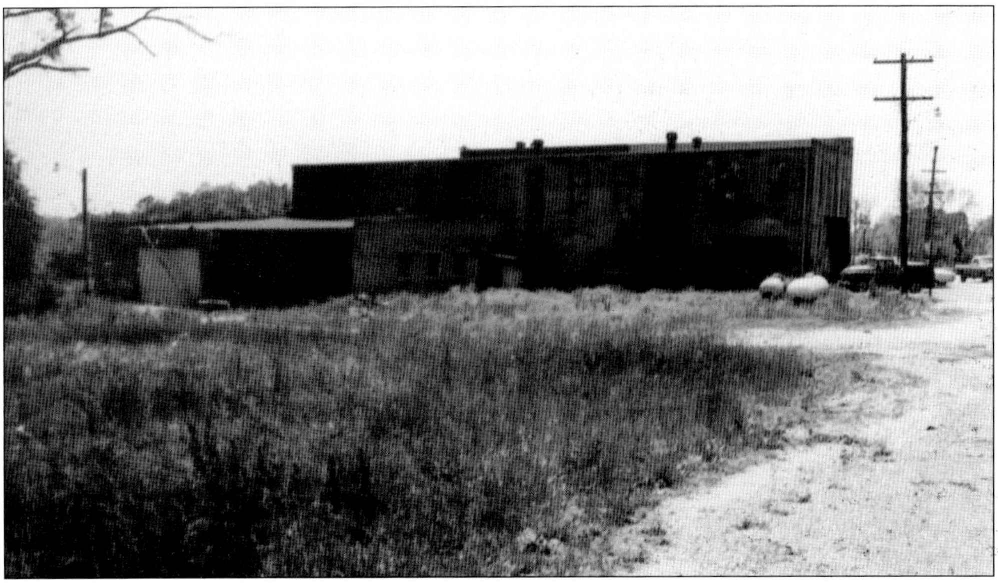

Vacant Building Burned. The vacant Pope Building was put up for auction in 1957. Unfortunately, while it was under consideration for the Alabama Register of Historic Places years later, the building burned. The history of one of Shelby County's largest general stores, which saw its way through the aftermath of the Civil War and the Great Depression, was lost in the fire. (Courtesy of SCHS.)

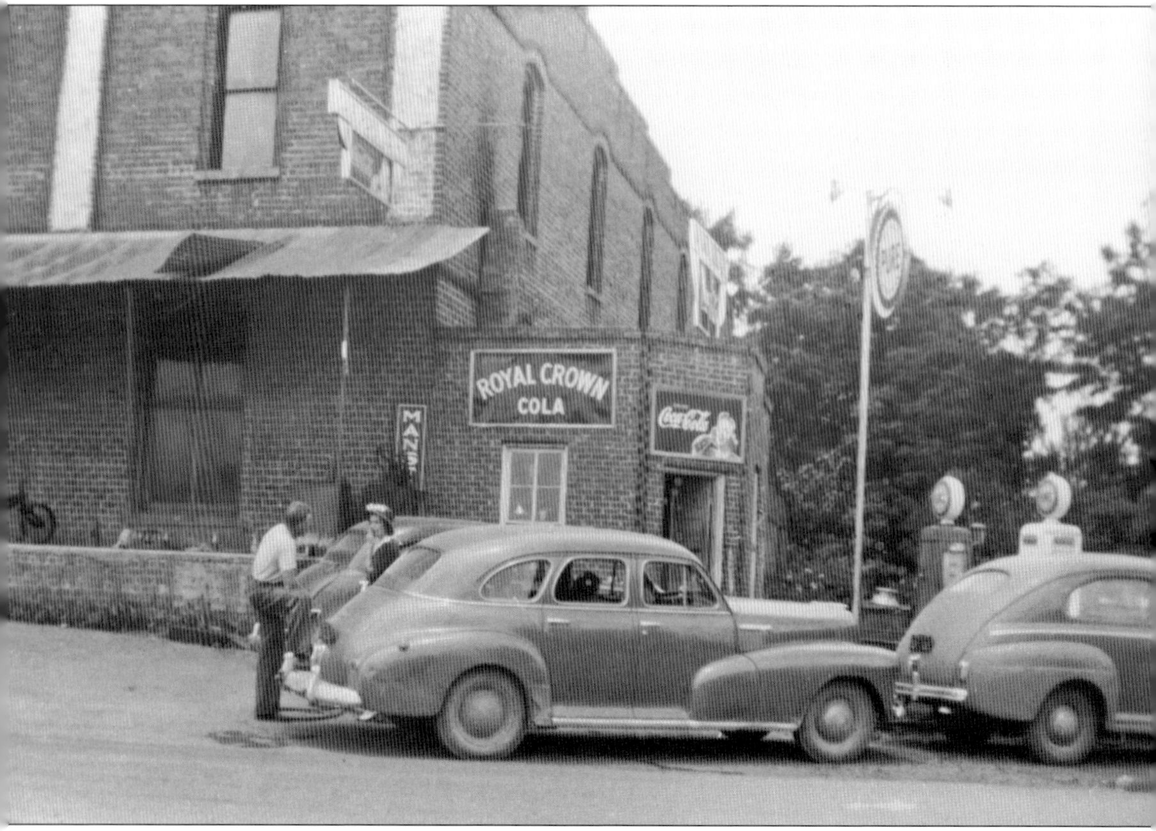

Service Station. The J.L. Batson Service Station stood at the corner of the popular J.F. Pope Building in downtown Wilsonville. Note the Royal Crown Cola sign. In 1934, Chero-Cola was reformulated and re-released as Royal Crown Cola. In the 1950s, Royal Crown and MoonPies were known as the "working man's lunch" in the South. Royal Crown was the first company to sell soft drinks in a can. (Courtesy of SCHS.)

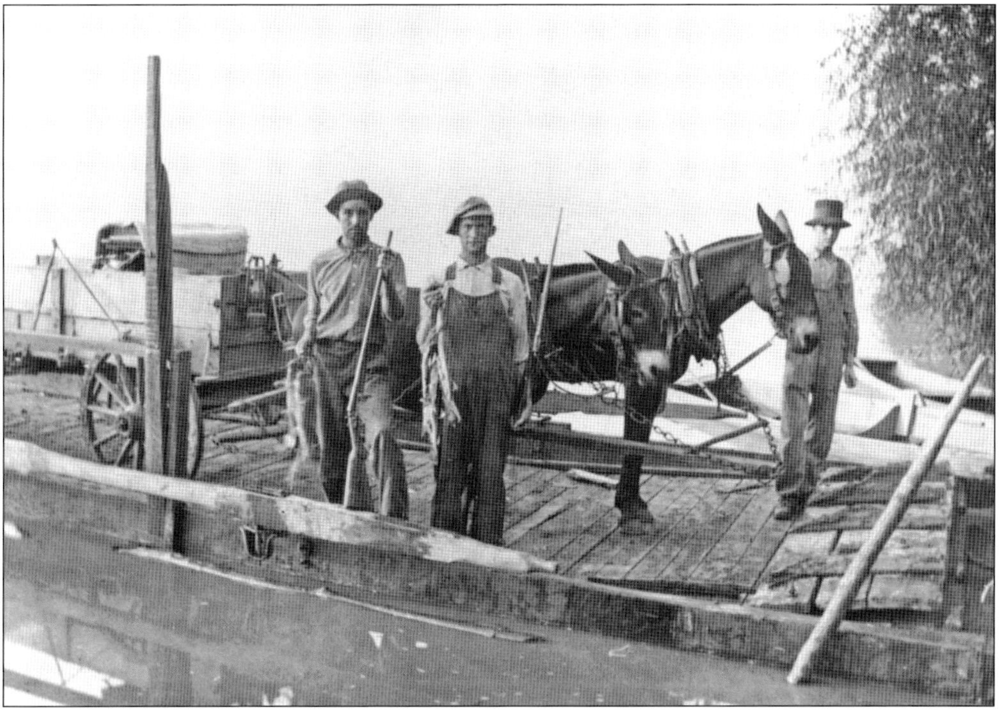

McGowan Ferry. The McGowan Ferry was on the Coosa River, one mile from Wilsonville. Several ferries operated in the area at the time. McGowan Ferry ceased operations in 1939. Marde's Ferry was operational until 1942. The ferry was also often used to transport grain for the Wilsonville wheat mill and gristmill. (Both, courtesy of SCHS.)

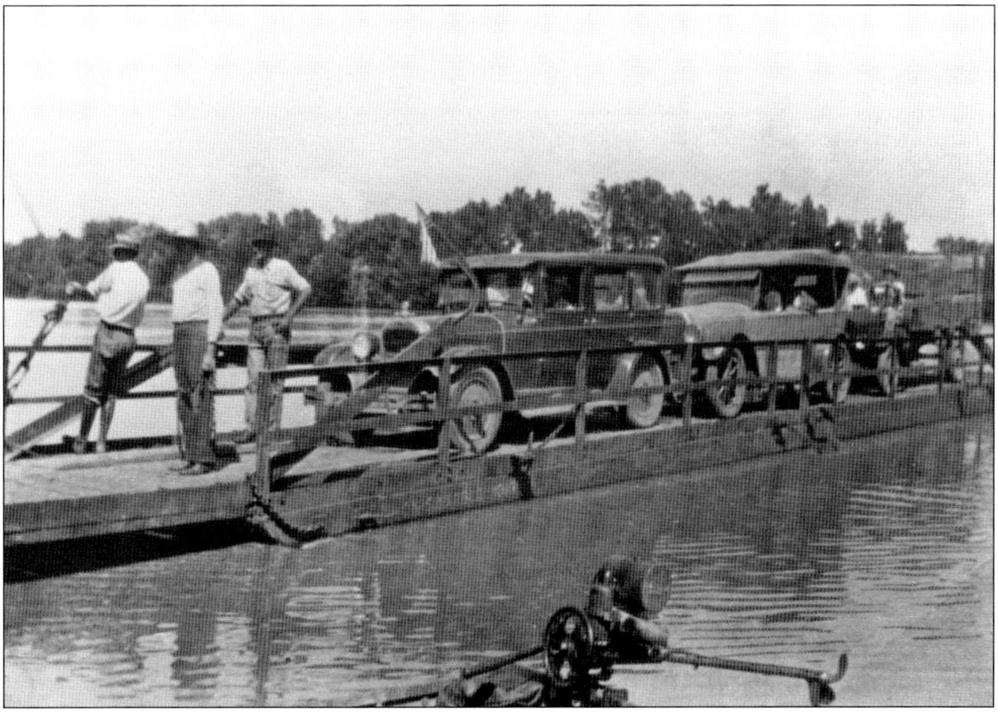

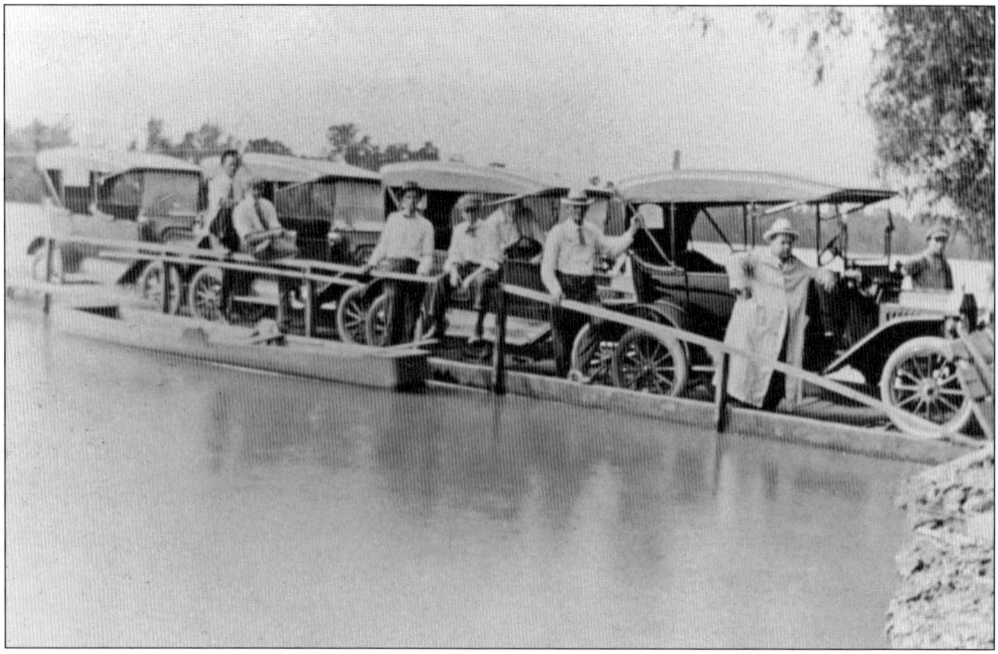

Model Ts on McGowan Ferry. Four Model T Fords are loaded onto McGowan's Ferry in Wilsonville to cross the Coosa River. Frank Bazemore helped operate the ferry. Those who drove these cars, like the man pictured near the front of the car at right, often had to wear large coats to protect their clothes from the dusty roads. (Courtesy of SCHS.)

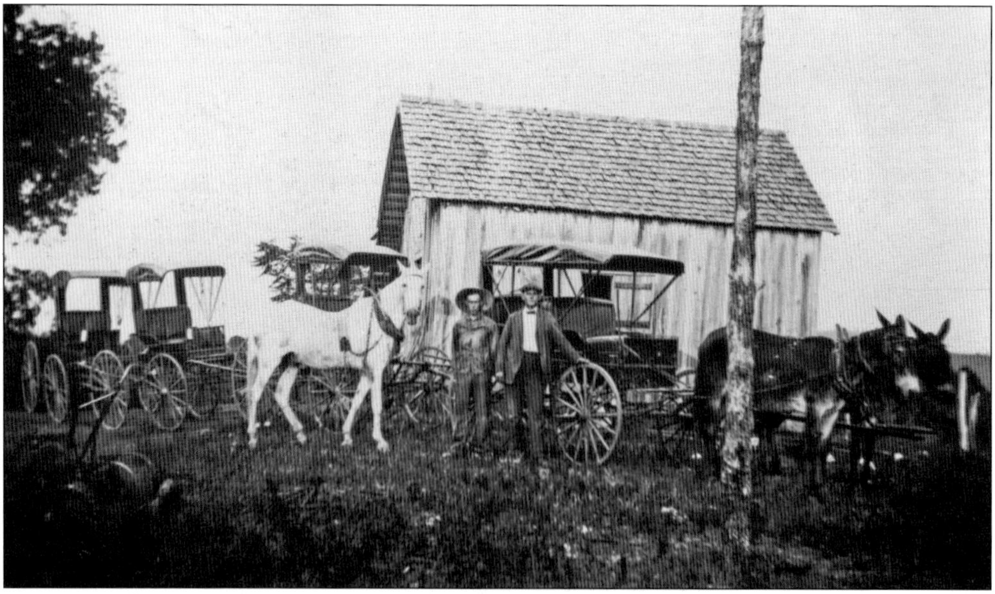

Bazemore Barn, Horse and Buggy. Even after the introduction of the Model T, the horse and buggy was still a popular means of transportation in Wilsonville. This photograph at the Bazemore family barn near McGowan Ferry shows the prevalence of the horse and buggy. The Bazemore family took root in Wilsonville in the early 1900s. William Blount Bazemore could not farm due to health reasons and operated a ferry from Wilsonville across the Coosa River. (Courtesy of SCHS.)

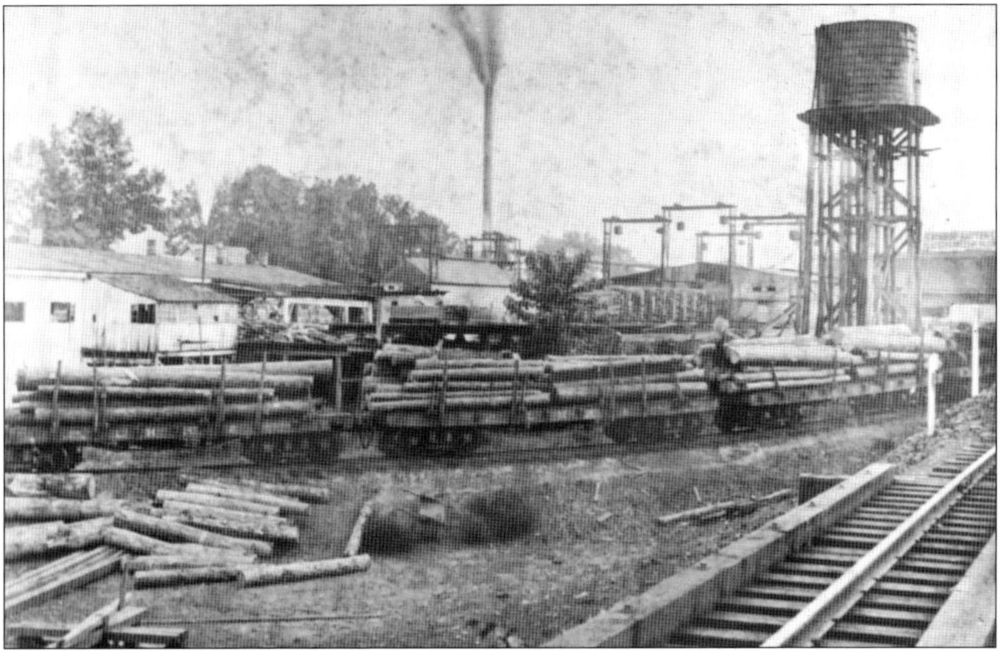

THE RAILWAY. Wilsonville was located on the important Old Montgomery Stagecoach Road. It also housed the county's first depot. After the town was settled, a railroad with wooden rails was built through the area. Since the bridges were wooden, watchmen were needed to keep them from burning. Shipments coming from the North had to be reloaded onto cars that the new rails could accommodate. This photograph shows flatbed railcars loaded with logs ready for transport. By the 1880s, a narrow-gauge track was laid and steel rails replaced the wood. All travel to and from Wilsonville in the early 1900s was done by train. (Courtesy of SCHS.)

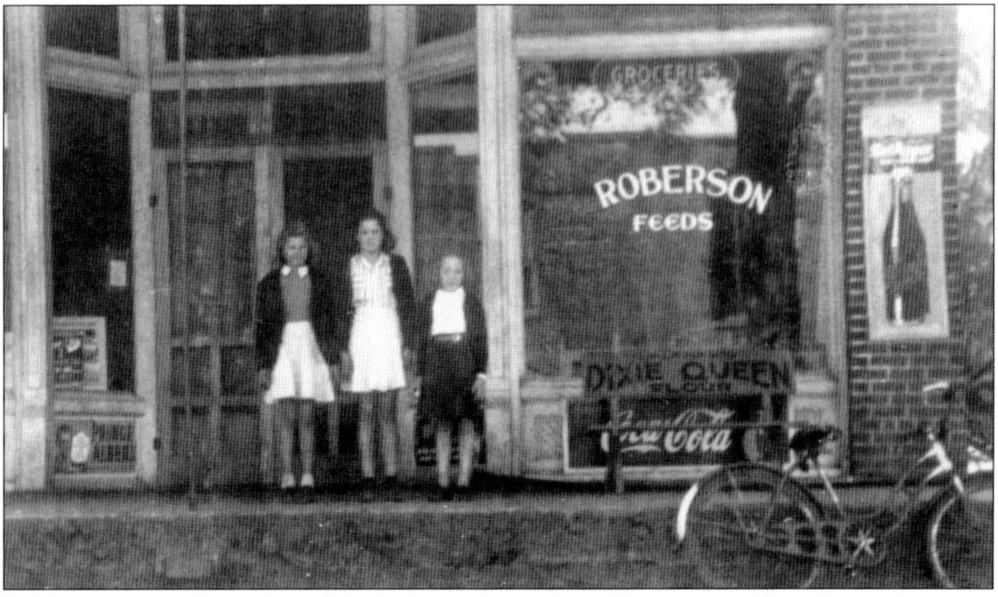

ROBERSON GROCERY, 1935. Roberson Grocery in Wilsonville is pictured here during the 1930s. The girls standing in front are, from left to right, Jonnie Sue Hill, Birdie Jean Baker, and Edna Roberson. (Courtesy of SCHS.)

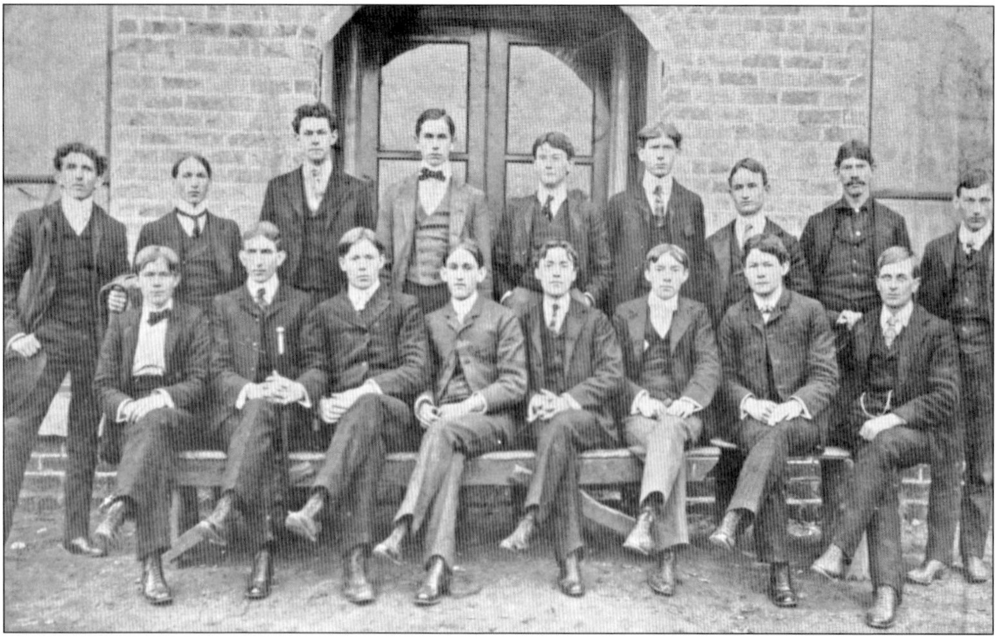

Men at Weldon Store. A group of young men pose in front of the popular Weldon Store in Wilsonville. From left to right are (seated) John ? , John Bolin, Jim Kimbrough, Lon Smith, Floyd Wilkins, Eugene Wilkins, Calvin Weldon, and Ben Berham; (standing) Charlie Bolin, O.C. Wolfe, Charles Niven, Olie Tinney, Roy Smith, Jerry Strickland, Earl Williams, and Duncan Wilkins. From its beginning in the early 1800s, the population and popularity of Wilsonville steadily increased. In 1900, the population was around 1,600. Resident Ress Weldon bought the Farmer's Alliance and turned it into a general store. (Courtesy of SCHS.)

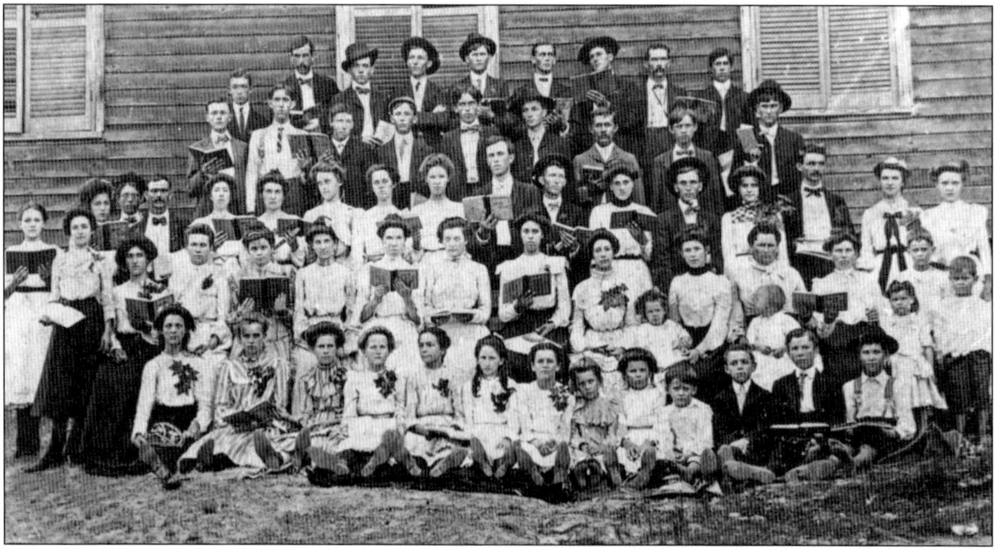

Singing School. This is the Singing School at Old Kingdom Church near Wilsonville. Included in the photograph are Houston Richard, Tom Horter, Carl Jackson, Charley Farris, Walter Almon, Claude Heaton, Tom Crumpton, Andie Crumpton, Cecil Crumpton, Jennie Bennet, Minnie Crawford, Mattie Crumpton, Minnie Templin, Beatrice Crumpton, Delilah Crumpton, Henry Crumpton, and William Rohards. (Courtesy of SCHS.)

Wilsonville Church, 1918. One of the oldest churches in Wilsonville, Wilsonville Baptist was assembled in 1879. Dr. E.B. Teague was asked to organize the church. Teague was an Alabama minister and influential education leader in the 19th century. Dr. Teague served as pastor from 1879 until 1887. Col. W.T. Smith, who moved from Virginia and ran a lumber mill, donated land for the church. Colonel Smith also ran the first cotton gin. Wilsonville Baptist is still operational today. (Courtesy of SCHS.)

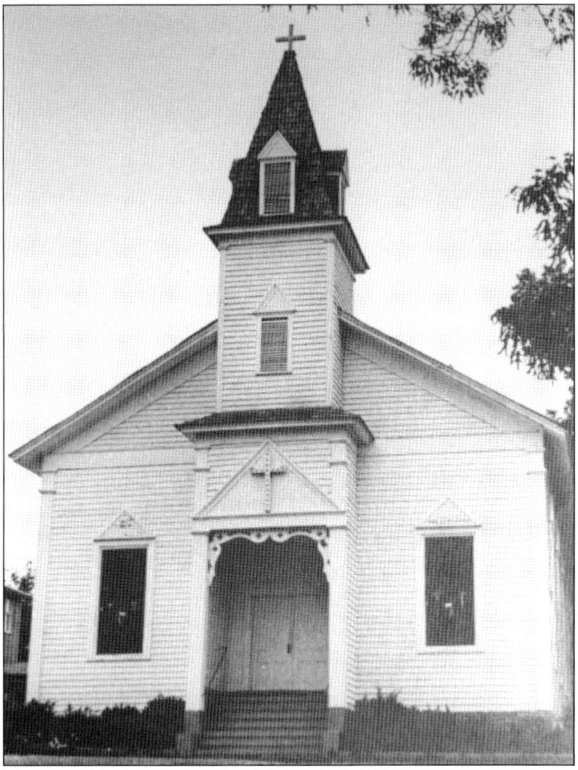

Old Chapel Church, Wilsonville. The Methodist Church is the oldest church in Wilsonville. The first building stood in an old part of the cemetery. Another building was built later, on a hill across from the cemetery. In 1946, the church was remodeled and rooms were added, such as a kitchen and Sunday school rooms. (Courtesy of SCHS.)

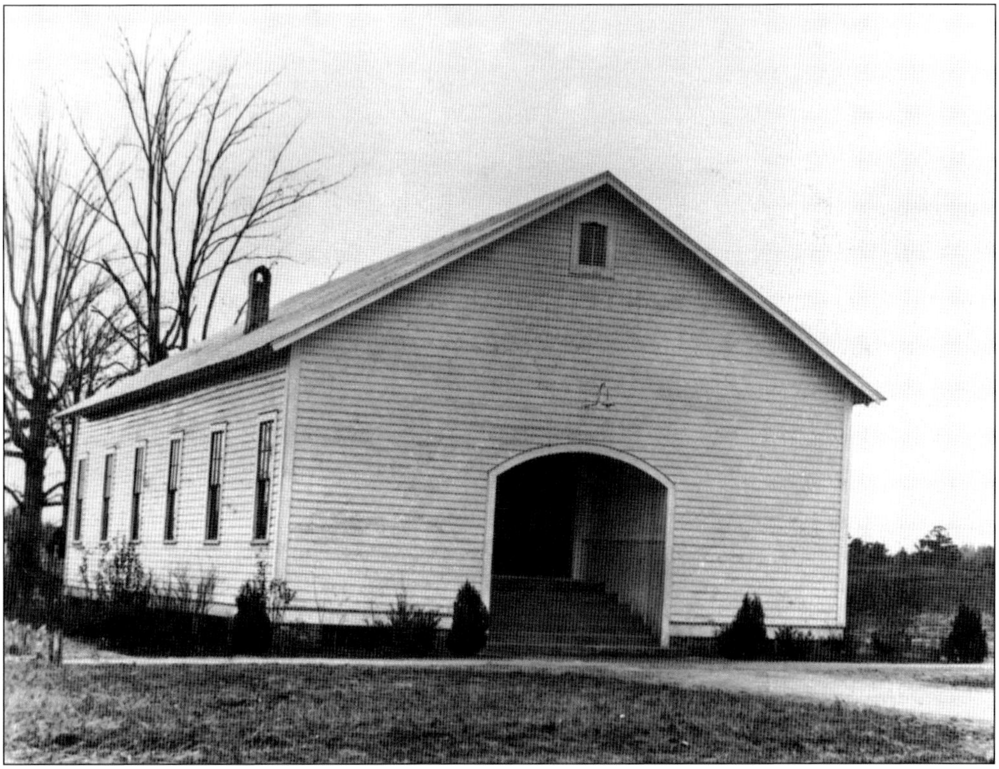

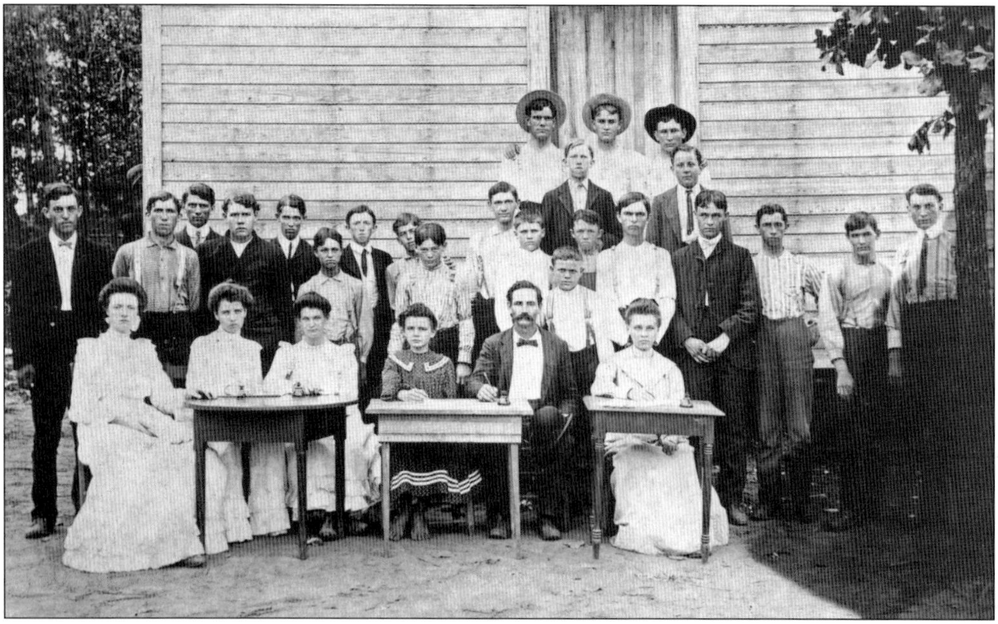

McGowan School. McGowan School was located on Highway 25 near Wilsonville. The school has been converted to a private residence. From the early 1800s to 1916, however, McGowan School was highly reputable and teachers considered themselves fortunate to teach in the school. There was one teacher for about 40 students, and they were paid about $60 per month. (Courtesy of SCHS.)

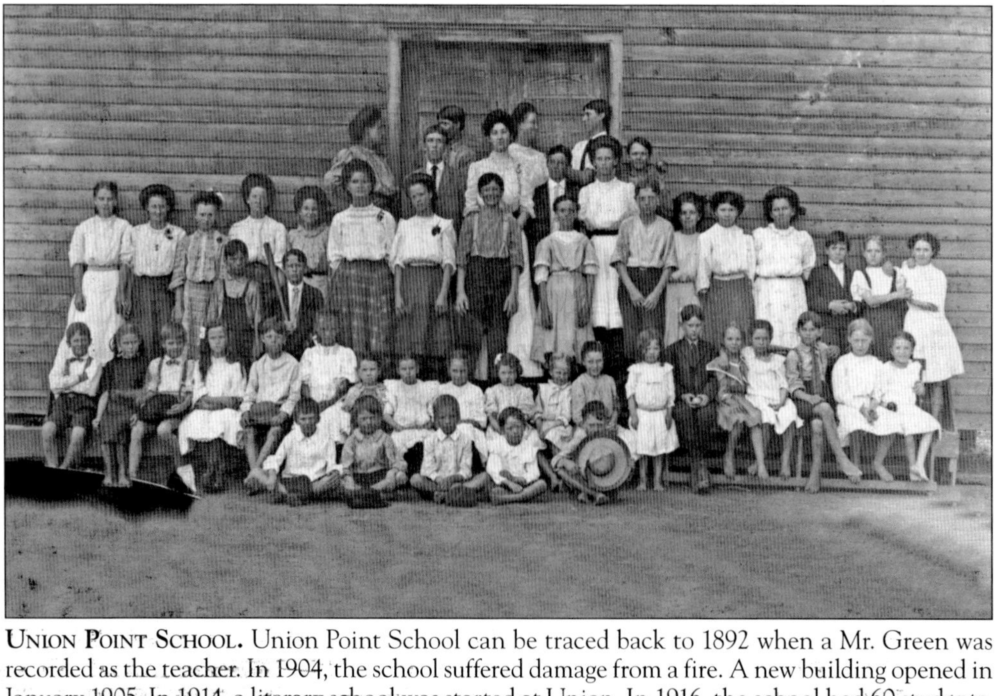

Union Point School. Union Point School can be traced back to 1892 when a Mr. Green was recorded as the teacher. In 1904, the school suffered damage from a fire. A new building opened in January 1905. In 1914, a literary school was started at Union. In 1916, the school had 60 students. The school was consolidated in 1927, and students transferred to Crossroads School, also known as the Old Rock School since it was built from native rocks. (Courtesy of SCHS.)

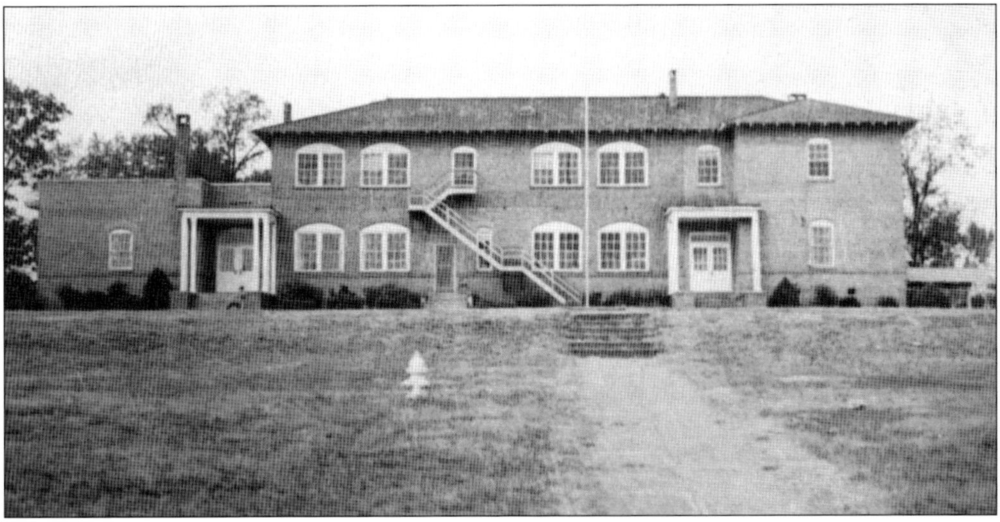

Wilsonville Junior High School, 1955. The history of the Wilsonville school systems involves many schools and buildings until the 1950s. One of the earliest schools was in the Chapel Meetinghouse, used from the early 1800s to 1900. Instructors such as Frank Lyon, Will McEwen, Isla Farr, and Delilah King were considered "good instructors" because it was rare a good instructor withheld whippings for misbehavior. Over time, schools were consolidated into the Wilsonville area. Wilsonville Junior High School served grades one through nine. Today, Wilsonville serves kindergarten to fifth grade; after the fifth grade, students are transferred to Columbiana. The main building of the present school was erected in 1919. It was bricked after fire destroyed the wooden structure. (Courtesy of SCHS.)

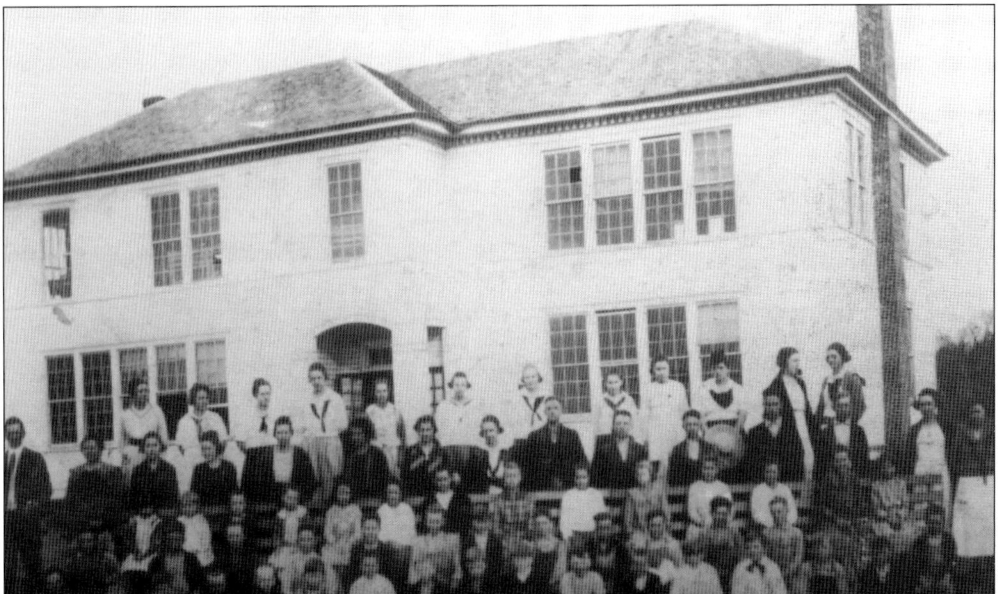

Fourmile School. Fourmile School was once a highly credible teaching institution. Fourmile was located near Wilsonville, and at the turn of the 20th century, it was a trading point for two prosperous farming sections. One was Fourmile, and the other was the Kingdom. Children walked two to four miles to attend school there. (Courtesy of SCHS.)

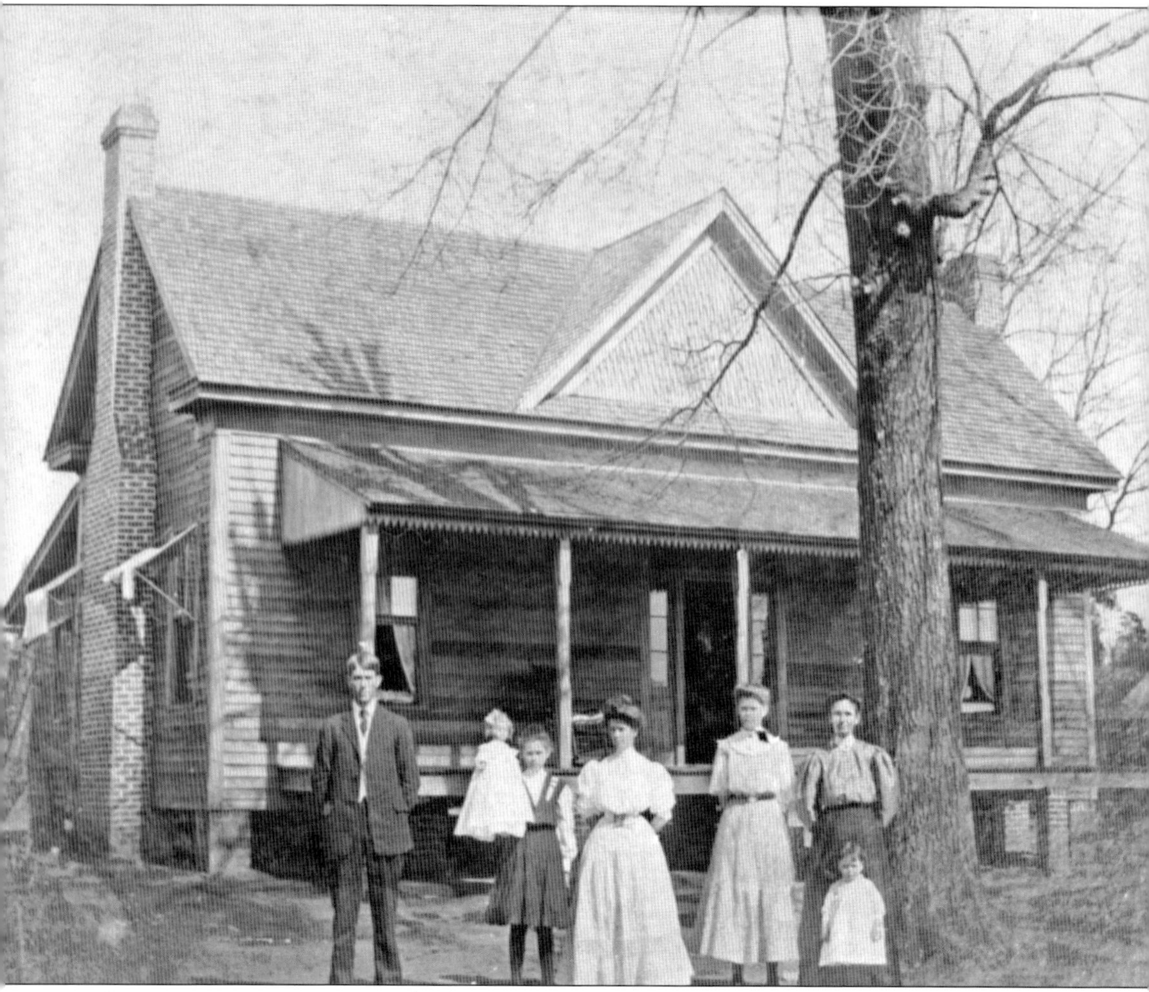

STRICKLAND FAMILY HOME. The family home of B.M.T. Strickland on McGowan Ferry Road is seen here. From left to right are Otis, Gaudia, Effie, Cammie, Mrs. Strickland, and an unidentified child. While churches were forming in Wilsonville. Dry Branch Baptist was organized in 1894. The building was blown down in 1923 and rebuilt a year later. B.M.T. Strickland built the steeple for it. It was remodeled in 1962, and the name was changed to First Baptist Church. (Courtesy of SCHS.)

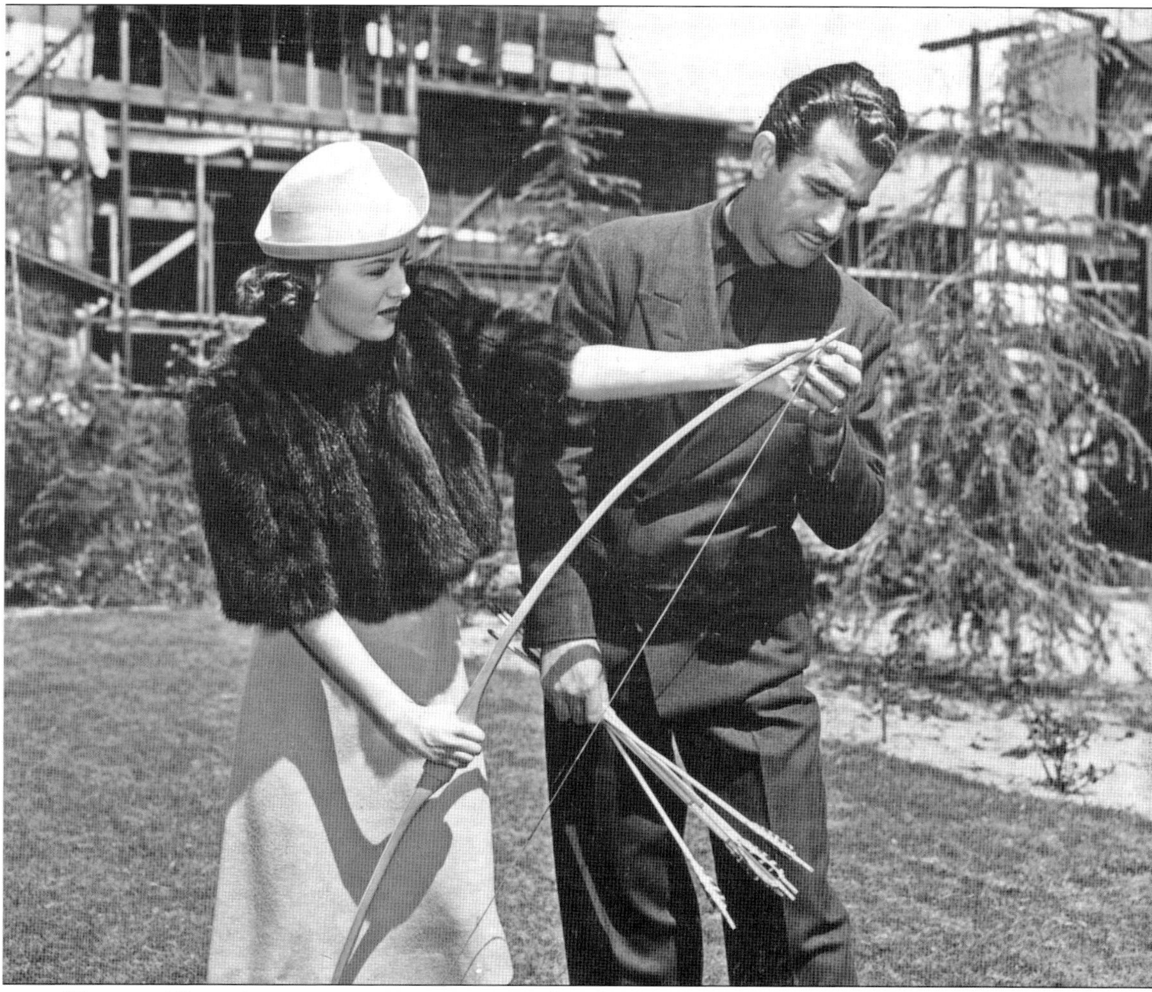

Howard Hill, Actor and Archer. Howard Hill, who hails from Wilsonville, is still widely considered the "World's Greatest Archer" with incredible achievements over a 50-year span. He also incorporated acting into his love for the sport that he discovered as a young boy. Hill was born in Wilsonville in 1899 and raised on a farm. He went to Auburn University, where he excelled at other sports, like football. But it was archery that was his passion and greatest achievement. Hill was inducted into the Alabama Sports Hall of Fame in 1971 for his archery skills. He is the only person to win 196 archery field tournaments in a row. During his career, he also produced 23 films related to archery and shot 10 different movies. He became the first white man to kill an elephant with a bow and arrow. He is also in the Bow Hunter's Hall of Fame. Hill said, "It takes more work to stay on top than it does to get there." Hill and his wife, whom he was married to since he was 21 years old, retired and moved back to Shelby County and lived in Vincent until his death in 1975. (Courtesy of SCHS.)

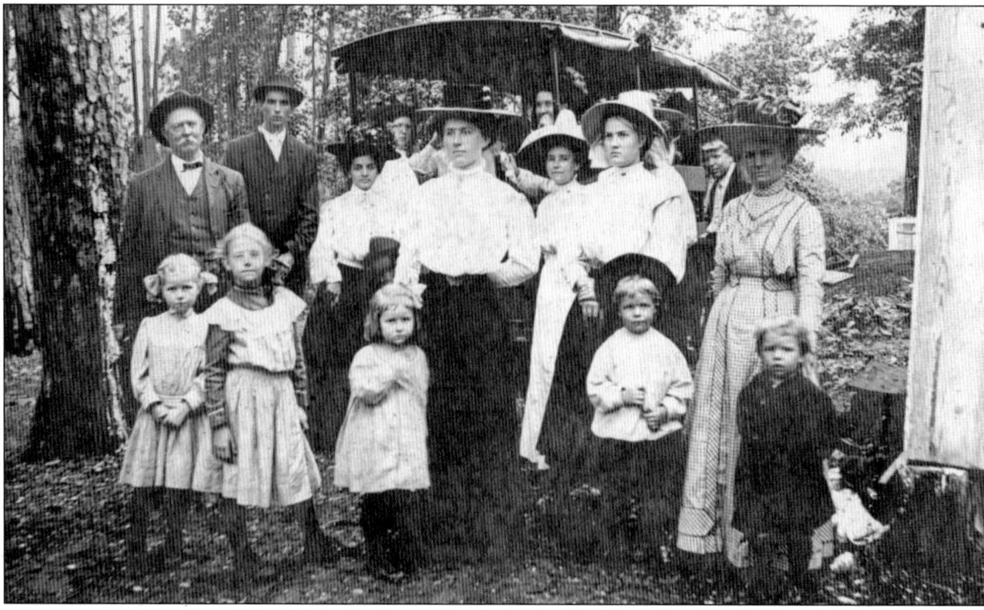

The Jitney Bus. In a Columbiana newspaper in 1915, an advertisement appeared about a new, convenient means of transportation. It touted that a jitney bus was available between Columbiana and Vincent. The jitney left Vincent in the morning and returned in the afternoon. People could ride for 5¢ per mile. In this 1915 photograph are Marjorie Nell Seal, Margurite Averyt, Mary Louis Seal, Alice Lena Browning, George Averyt, and Grady Curly. (Courtesy of SCHS.)

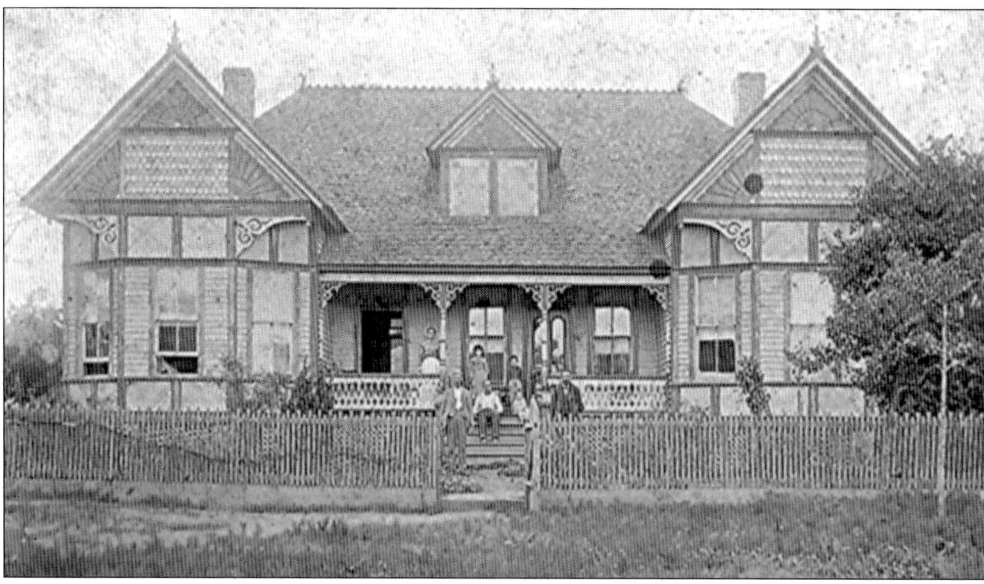

Raley House. The Raley House in Vincent was designed and constructed by George Bilbry in 1890. Ornate woodwork adorns the gables, and all the doors have their original wooden spindle screens. A log smokehouse and servant's quarters remain on the site. The home was owned by William Daniel Raley, who was a farmer and owner of a sawmill, Raley & Davis Lumber Company. Raley was once the mayor of Vincent. His gifts of lumber helped build a school and the Methodist church in 1891. The Raley home was added to the Alabama Register of Landmarks and Heritage in 1978. (Courtesy of SCHS.)

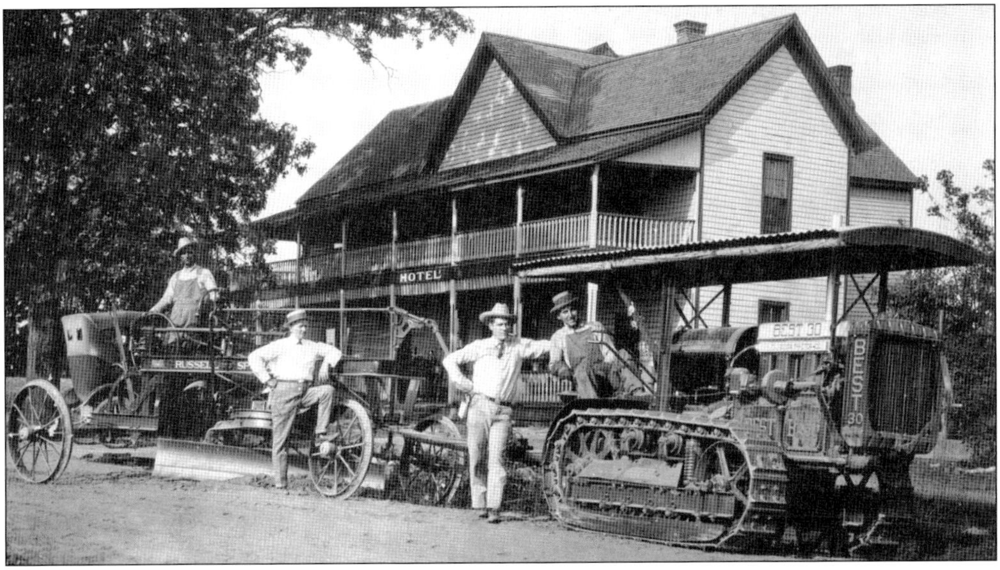

THE FREEZE HOTEL. James "Big Bud" Fluker McGraw, a member of the Shelby County Commission, and his son Richard Thomas McGraw are pictured in front of the Freeze Hotel in Vincent. Vincent resident Ada Freeze operated the hotel. While Vincent was a thriving farming town after the railroad was built, McGraw and his sons opened McGraw Brother's Store. The tractors seen here are the C.L. Best 30 brand, which provided some of the first mechanized equipment used in the country. Tractors drove the mechanization revolution, drastically changing farming. A job like planting and harvesting corn that could take 40 hours was cut to three hours. (Courtesy of SCHS.)

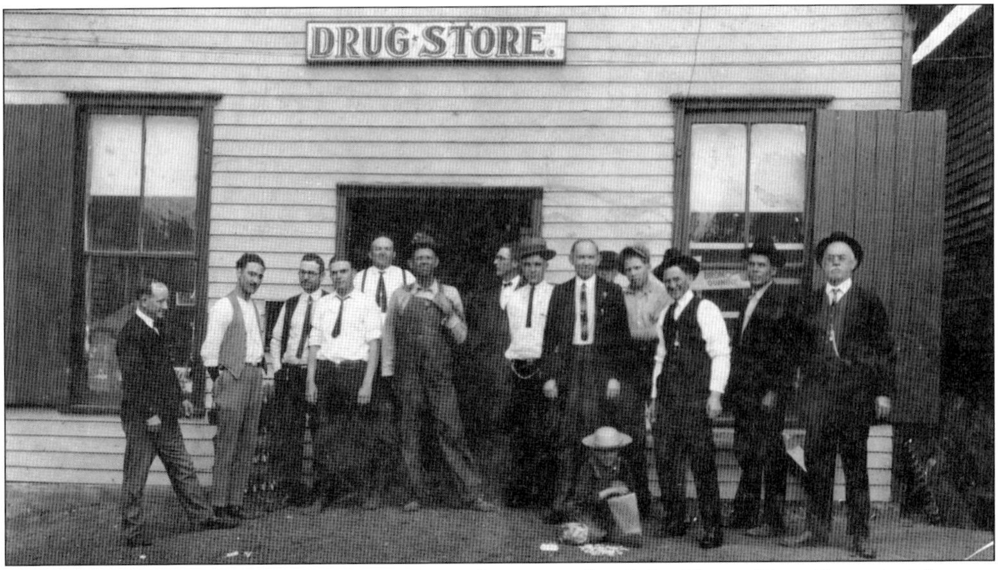

FLOREY DRUGSTORE, 1910. Patrons are standing outside of the Florey Drug Store in Vincent in 1910. Before the train made stops in Vincent, there was not much growth in the area except farming, mills, and a few stores. After the railway, however, there was a cotton gin, several more stores, and the Vincent Mercantile, which was operated by the Florey family. Carroll H. Florey, who was in education, was instrumental in getting the Town of Vincent's charter enacted into law by the state legislature in 1897. (Courtesy of SCHS.)

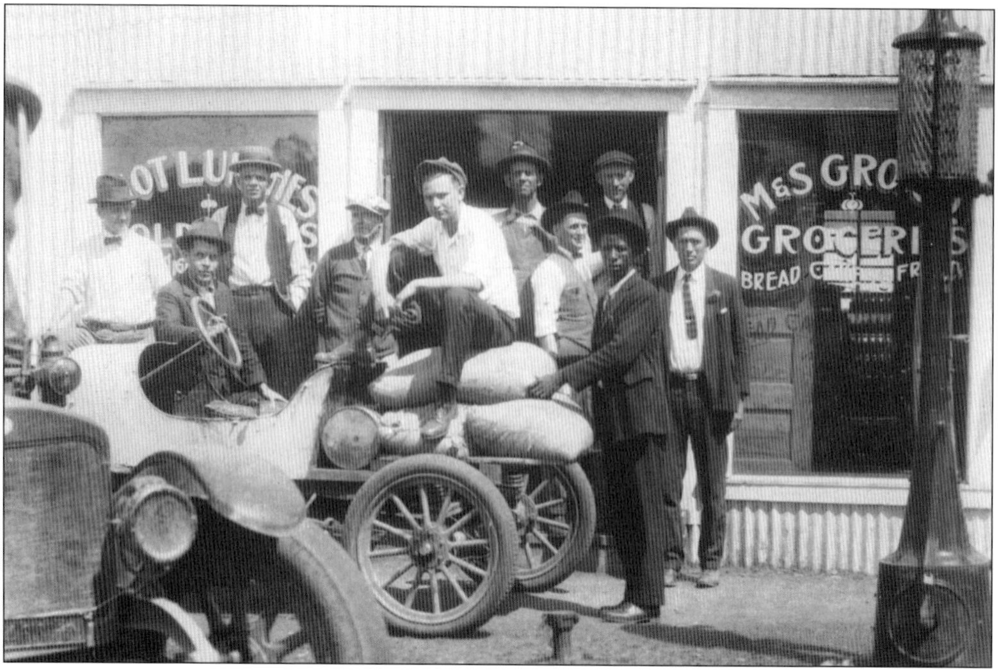

McGraw Shealey Grocery Co., 1920. Above, a 10-gallon gas pump sits to the right of a group of men in front of the McGraw Shealey Grocery Store in 1920. From left to right are unidentified, Tom Lacky, Amos Smith, Richard T. McGraw, E.C. Clyde, "Hobo" Glaze, W.E. Eastis, and Parker Shealy. The men are posing with a cut-down Model T. (Both, courtesy of SCHS.)

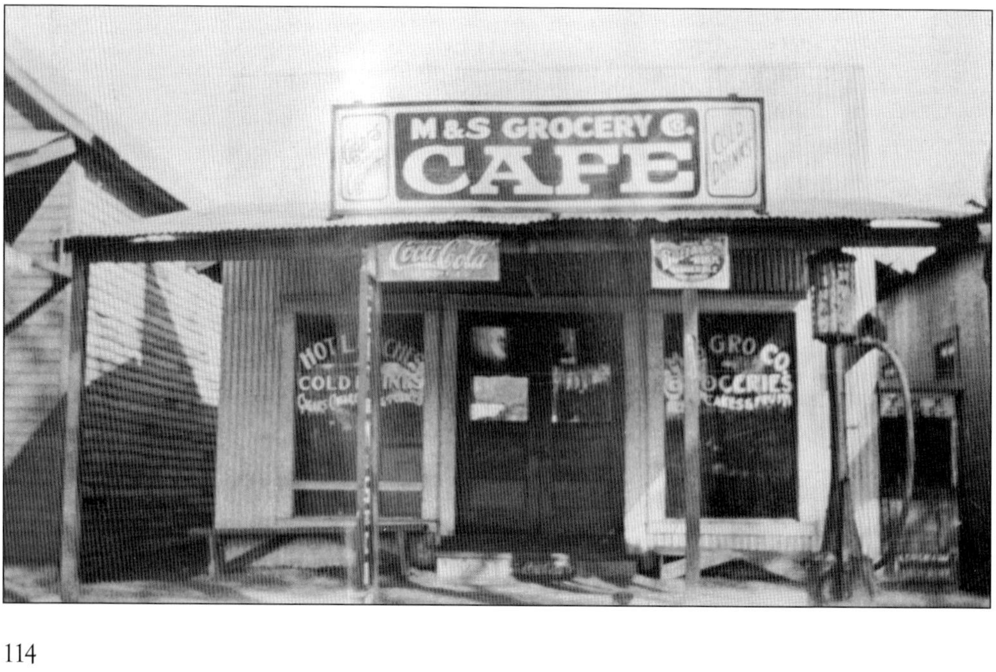

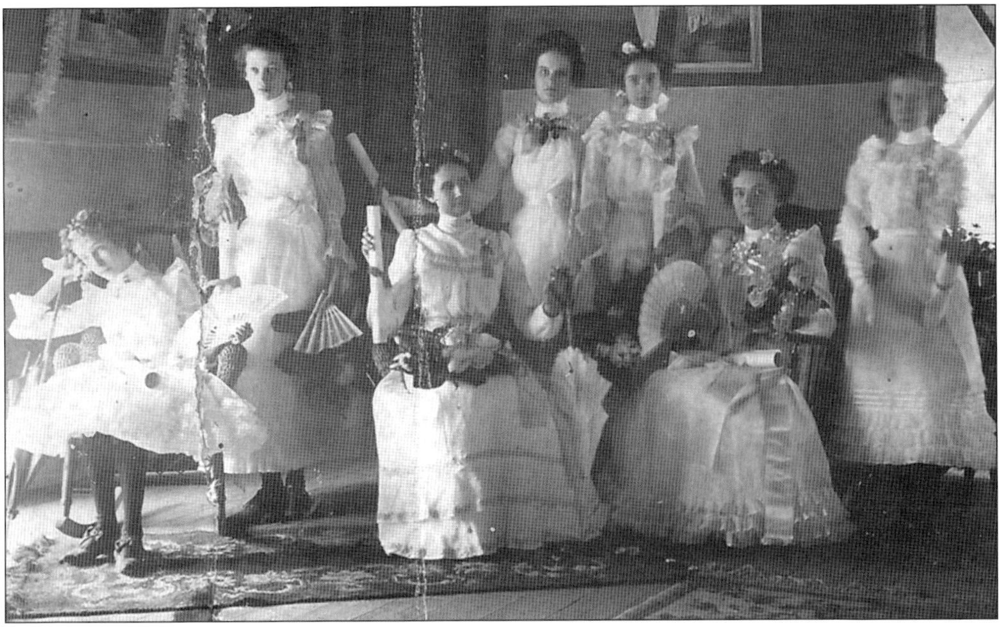

Vincent Class, 1901. A group of ladies in Vincent's 1901 graduating class pose for their class photograph. Regular school terms in the first school in Vincent lasted three months. The Central of Georgia Railroad was built on land owned by the Vincent family. A school, adopting the name of the town of Vincent, was built on the property. The new school consisted of four rooms with one serving as a music room. The building was crafted by the townspeople, and the desks were handmade. (Courtesy of SCHS.)

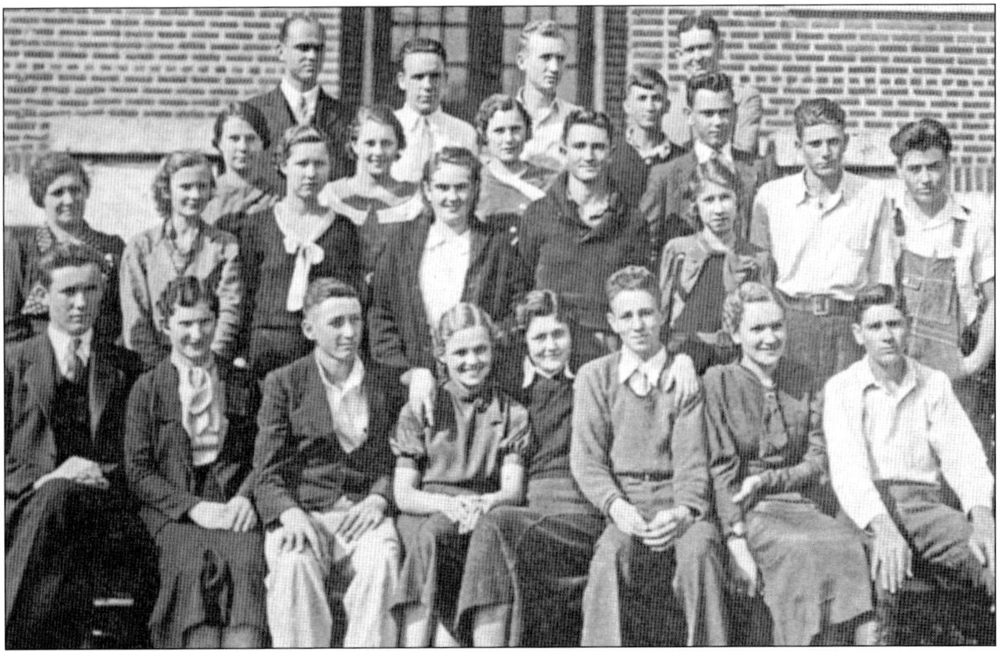

Vincent High School Class of 1930. In 1904, Vincent School was moved to a location near the railroad tracks. The land was donated by J.C. Elliott. Schools began to consolidate, and the building was occupied in January 1927. The building burned in 1945.

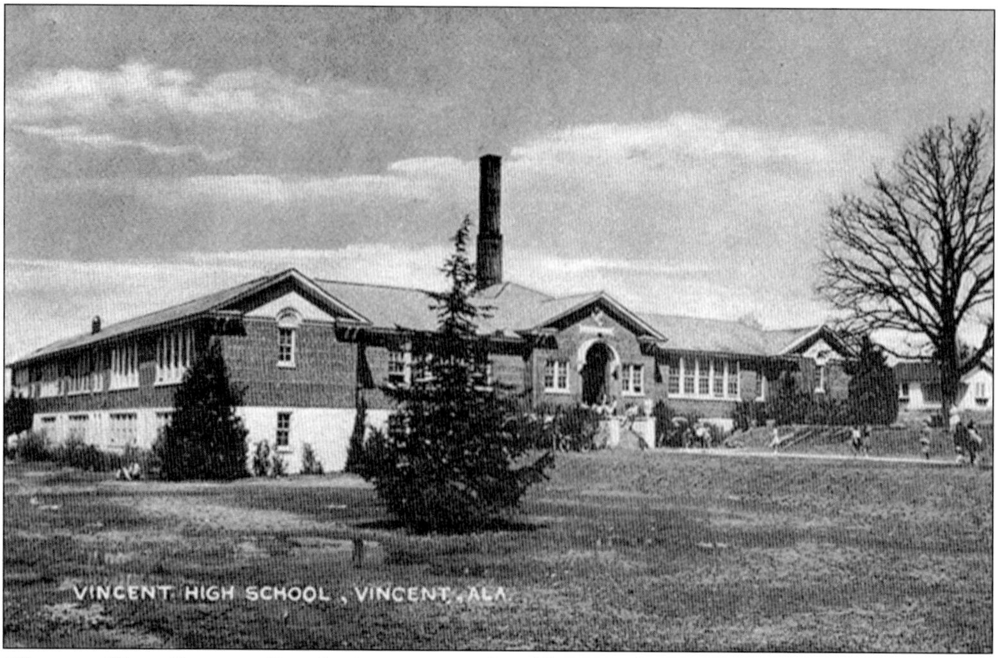

VINCENT HIGH SCHOOL. Standards were considered high in the Vincent system as early as 1900. The elementary school made history when it became the first school to implement a revised calendar. After each nine-week session, there was a three-week break. (Courtesy of SCHS.)

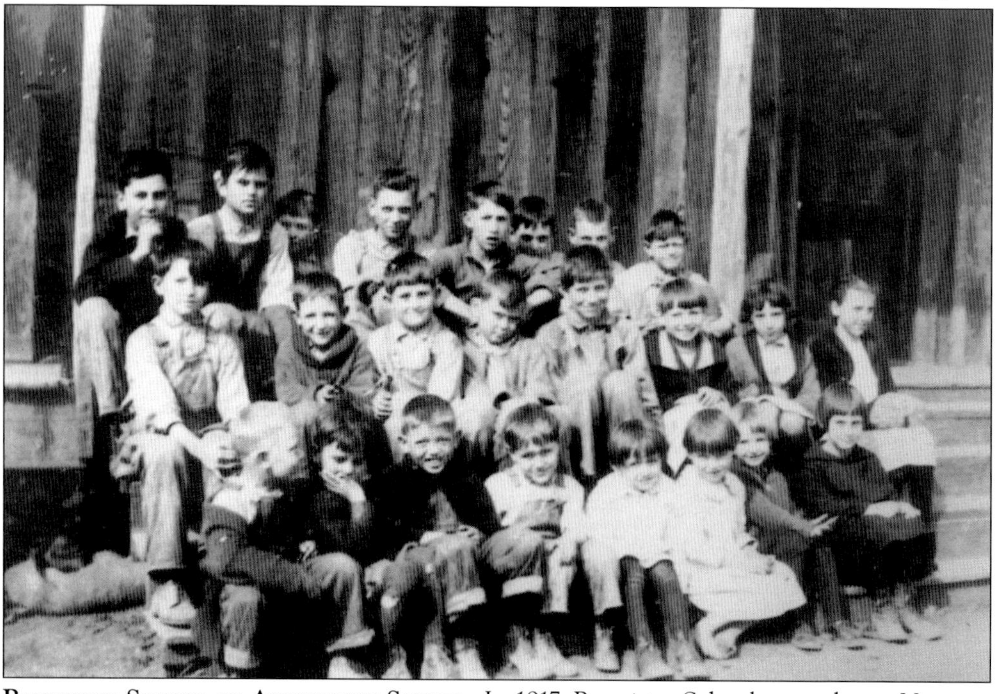

BANNISTER SCHOOL OR ARKWRIGHT SCHOOL. In 1917, Bannister School opened near Vincent. There were two teachers for 75 students, with grades one through nine offered. School opened at 8:00 a.m. and finished at 4:00 p.m. Operational for 10 years, the school was consolidated with Vincent School in 1927. (Courtesy of SCHS.)

ARKWRIGHT BAPTIST. Arkwright Baptist Church, organized in 1911, is now in the Alabama Register of Landmarks and Heritage. Services were originally held in a small building known as "Pop Ray's Old Store." The Coosa River and Locust Creek served for baptisms. Around 1919, the church began to meet in the old Bannister School in Vincent. In 1957, the congregation put brick around the building and expanded it. Stained-glass windows were donated by family members in memory of loved ones. (Courtesy of SCHS.)

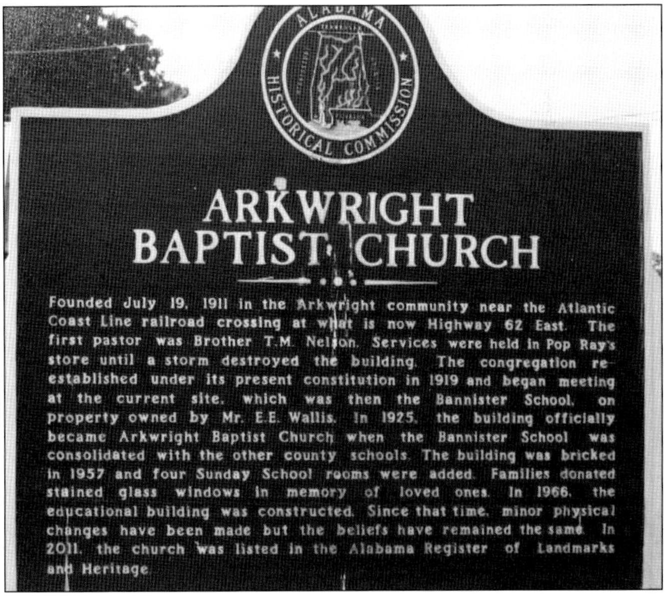

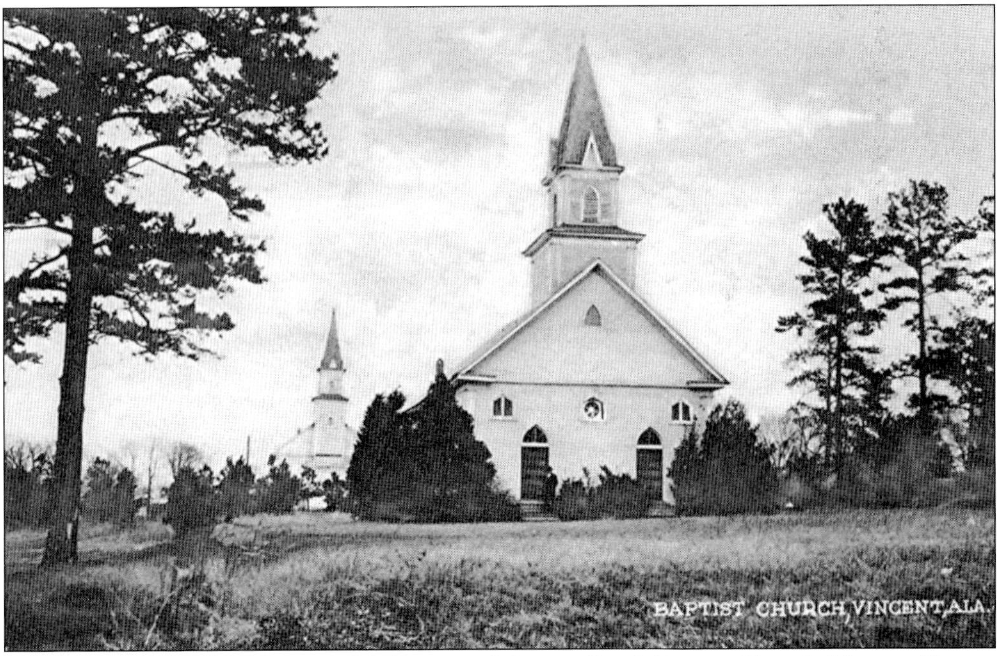

VINCENT BAPTIST CHURCH. Originally named Spring Creek Baptist Church, Vincent Baptist Church was founded in 1845. It was first located near two streams, which were used as pools for baptisms. In the 1850s, the church moved to land deeded by James Lindsey Elliot. It was closer to what would become the town of Vincent and near a spring that furnished water for Vincent. Church members provided most of the material for the building, and most work was done by hand. Candelabras were hung from the ceiling to provide light. In 1894, as Vincent grew, the building was torn down and moved again, this time into Vincent. The name Vincent Baptist Church became official in 1902. (Courtesy of SCHS.)

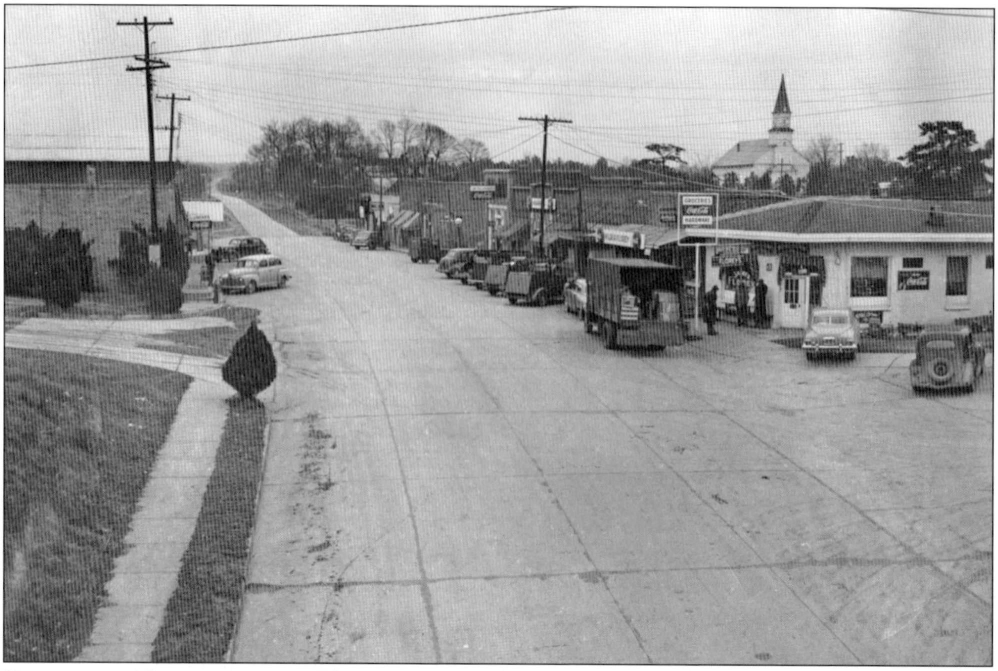

Downtown Vincent, 1930s. This is a view of what downtown Vincent looked like in 1935. The town began after land was granted to the Kidd family by the governor of Alabama in the 1800s. The land was willed to three daughters in the Kidd family in 1859. One of them was named Anna Vincent. After the railroad arrived, the town began to thrive. The post office was first named Propel, but it was changed to Vincent in 1888. (Courtesy of SCHS.)

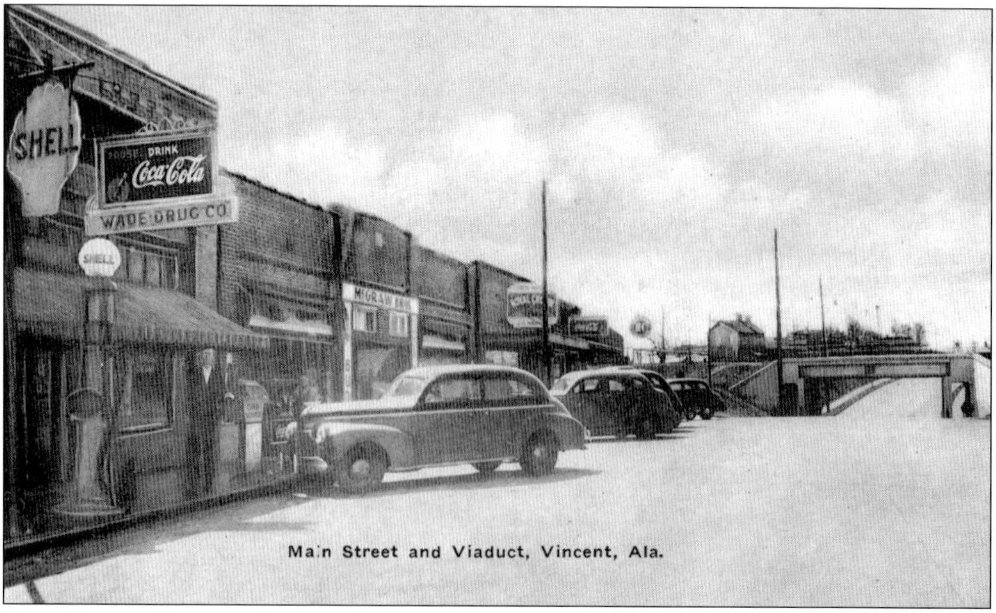

Main Street, Vincent. In the early days of Vincent, some of the popular places were Pitts Bros. & Co., C.P. Flemings and Co., McGraw Hotel, and the railroad depot. McGraw "Big Bud" Bros. Store sat next to Citizens Bank. This c. 1930s photograph of Vincent shows the viaduct in the background. (Courtesy of Martin Everse.)

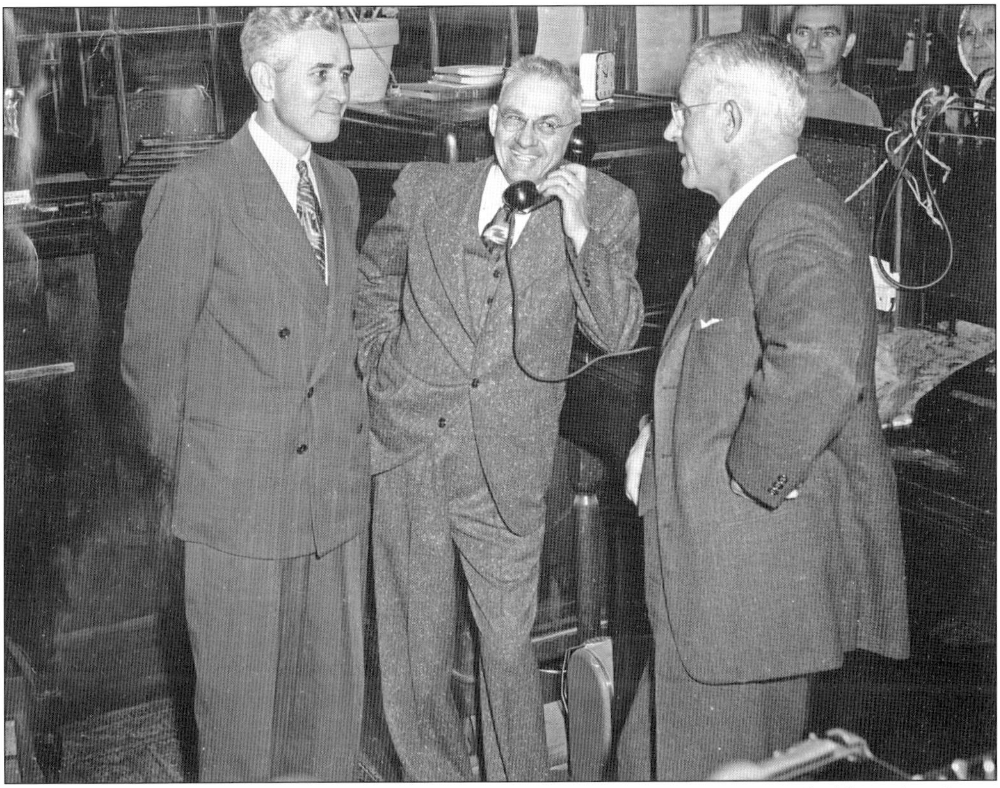

First Call, Southern Bell. The mayor of Vincent, S.E. McGrawis, is seen holding the phone and making the first official phone call on the Southern Bell telephone system after service was installed. Telephone company representatives are standing with McGrawis. Southern Bell and Telegraph Company began in 1879. (Courtesy of SCHS.)

Freight Train Wreck, 1955. Nearly 30 cars derailed, presumably caused by a split switch, causing a pileup on the tracks in Vincent in 1955. Flames could be seen for more than 30 miles after two tanks carrying liquefied petroleum exploded. No one was hurt in the incident. (Courtesy of SCHS.)

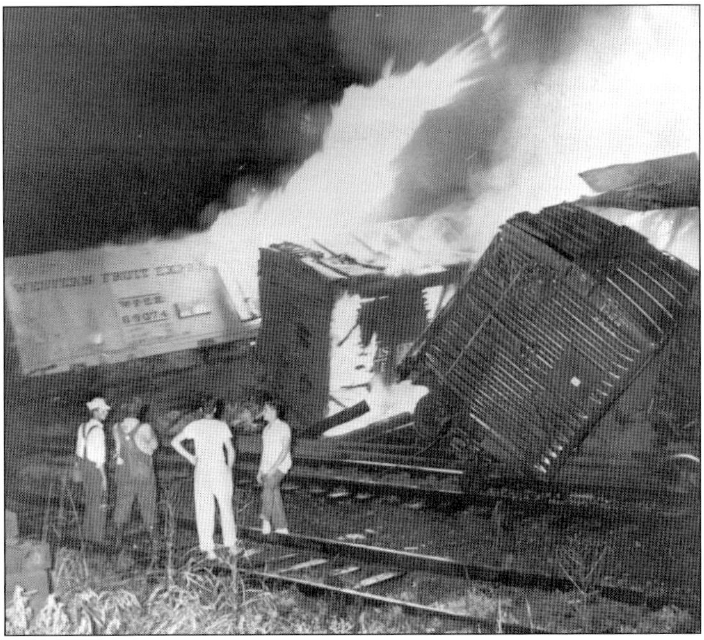

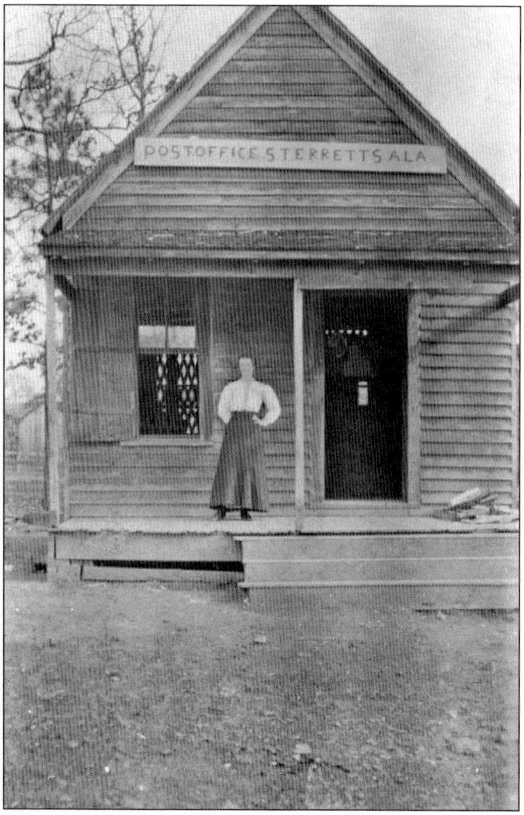

Sterrett Postmistress. Etta Monroe Walker stands in front of the Sterrett Post Office in the early 1900s. Walker was the postmistress at the time. (Courtesy of SCHS.)

US Parcel Post Delivery. This is an early post office delivery wagon. J. Elmer Faulkner was the rural mail carrier for Sterrett and Vandiver. (Courtesy of SCHS.)

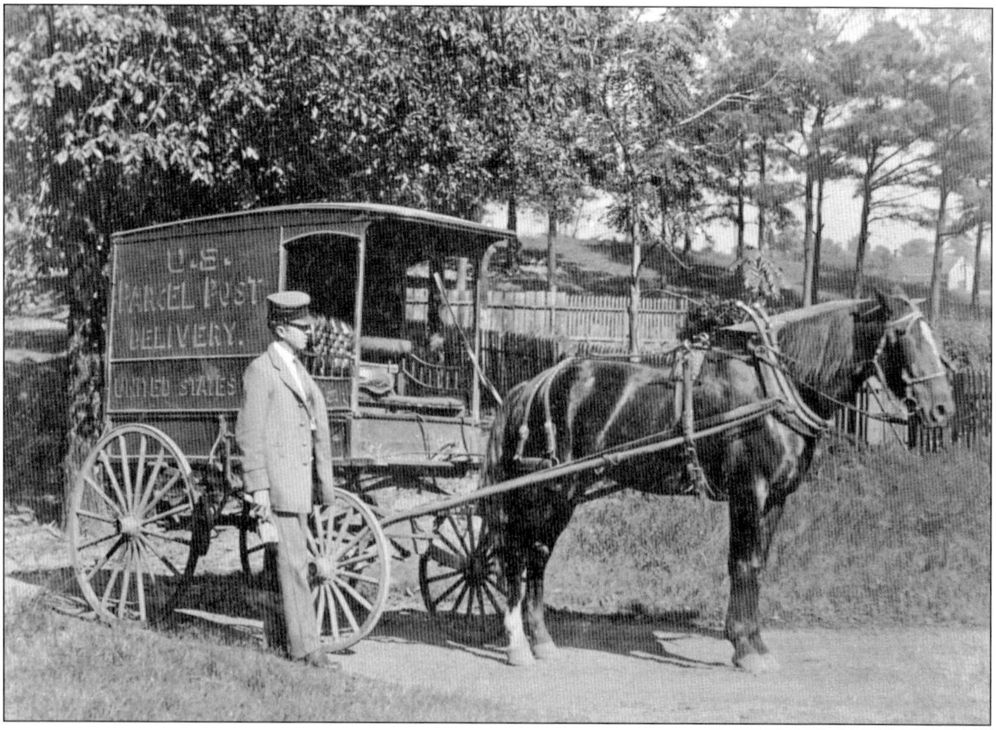

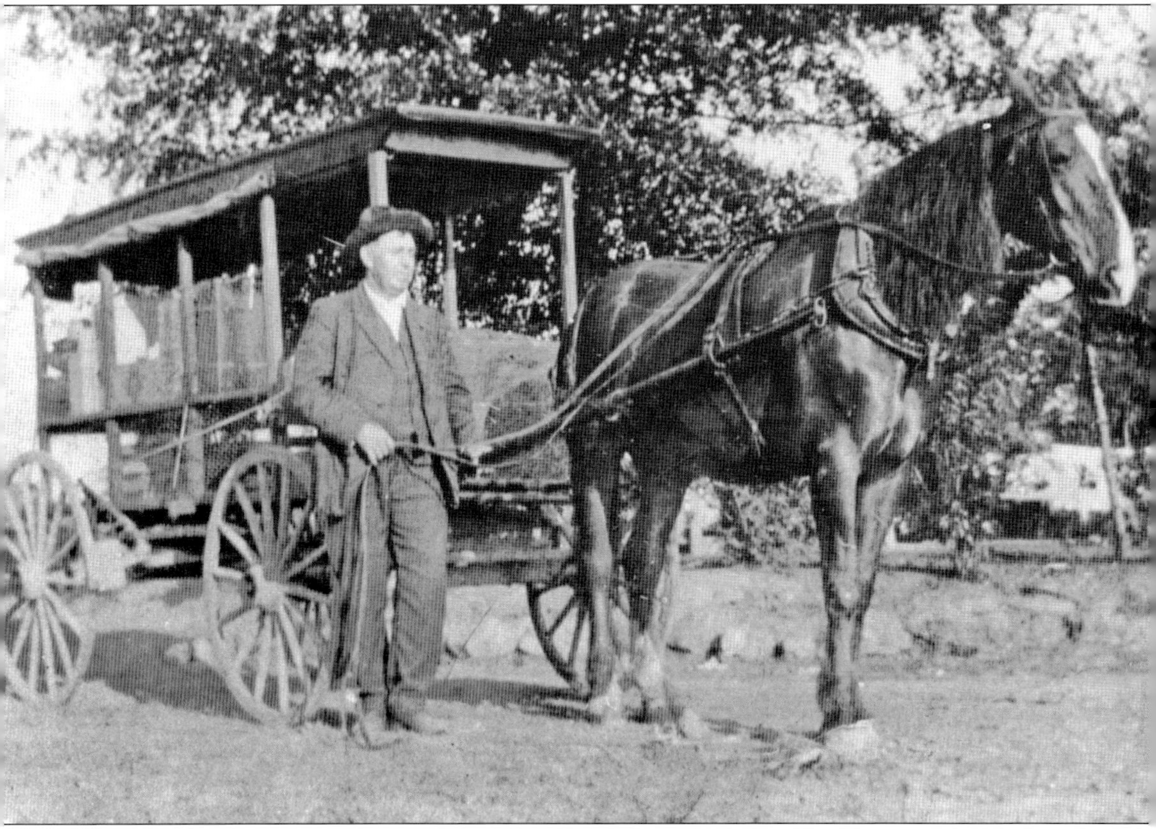

First Rolling Store. Operated by a Mr. Spearman, this was the first "rolling store" for east Shelby County. Spearman sold goods from the horse-drawn open buggy to Shelby County communities. (Courtesy of SCHS.)

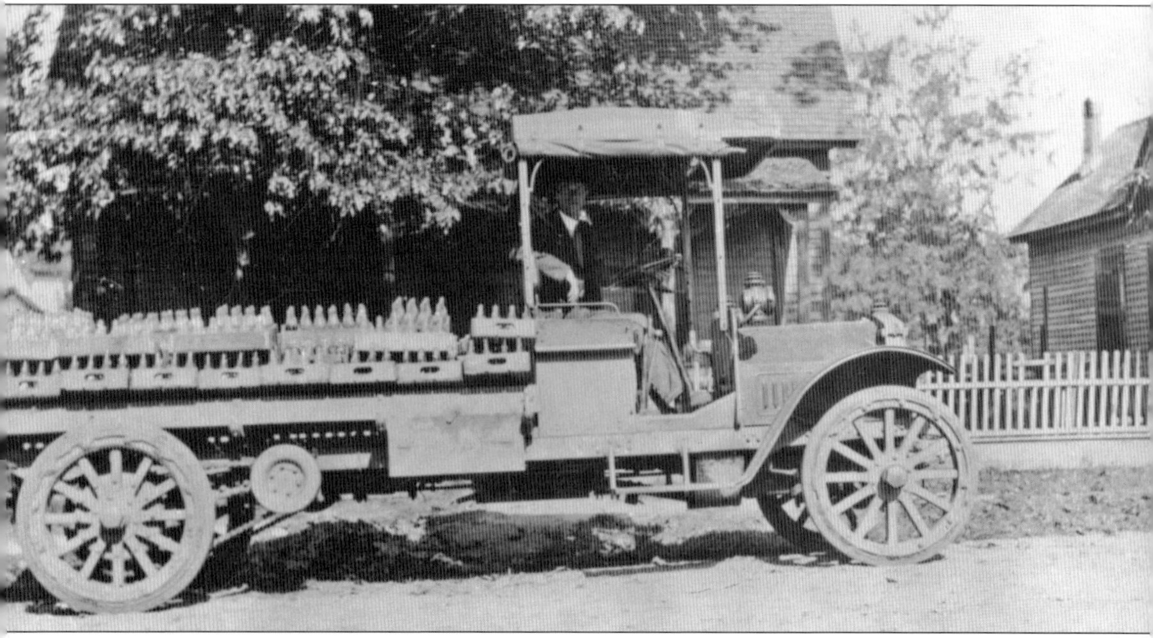

Delivery Truck. This delivery truck is believed to belong to Coca-Cola. It is delivering to businesses in the Sterrett area around the turn of the 20th century. (Courtesy SCHS.)

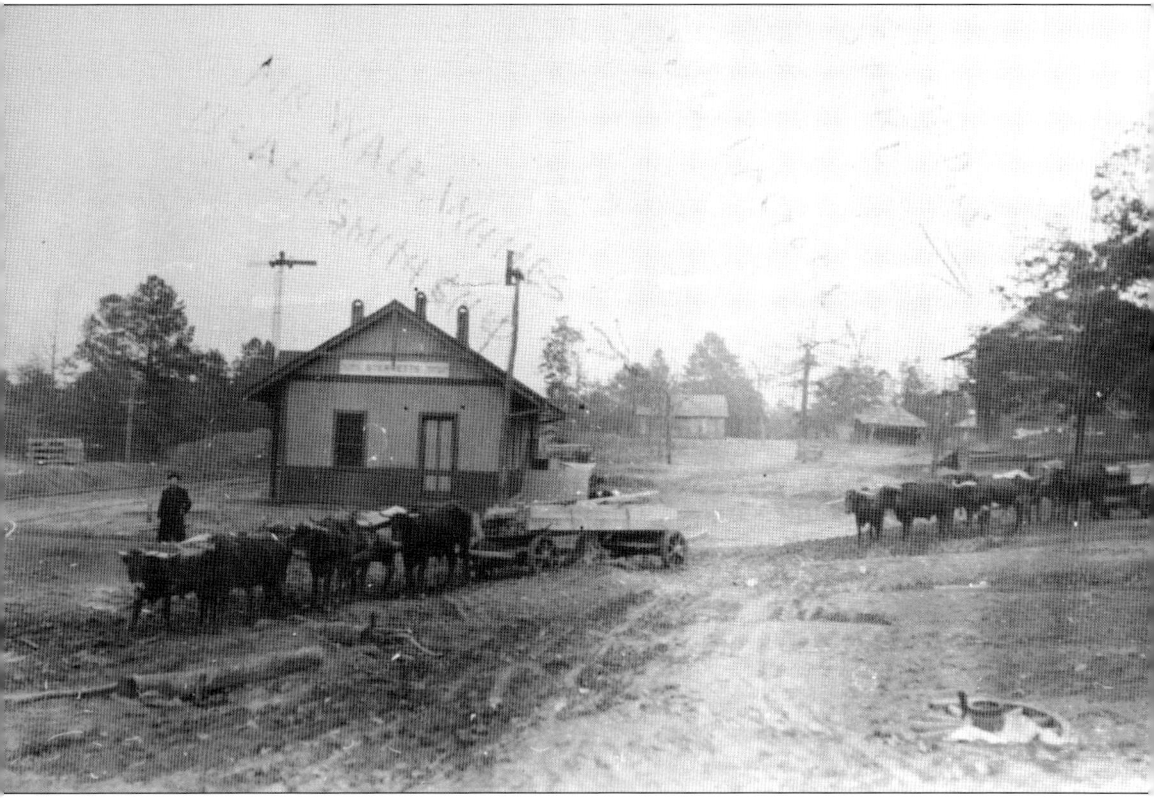

Sterrett Depot. Here is a view of what the train depot looked like in Sterrett in 1900. Note the working oxen pulling the wagons of wood parallel to the railroad tracks. (Courtesy of SCHS.)

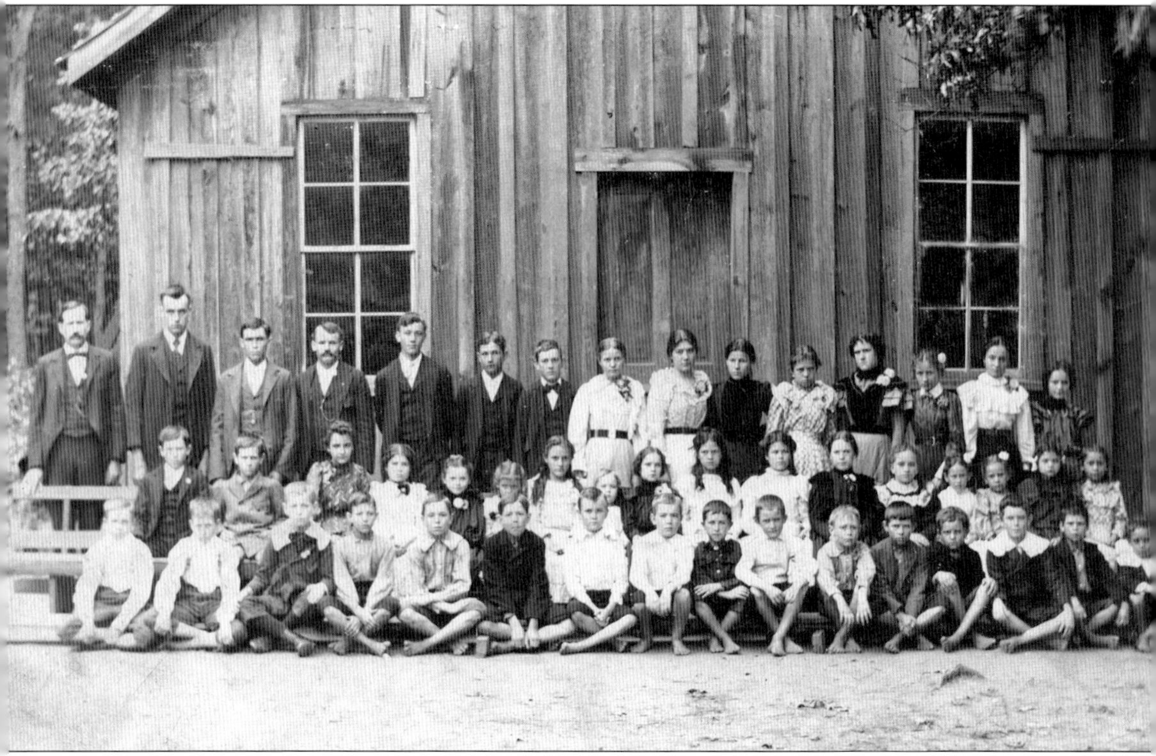

Sterrett School. Sterrett School began around 1890 and was located near "Jugtown." Jugtown's name came from the area's heavy pottery production. In 1902, a school was built on land donated by Hillarde Faulkner. In the beginning, the school consisted of just three classrooms. (Courtesy of SCHS.)

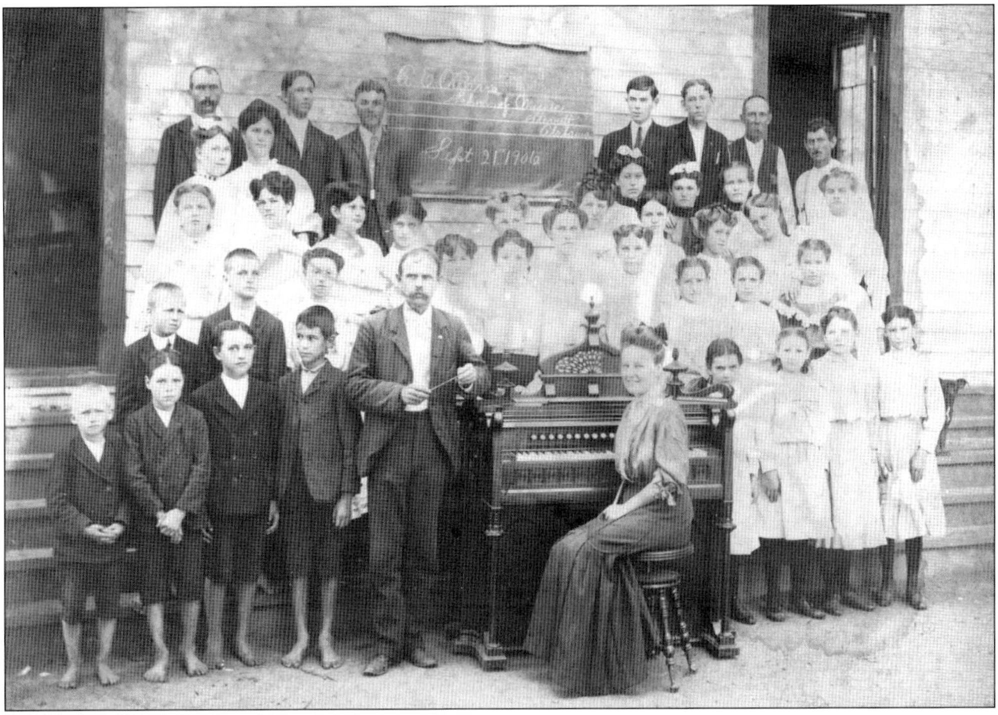

Sterrett Music School. Taken on September 21, 1906, this photograph shows A.E. O'Barr's School of Music in Sterrett. (Courtesy of SCHS.)

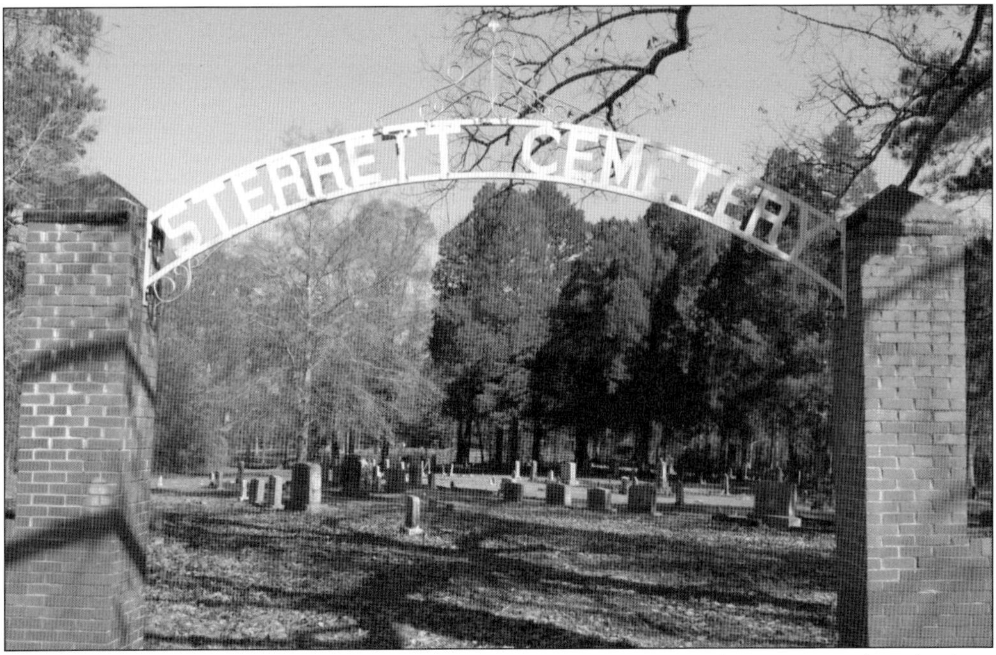

Sterrett Cemetery. Also known as the "Old Sterrett Cemetery," this cemetery dates back to 1841. It is listed in the Alabama Historic Cemetery Register. The oldest marked grave is for Polly Webster, the daughter of Beulah Land founder Henley Webster, who was born in South Carolina. Webster acquired the land and the surrounding 40 acres in 1824. (Courtesy of SCHS.)

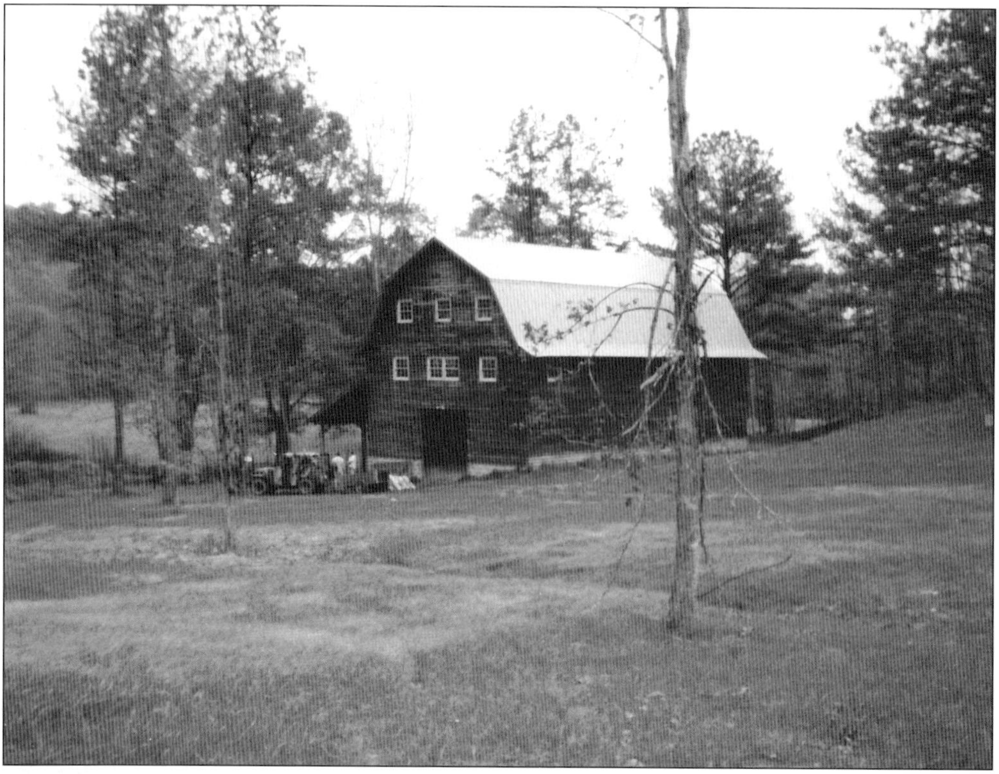

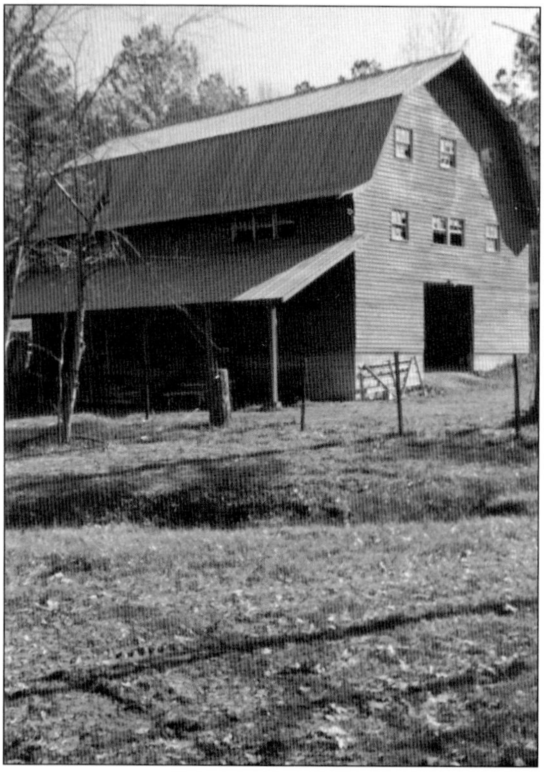

VINCENT BED-AND-BREAKFAST. What became affectionately known as Blue Spring Manor Bed-and-Breakfast in Vincent began as a small barn off of a desolate stretch of Highway 280. The local Byers family bought the barn and property in the 1980s to reconstruct as their family home. (Both, courtesy of Mary Ann Byers.)

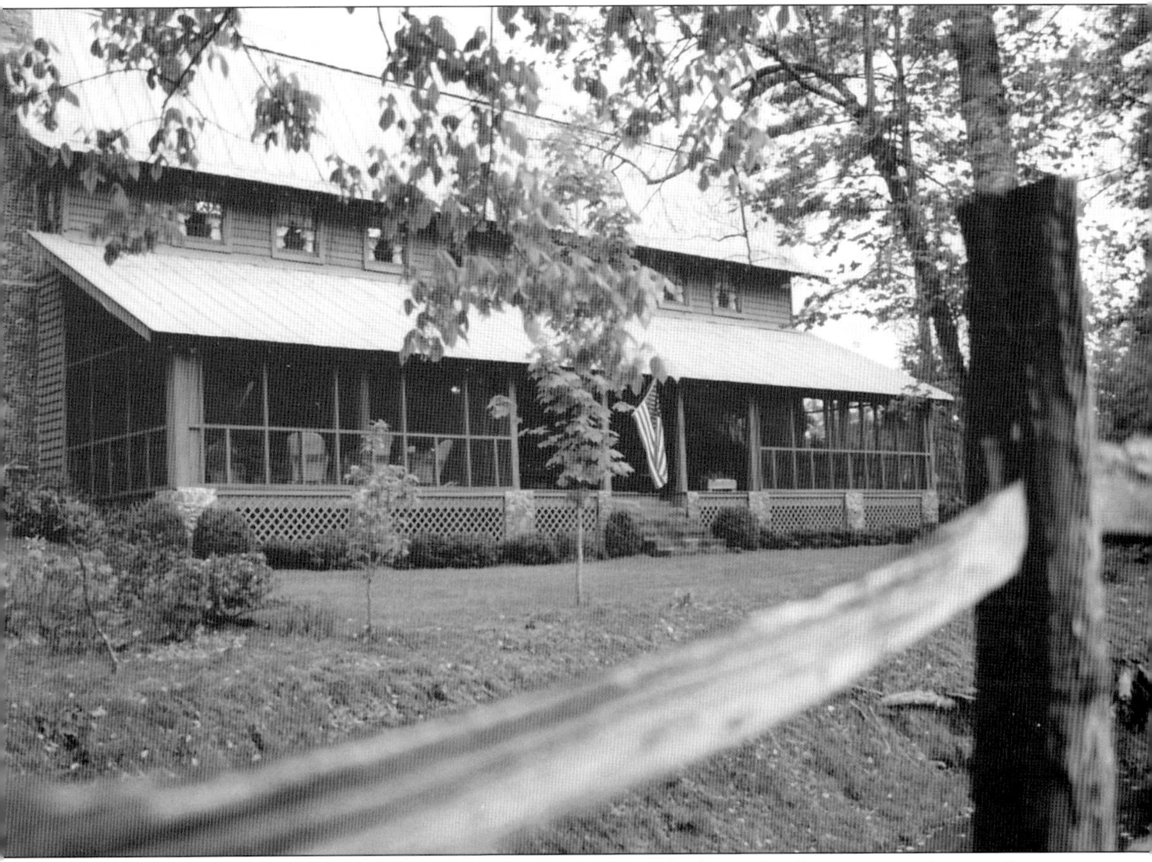

The Finished House. After much hard work, additions to the barn, landscaping, and time, the home became a beautiful dwelling. The Byers family lived in the house before selling it for the progress of the Greystone area. The renovated barn was purchased and moved to Vincent on 10 acres of land. Many of the pine walls were left intact. The home became the tucked-away, beautiful Blue Spring Manor Bed-and-Breakfast on Highway 83. (Courtesy of Mary Ann Byers.)